THE DEVIL

BOOKS BY JEFFREY BURTON RUSSELL

Dissent and Reform in the Early Middle Ages (1965)
Medieval Civilization (1968)
A History of Medieval Christianity: Prophecy and Order (1968)
Religious Dissent in the Middle Ages (1971)
Witchcraft in the Middle Ages (1972)
The Devil: Perceptions of Evil from Antiquity to Primitive Christianity (1977)
A History of Witchcraft: Sorcerers, Heretics, Pagans (1980)
Medieval Heresies: A Bibliography (with C. T. Berkhout) (1981)
Satan: The Early Christian Tradition (1981)
Lucifer: The Devil in the Middle Ages (1984)
Mephistopheles: The Devil in the Modern World (1986)
The Prince of Darkness: Radical Evil and the Power of Good in History (1988)

THE DEVIL &

Perceptions of Evil from Antiquity
to Primitive Christianity

JEFFREY BURTON RUSSELL

Cornell University Press ITHACA AND LONDON

First published 1977 by Cornell University Press
First printing, Cornell Paperbacks, 1987

Printed in the United States of America

Library of Congress Cataloging-in-Publication Data
(For library cataloging purposes only)

Russell, Jeffrey Burton.
  The Devil.

  Bibliography : p.
  Includes index.
  ISBN-13: 978-0-8014-9409-3 (pbk. : alk. paper)
  ISBN-10: 0-8014-9409-5 (pbk. : alk. paper).
  1. Devil—History of doctrines. 2. Good and evil. I. Title.
BL480.R86   291.2'16   77-3126

Paperback printing   10

For Penelope

Contents

Preface		11
1.	The Question of Evil	17
2.	In Search of the Devil	36
3.	The Devil East and West	55
4.	Evil in the Classical World	122
5.	Hebrew Personifications of Evil	174
6.	The Devil in the New Testament	221
7.	The Face of the Devil	250
	Select Bibliography	261
	Index	271

Illustrations

M. C. Escher, "The Scapegoat," woodcut	20
Concentration camp victim	33
Alchemical androgyne, drawing, Germany, fifteenth century	39
Head of Dionysos, Roman sculpture	45
Gustave Moreau, "Zeus and Semele," painting	53
Quetzalcoatl, sculpture, Mexico	57
The asura Sumbha, painting, India, eighteenth century	59
Shiva and his family, painting, India, eighteenth century	61
Kali, painting, India, eighteenth century	63
The wheel of becoming, painting, Tibet, eighteenth century	65
Ouroboros, relief, Dahomey, nineteenth century	69
The dancing sorcerer, paleolithic drawing, France	71
Goat or ram, golden statue, Ur, third millennium B.C.	72
Buddhist hell, painting, Japan, sixteenth century	74
Seti I with Seth and Horus, rendering from Egyptian source, nineteenth dynasty	77
The dual Horus-Seth god, rendering from Egyptian source	79
Isis, relief, nineteenth dynasty	81
Hathor, copy of statue, twenty-sixth dynasty	83
Sekhmet, rendering from Egyptian source	85
Assyrian deity, relief, ninth century B.C.	87
Pazuzu, statue, Mesopotamia, second millennium B.C.	91
Lilitu, relief, Sumer, second millennium B.C.	93
Anath, relief, Ugarit, 1400–1200 B.C.	96
A shitenno, Japan, eighth century	100
Parthian goddess, statue, Persia, first or second century A.D.	103

Ahura Mazda, relief, Persepolis, sixth or fifth century B.C.   106

Birth of Ohrmazd and Ahriman, relief, Luristan, eighth century B.C.   109

Zurvan, Hellenistic statue   110

The Chinvat Bridge, painting, India, sixteenth century   118

Pan, Coptic relief, sixth century   125

Artemis, statues, Greece, fourth century B.C., and Ephesus, first century B.C. or A.D.   128

Hecate, rendering from engraved gem, Rome   130

Dionysos, relief, Boeotia, early fourth century B.C.   138

Maenad, Coptic relief, sixth century   140

Pan and nymphs, fresco, Pompeii, first century B.C. or A.D.   151

Head of Mithras, Romano-British sculpture   153

Mithras slaying the bull, Roman relief, second century A.D.   155

Charun, Etruscan fresco, fourth century B.C.   156

Head of Charun, Tarentum, fourth century B.C.   159

Tetradrachm of Demetrios, Hellenistic coin, second century B.C.   169

Pan and Olympus, sculpture, Pompeii, first century A.D.   171

Moses presenting the law to the Jews, manuscript illumination, France, fourteenth century   177

William Blake, "Satan before the Throne of God," watercolor   187

Eugene Delacroix, "Jacob Wrestling with the Angel," painting   201

Gustave Doré, "Satan Enthroned in Hell," engraving   210

Christ exorcising a demon, Coptic manuscript illumination, sixth century   230

The harrowing of hell, manuscript illumination, Germany, tenth century   233

Exorcism, illustration from a picture Bible, Germany, fifteenth century   238

"The Worship of the Beast," illustration, De Quincey Apocalypse, thirteenth century   244

M. C. Escher, "The Encounter," lithograph   258

Preface

This is a work of history, not of theology. It is a study of the development of a concept in the human mind, not a metaphysical statement. Historical scholarship cannot determine whether the Devil exists objectively. The historian may, however, suggest that men and women have seemed to act as if the Devil did exist. Evil—the infliction of pain upon sentient beings—is one of the most longstanding and serious problems of human existence. Frequently and in many cultures evil has been personified. This book is a history of the personification of evil, which for the sake of clarity I have called "the Devil."

I am a medievalist, but when I began some years ago to work with the concept of the Devil in the eleventh and twelfth centuries, I came to see that I could not understand the medieval Devil except in terms of its historical antecedents. More important, I realized that I could not understand the Devil at all except in the context of the problem of evil. I needed to face the issue of evil squarely, both as a historian and as a human being. The story of evil and its personification is a long one, and I am obliged to terminate this book at the end of the period of the New Testament. A second volume, dealing with the Devil in the Middle Ages, is planned to follow.

This is a work of synthesis, dealing with the large problem of the personification of evil over a broad span of time in a number of diverse cultures. The current tide of historical scholarship is in the direction of analysis rather than synthesis. But a balanced view recognizes the need for both. We need detailed studies; we also need studies that place the details in their contexts and relate the historical evidence to human life and experience as a whole.

The historian faces special difficulty in a history of values, which are always in flux, and the difficulty is compounded in a cross-cultural study, where terms relating to values must be translated from one language and one cultural context to another. The inevitability of error and disputable interpretations should not, however, deter a writer from dealing with what he perceives as a problem central to humanity and to himself. A work of scholarship should be more than an exercise. In writing, the writer should himself change; and his best hope is that, in reading, the reader may change also.

I would like to make completely clear in this book a point that was sometimes misunderstood in my history of witchcraft. It is this: the historical evidence can never be clear enough for us to know what *really* happened (*wie es eigentlich gewesen*), but the evidence as to what people *believed* to have happened is relatively clear. The concept—what people believed to have happened—is more important than what really did happen, because people act upon what they believe to be true.

In a wide work such as this I have necessarily drawn upon the assistance of many colleagues, students, friends, and relations. I am grateful to each in a special way that each will understand. None of them is responsible for any error in this book, and none should be assumed to subscribe to the interpretations it offers. My sincere thanks, then, to Carl T. Berkhout, Joseph R. Blenkinsopp, Edmund Brehm, Helen E. Conrad, Frank Cook, Clara Dean, Edwin S. Gaustad, Norman Girardot, Barbara Hambly, Bernhard Kendler, Helen Logue, Donald M. Lowe, Eileen MacKrell, Leon McCrillis, Ralph McInerny, Francis J. Marcolongo, William Mathews, June O'Connor, Douglas Parrott, Johnnie Ann Ralph, Diana Russell, Jennifer Russell, Kay Scheuer, and Mark W. Wyndham. I am grateful also to the following institutions, which have given me financial and other assistance: the Research Committee of the University of California, Riverside, the Michael P. Grace Chair of Medieval Studies at the University of Notre Dame, the Index of Christian Art, the National Endowment for the Humanities, and the Warburg Institute.

Chapter 1 appeared in an earlier version in *Listening/Journal of Religion and Culture*, vol. 9, no. 3 (1974), 71–83. Chapter 2 appeared in an earlier version in *Indiana Social Science Quarterly*, vol. 28 (Winter 1975/76), 24–37. I thank the editors for permitting their appearance in revised form here.

JEFFREY BURTON RUSSELL

Notre Dame, Indiana

THE DEVIL

Der Teufel, der ist alt.

—GOETHE

*He who plucks a flower
disturbs the farthest star.*

—THOMAS TRAHERNE

1   The Question of Evil

Did heaven look on and would not take their part?

—Macduff

The essence of evil is abuse of a sentient being, a being that can feel pain. It is the pain that matters. Evil is grasped by the mind immediately and immediately felt by the emotions; it is sensed as hurt deliberately inflicted. The existence of evil requires no further proof: I am; therefore I suffer evil.

Evil is frequently and in many societies felt as a purposeful force, and it is perceived as personified. For the sake of simplicity and clarity I have called this personification "the Devil." Evil is never abstract. It must always be understood in terms of the suffering of an individual. No better description of the immediacy of evil exists than Ivan's discourse to Alyosha in *The Brothers Karamazov*:

Imagine a trembling mother with her baby in her arms, a circle of invading Turks around her. They've planned a diversion; they pet the baby, laugh to make it laugh. They succeed, the baby laughs. At that moment a Turk points a pistol four inches from the baby's face. The baby laughs with glee, holds out its little hands to the pistol, and he pulls the trigger in the baby's face and blows out its brains. Artistic, wasn't it? . . . I think that if the Devil doesn't exist, but man has created him, he has created him in his own image and likeness.

And again:

There was a little girl of five [who] was subjected to every possible torture by [her] cultivated parents. [They] shut her up all night in the

cold and frost in a privy, and because she didn't ask to be taken up at
night [and so wet herself], they smeared her face and filled her mouth
with excrement, and it was her mother, her mother did this. And that
mother could sleep, hearing the poor child's groans! Can you understand why a little creature, who can't even understand what's done to
her, should beat her little aching heart with her tiny fist in the dark
and the cold, and weep her meek unresentful tears to dear, kind God
to protect her? . . . Why should mankind know that diabolical good
and evil when it costs so much? Why, the whole world of knowledge
is not worth that child's prayer to "dear, kind God!"[1]

On August 22, 1976, according to UPI,

A sixteen-year-old girl, apparently high on LSD, slashed her wrists
and arms and then rushed to the steps of a Roman Catholic church,
poking a razor to her throat while a crowd of 300 persons cheered and
screamed, "Do your thing, sister!" Police called the crowd's cheering
"disgusting". . . . "They were yelling, 'Do it, sister!' 'Right On!' "
the officers told the detective. . . . The crowd cheered when the girl
finally fainted and collapsed from loss of blood from her cuts.

Wanton cruelty and destructiveness are commonplace in everyday news stories, just as they are commonplace in the history of humanity. Almost three millennia ago, Ashurnasirpal
II, king of Assyria, when capturing an enemy town, would
order his soldiers to take all the inhabitants, cut off their hands
and feet, and pile them up in the city square to bleed and suf-
focate to death.

Most of the examples of evil presented in this chapter are
physical, because physical hurts are more obvious than mental
and spiritual abuses. Yet mental and spiritual abuses are as
common, as destructive and painful, and partake fully of the
spirit of evil.

What is evil, and how did it come to be? These are among
the most ancient and intricate of human questions. Nor has the
problem of evil declined with time: in the twentieth century it
seems more pressing than ever.

1. Feodor Dostoevsky, *The Brothers Karamazov* (New York, 1936), pp. 283,
287. For a current example dealing with boundless human cruelty, see Colin
M. Turnbull, *The Mountain People* (New York, 1973).

What *is* evil? Evil is as people have perceived it. But perceptions of evil are so diverse that the concept cannot be defined satisfactorily. Arbitrary definitions may be assigned the word for the purpose of limited communication. But evil is not merely a fuzzy-bordered concept; it has no internal coherence at all. Consequently we must consider evil as perceived immediately, directly, and existentially, rather than defined categorically.

The perception of evil is a direct, immediate experience of something done to an individual. You experience immediately evil done to you; by empathy you experience directly evil done to those you love, to your friends and neighbors, or even to those you do not know personally at all. Evil is not an abstraction. You know, and understand by analogy from your own suffering, the pain of Anne Frank in the concentration camp, of the napalmed child in Vietnam, of the Assyrian soldier dying in the heat. Though the pain is 10,000 miles or 5,000 years away, the distance does not matter. The voice cries out, and it is heard. The Jew in the gas chamber; the heretic at the stake; the lonely old man mugged in the city street; the woman raped; that *one* of these, just *one*, should suffer is intolerable. That one should suffer imposes the absolute obligation of trying to understand and so grapple with the problem of evil.

And it is seldom only one who suffers. After the execution of one victim of the NKVD, his eight-year-old daughter Zoya lived only one year. "Up to then she had never been ill. During that year *she did not once smile*; she went about with head hung low. . . . She died of inflammation of the brain, and as she was dying she kept calling out: 'Where is my papa? Give me my papa!' When we count up the millions of those who perished in the camps, we forget to multiply them by two, by three."[2]

From the basic perception of individual evil you extrapolate to the general, moving from the realm of experience to the realm of conscious construction and conceptualization. From the death of the Assyrian soldier you can form a concept of the

2. Aleksander Solzhenitsyn, *The Gulag Archipelago* (New York, 1974), p. 431.

M. C. Escher, "The Scapegoat," 1921. The Devil appears as the shadow of God, the dark side of the divine nature. Courtesy Escher Foundation, Haags Gemeentemuseum, The Hague.

horror of Assyrian wars and of all wars. From the suffering of Anne Frank you form a concept of the terror of life under a cruel and self-righteous regime. From the pain of the napalmed Vietnamese child you construct an idea of the agony caused by ideologies senseless of their destruction of human beings. General notions, general concepts of evil arise. But these are impossible to define theoretically; they speak to our consciousness from our direct perceptions of individual suffering.

From your consciousness of general evil arises yet another level of understanding. You see that evils are not only general, but universally present in human experience. Evil has touched all places, all times, and the life of every mature individual. We understand that evil is cosmic. With a better world in our minds, we sense the fundamental insufficiencies of this one. The perception of a flawed world is radical—deeply rooted—in each individual soul. The perception of the flaw is as widespread a perception as any that can be ascribed to mankind. When we ask the question: how is it that the world is flawed (perhaps incurably), we are raising the problem of evil in its full form.

But "flaw" is a metaphor. And questions of ontology and etiology are metaphysical speculations. Always if we are to make sense of evil, we must return from metaphor and metaphysic to the individual. Numbers only disguise reality. Six million Jews exterminated by the Nazis become an abstraction. It is the suffering of one Jew that you understand, and your powers to extrapolate beyond that are limited. That is why Milton's Satan can seem so proud: the evil he personifies is disguised by abstraction. Ivan's one tortured child alone in the darkness reveals the true nature of the spurious glory of Satan, a glory that we feel only if we allow our minds, borne aloft by abstract considerations, to forget the suffering of the individual. Abstractions loosed from their ties to the individual can kill. How many blood offerings have the Church, and Democracy, and the People not demanded? Abstractions kill when we pretend that they are more than human constructs, when we falsely imagine that they are real phenomena. The National Socialism to which Anne Frank was sacrificed and the Democracy to which the Vietnamese child was offered are not real. The children's pain is real. It is real to you because you know their pain with an immediate certainty derived from your own.

Many were shot—thousands at first, then hundreds of thousands. We divide, we multiply, we sigh, we curse. But still and all, these are just numbers. They overwhelm the mind and then are easily forgotten. And if someday the relatives of those who had been shot were to send one publisher photographs of their executed kin, and an album of those photographs were to be published in several volumes, then just by leafing through them and looking into the extinguished eyes we would learn much that would be valuable for the rest of our lives. such reading, almost without words, would leave a deep mark on our hearts for all eternity.[3]

Returning to the individual in another way is necessary. So far I have been speaking of evil as something done *to* me. But it is also something done *by* me. As none of us has a life in which no evil befalls him, none of us has a life in which he does no evil. The worm is in my rose too. In each of us, somewhere, are the feelings that, improperly developed, can produce the torturer, the killer, the ravisher, the sadist. And always, to some small extent at least, I allow those feelings play. At least part of the answer to the question of evil lies within me. And yet I almost always perceive that evil as coming from outside. Seldom does anyone admit that he is evil; seldom does he even admit that he does evil. One of the great dangers to humanity is our tendency to project our own evil onto others.

If only it were all so simple! If only there were evil people somewhere insidiously committing evil deeds, and it were necessary only to separate them from the rest of us and destroy them. But the line dividing good and evil cuts through the heart of every human being. And who is willing to destroy a piece of his own heart? . . . At times [one human being] is close to being a devil, at times to sainthood. But his

3. Solzhenitsyn, p. 442.

name doesn't change, and to that name we ascribe the whole lot, good and evil.[4]

We think of evil as inflicted on us, either in the sense of being done to us or in the sense of an alien force causing ugly actions on our part. How could I have done that, we ask; or we say, Something must have come over me.

But what is that something? What, really, is evil? What follows in this paragraph is a statement of what evil means to me. And yet the statement is not wholly solipsistic, for it finds validation in the perception of many others. Evil is meaningless, senseless destruction. Evil destroys and does not build; it rips and it does not mend; it cuts and it does not bind. It strives always and everywhere to annihilate, to turn to nothing.[5] To take all being and render it nothing is the heart of evil.[6] Or, as Erich Fromm puts it, evil is "life turning against itself" or "at-

4. Solzhenitsyn, p. 168.
5. A humanly convincing statement of evil is Madeleine L'Engle's *A Wind in the Door* (New York, 1973). The Echthroi, or enemies, attempt to "X", to annihilate the Universe, and nothing from a galaxy to a mitochondrion escapes their attention. To make everything into nothing is their only wish. By destruction I do not mean "destruction of illusion" or "destruction of the undesirable," or "purification." I mean absolute *destruction:* annihilation.
6. Even oriental thought, if understood properly, does not really postulate nothingness as desirable. The negating of the material world and even of the self which is the ideal of much Hinduism and Buddhism is not really destruction. For in Hinduism what is destroyed is Maya, illusion, and what remains is Atman, which is Brahman, true reality. Hinduism calls for the destruction of apparent reality, not for true nothingness. When a Buddhist says, "Buddha nature is intrinsic Non-being as Absolute Good" (Akiyama), he does not mean nothingness in the Western, ontological sense. By Nonbeing he means direct, selfless perception, no differentiation between subject and object. He means the removal of the self from the process of perception, so that the subject can become one with the object and with all objects, so that all will be one. The Buddhist concept of emptiness is similar to that of Nonbeing. Both aim at a destruction of selfness, but not a destruction of Being (in the Western philosophical and religious sense). Thanks to Francis H. Cook for a discussion of this point.
The concept of Nonbeing in the East is in effect equivalent to that of Being in Christian tradition: both imply ultimate reality. It is an assumption that Being is superior to Nonbeing even in Western terminology. I make that assumption here on two grounds. One: if God exists, God is Being by definition. Further, if God did not want anything other than himself to exist he

traction to what is dead, decaying, lifeless, and purely mechanical."[7]

Evil is sometimes deliberately malicious. Sometimes it is the product of rationalization or weakness: I am most likely to be arrogant, bitter, or hostile at times when I feel exposed and vulnerable. Questions of motivation are difficult, and perhaps unnecessary. We can judge the deed without judging the doer of the deed. A torturer may be acting from fear or from misled rationalization; but torture remains an absolute objective evil.

A distinction is conventionally made between "natural evil" and "moral evil." Natural evil consists of destructive "acts of God" or of nature, such as tornadoes or cancer, and moral evil proceeds from the will of a human or other intelligent being. But if one reflects seriously upon the concept of the God, the distinction fades, for God is a sentient being inflicting suffering upon other sentient beings. You suffer if you are struck down by a wooden beam, whether the beam is a club that I wield or a roof falling on you in the course of an earthquake. It may be that the motive of God in striking you down is to make a better universe by doing away with you; it may be that my own intentions in striking you are good. But human motivations are difficult to plumb, and those of the God are impossible to discern. Natural and moral evil are two facets of the same problem.

It may also now be time for humanity to consider that its responsibilities go beyond humankind and extend to other beings as well—to animals and even to plants. What is the basis of the

would not have created anything. Since he did create (or at least maintains) something, that something must be inherently good. Two: it is the common experience of humankind that except in extreme circumstances being is preferable to nonbeing for ourselves and for our surroundings. The urge to annihilation is commonly perceived as an aberration. Aquinas observed that we hardly ever really choose nothingness—usually we do evil by seeking a good in the wrong way.

7. Erich Fromm, *The Anatomy of Human Destructiveness* (New York, 1973), pp. 9–10. Both Fromm and Rollo May have made the distinction between positive aggression, which is creative and adaptive, and wanton, destructive, aggression, which is the heart of evil. See Fromm, *passim*, and May, *Power and Innocence* (New York, 1972).

assumption that I have the right to cut down trees that were growing before I was born? What gives me the right to deprive animals who live in the forest of their sustenance? The Judeo-Christian tradition says that God gave the creatures of the world into Adam's hands for his use; but other traditions have viewed God's purposes differently. At any rate, the continued exploitation of nature by those who have ceased to believe in God or in the Book of Genesis reveals the real basis for this human "right." It is might, sheer might and might alone. Because we have the power to exploit other beings to slake our greed, we do it, and until very recently we have done it without thought or consideration. It may be that there is virtue in the Hindu principle of *ahimsa*, respect for every living being, for every creature that can feel. Richard Taylor writes:

What but a narrow and exclusive regard for themselves and a slavish worship for rational nature would ever have led moralists to think otherwise? That men are the only beings who are capable of reason is perhaps true, but they are surely not the only things that suffer. . . . The heart is no less evil that takes delight in the suffering of a cat, than one that extracts similar delight from the sufferings of men.[8]

Whether or not you are fond of cats, your sense of evil is aroused by an account such as this:

A group of boys, wandering aimlessly about in search of amusement, found a dirty and emaciated old cat asleep in a barn. One of the boys was sent off with a tin can for some kerosene while the others tied the cat up in a bag and sat around waiting. The kerosene finally supplied, it was sprinkled liberally over the squirming animal, precautions being taken not to get any into its face and eyes, and then a match was applied to the tail. The effect was spectacular: a howling torch, streaking over the field, culminating in a series of wild gyrations and leaps, and finally into a twitching mass whose insides burst forth in wet sputters, the eyes bulging to the size and brilliance of agates.[9]

A new machine has been invented for killing trees, a "harvester [that] grabs each tree with huge steel hands and pulls it

8. *Good and Evil* (New York, 1970), pp. 215–217. See also Peter Tompkins and Christopher Bird, *The Secret Life of Plants* (New York, 1973).
9. Taylor, p. 207.

from the soil like a carrot."[10] The Judeo-Christian ethic cut man and God off from nature; modern materialism has now compounded the problem by eliminating God and leaving man entirely alone.

To trees and to cattle it is humanity, not nature, that is red in tooth and claw. Perhaps we might consider whether the denaturing of nature is as great a violence as the dehumanization of human beings. And indeed whether it encourages it. We have made the universe so much an *It* that we reduce people to the status of an *It* as well. The essence of evil remains deliberate violence done to a being that can feel pain.

Of all evils, the calm, institutionalized evils are the worst. In *The Exorcist*, William Blatty presents a Devil who is stupid enough to choose to possess a little girl rather than a national government, which would enable him to do much greater harm to the world.[11] Everyone knows the strikingly impersonal and bureaucratized form that the Nazi death camps took. A more recent example is provided by the military government of Chile, where a torturer and his victim enjoyed the following conversation:

"If you ever find me outside, Giorgio," the torturer asked, "what will you do to me?" Solimano said he would do nothing—he was a doctor, he helped people. The torturer responded: "Don't you see? This is a profession, just like yours."[12]

What is the cause of evil? One answer, recently popular, is that it is genetic. Simply stated, this argument asserts that the violence of mankind springs from our animal nature. Like other animals, primitive humans had to struggle endlessly against an indifferent or hostile environment, and the merciless habits learned during those long eons, now veneered only thinly by civilization, frequently and easily burst forth destructively from beneath their tenuous covering. This unconscious, "genotypal"

10. John Dillin, The Christian Science Monitor News Service, December 22, 1974.

11. See the critique by Richard Woods, *The Devil* (Chicago, 1974), pp. 111, 120.

12. Anthony Lewis, column, *New York Times*, January 27, 1975.

aggressiveness is universal and powerful enough to destroy us completely when coupled with runaway technology.[13] The tendency of much recent research has been to place more weight upon the genetic and less upon the social. Yet there is no convincing evidence that any somatically rooted instinct is the cause of spontaneous destructive aggression in man. Even if such evidence existed, it would not explain the human violence and evil that go well beyond the bounds of defense of life or territory. Nor would it explain the range of different forms that evil takes in different circumstances. Genetics can offer explanations of certain problems within the limitations imposed by the framework of biological science, and in so doing it contributes to our total understanding of evil. But genetics cannot deal with the many aspects of evil that lie beyond its competence; much less can geneticists maintain that only their own explanations can enlighten.

The great opponents of the genetic argument (the argument from "nature") are the proponents of "nurture," who argue from a behaviorist or behaviorist/sociological point of view. (I do not of course mean to imply that all sociologists are behaviorists.) Briefly stated in its strong form, the argument is that your surroundings—family, peers, institutional and cultural environment, and so on—determine your behavior. The familiar popularization of the position is the statement that society, not the individual, produces evil.[14] The sociological approach of

13. This is a highly simplified summary of views expressed by Konrad Lorenz, *Das sogennante Böse—zur Naturgeschichte der Aggression* (Vienna, 1963), translated as *On Aggression* (New York, 1966); Robert Ardrey, *African Genesis* (New York, 1961); Ardrey, *The Territorial Imperative* (New York, 1966); and Desmond Morris, *The Naked Ape* (New York, 1967). For some opposing views see Hannah Arendt, *On Violence* (New York, 1970), especially pp. 62–65; M. F. Ashley Montagu, ed., *Man and Aggression* (New York, 1968; and Fromm, *The Anatomy of Human Destructiveness*. In my view, Fromm effectively destroys the genetic argument.

14. The behaviorist position is stated most strongly by B. F. Skinner, *Beyond Freedom and Dignity* (New York, 1971), and *Walden Two* (New York, 1948). Some excellent discussions of evil from a sociological point of view are in Nevitt Sanford and Craig Comstock, *Sanctions for Evil* (San Francisco, 1971); J. Glenn Gray, *The Warriors* (New York, 1969); and Kai Erikson, *Wayward Puritans: A Study in the Sociology of Deviance* (New York, 1966). In a brilliant

course offers explanations of group and societal evil as well as of individual evil. Some conditions are more conducive to violence than others. A social order "seized by convulsive change, dislocation of values, and spiritual uncertainty, inevitably invites" the kind of alienation that produces evil.[15] Apart from behaviorism, the sociological explanations of evil from "nurture," within the limitations of the conceptual framework of their own discipline, add to our understanding.

But the orthodox, Skinnerian behaviorists, like the orthodox proponents of the genetic argument, not only obscure the problem with their dogmatic reductionism but threaten through social engineering to do great practical harm to human society. Both the biological and the behaviorist arguments tend to obscure the most important element in the discussion. That is the specifically human element, the element of responsibility, freedom, and consciousness (and even dignity). Skinner, for example, has never responded successfully to criticism that he is incapable of providing any basis for values that is not arbitrary. In *Walden Two*, the leader of the commune, Frazier, calls for "positive reinforcement" to shape human behavior, a position that Skinner had not modified twenty-three years later in *Beyond Freedom and Dignity*. But who is to determine the values toward which human behavior is to be shaped? Adolf Eichmann was in his day positively reinforced by his government for killing Jews. Skinner admits that this problem exists—he could hardly fail to do so—and comments that "the problem is to free man, not from control, but from certain kinds of control."[16] But which kinds? Skinner dodges the question, asserting that man, though lacking an ethical sense, has somehow generated "a moral or ethical social environment."[17] How this could occur within the framework of Skinner's system is inex-

novel, *This Perfect Day* (New York, 1970), Ira Levin ironically and effectively disposes of Skinner's *Walden Two* behaviorism; and Erich Fromm destroys the argument from "nurture" as completely as he does the argument from "nature."

15. Robert A. Nisbet, ed., *The Sociological Tradition* (New York, 1966), p. 264.

16. Skinner, *Beyond Freedom*, p. 41.   17. *Ibid.*, p. 175.

plicable. The only answer that the system can ultimately provide is: that is undesirable which Skinner finds undesirable. The psychology professor has become God. And then has abdicated, for nowhere in either *Walden Two* or *Beyond Freedom and Dignity* does Skinner ever show what humanity's happiness, ultimate concern, or fundamental nature either is or ought to be. The claim of Skinner to divinity is clear enough in *Walden Two:* Frazier and the "Planners" have the power to accept into the community those they wish, to drive out those whom they do not wish, and to decide what activities are permitted within the commune and what are not. The assumption is made that the Leader (whether singular or plural, and whatever his or their identity) has the values and the right to impose them. The people can scarcely criticize them, since in a world without objective values absolutely no criteria remain by which to judge the values of the Leader. And, in a world without objective values, the values of the Leader can themselves be only arbitrary.[18] With behaviorism, you are beyond freedom and dignity, beyond good and evil, beyond pain and joy, beyond love and compassion, beyond originality and creativity, beyond humanity. My own assumption is that man has freedom, dignity, and responsibility.

A third approach to the problem of evil is that of humanistic psychology, the systems of those psychologists such as Freud, Jung, and Frankl who have insisted upon the necessity of taking the psyche, both conscious and unconscious, as real. To agree, one does not have to insist that mind is separate from brain and body—few people would so argue today—but rather to acknowledge that the ideas and feelings of the mind are what we experience directly and so are in a sense the only things we really know. The mind therefore has for our purposes as human beings an independence and a freedom beyond the boundaries set by the genetic or the behaviorist determinists.

The most eloquent recent defense of this position is Erich Fromm's *Anatomy of Human Destructiveness*. Fromm begins by

18. Skinner, *Walden Two*, esp. pp. 233, 249, 268–296.

rejecting both the argument from "nature" and the argument from "nurture." He distinguishes between "biologically adaptive aggression," which may be the result of instinct (the simplest example is a blow you strike to ward off a mugger), and "destructiveness and cruelty." The aim of the one is to protect; the aim of the other is to destroy. Fromm argues that destructiveness is "character-rooted." Genetic traits and environmental problems may promote, but they are not the sufficient cause of, destructiveness. He argues that there are basic human needs that one is free to respond to in a positive or in a negative way. The need for an object of devotion may result in the imitation either of Albert Schweitzer or of Adolf Hitler; the need for relatedness may be met either by love or by sadism, the need for stimulation and excitement either by creativity or by mindless pursuit of pleasures. If a person responds to these needs too often in a negative way, a negative syndrome is formed that may release itself in vengeance, "sadism" (the drive for total power over others), or "necrophilia" (the wish to reduce everything to the dead, the mechanical, the inert).

Other humanistic psychologists have approached evil differently. C. G. Jung and Erich Neumann, for example, argue that repression (as opposed to conscious suppression) of destructive feelings gradually creates a "shadow," a negative force in the personality that can burst out destructively without warning. I anger you and you want to hit me in the face. You may recognize that urge and decide not to act upon it. That is conscious suppression. Or you may refuse to recognize the urge, insisting that you are too nice a person to feel that way. That is unconscious repression. The feelings you repress do not disappear but are locked into the unconscious, where they may add to your hatred of yourself, producing ulcers or other such symptoms, or they may cause you to project your own repressed hostilities onto others. "The more [a person] represses his shadow, the blacker and denser the shadow becomes," says Moreno. And Solzhenitsyn says: "In keeping silent about evil, in burying it so deep within us that no sign of it appears on the surface, we are implanting it, and it will rise up a thousandfold in the future."[19]

It is the perspective of depth psychology, especially that of Jung, that is most suggestive in understanding the Devil. The Jungian psychic process is the process of individuation. In the beginning a person has only a chaotic, undifferentiated view of himself. As he develops, his good and evil sides are gradually differentiated one from the other. Ordinarily he represses the evil side, causing the growth of a shadow in his unconscious. If the repression mechanisms are too strong, his shadow will become monstrous and may eventually burst out and overwhelm him. In healthy people there is a third stage, the stage of integration, in which the good and evil sides are both recognized and then reintegrated on a conscious level.[20]

This three-stage development in the human psyche may produce a similar three-stage development of the human perception of the God himself. In other words, the God may appear at first undifferentiated. In the second stage, the benevolent Lord and the evil Devil are increasingly separated and the evil Devil repressed and banished. A third stage, which has yet to manifest itself clearly in the history of the concept, would be the integration of the Lord and the Devil. Jung expressed his belief in such a process in the deity in his "seven sermons to the dead": "Abraxas speaketh that hallowed and accursed word which is life and death at the same time. Abraxas begetteth truth and lying, good and evil, light and darkness in the same word and in the same act. Wherefore is Abraxas terrible."[21]

The study of the Devil indicates that historically, he is a

19. Antonio Moreno, *Jung, Gods, and Modern Man* (Notre Dame, 1970), p. 41; Solzhenitsyn, p. 178; See also Carl G. Jung, "Good and Evil in Analytical Psychology," in his *Civilization in Transition*, 2d ed. (Princeton, 1970); The Jung Institute, *Evil* (Evanston, Ill., 1967); Erich Neumann, *Depth Psychology and a New Ethic* (New York, 1969); Viktor Frankl, *Man's Search for Meaning* (New York, 1959). The variety of humanistic psychology is very great and permits only the briefest glance here.

20. See Hermann Hesse, *Demian* (New York, 1965), and "The Stranger" motif in Flannery O'Connor, *The Violent Bear It Away* (New York, 1955).

21. C. G. Jung, *Septem Sermones ad Mortuos* (London, 1925), pp. 17–24.

manifestation of the divine, a part of the deity. *Sine diabolo nullus Deus.* Yet, morally, his work is completely and utterly to be rejected. The paradox can be resolved in only one way: evil will be absorbed and controlled when it is integrated, and it will be integrated when it is fully recognized and understood. Not by *repression*, which only increases the shadow in the unconscious, but by conscious *suppression* of the evil elements that we have recognized in ourselves, will that element of the divine we call the Devil be brought out of chaos and out of opposition into order and under control. [22]

Older though still current interpretations of the origins of evil are well known. In much Christian and Buddhist thought, evil is nothingness, an absence of good. Another Christian explanation of evil is that it is the result of original sin and thus ultimately traceable to free will. Yet another, monism, insists that apparent evil is part of a greater good that lies beyond the power of poor mortals to perceive. Dualism posits two opposite principles of good and evil, attributing evil to the will of a malign spirit.

How and why is evil personified? The most basic answer is that it is personified because we feel it as a deliberate malignancy that intrudes upon us from outside ourselves. Not surprisingly, in view of the horrors that the twentieth century has produced, belief in the Devil, after a long lapse, is rapidly reappearing. A survey completed in 1974 indicated that in the United States positive belief in the Devil had risen since 1965 from 37 percent to 48 percent, with another 20 percent considering his existence probable. [23] Whether one perceives the Devil as a supernatural being, or as an uncontrollable force arising in the unconscious, or as an absolute aspect of human nature is less important than the essence of the perception, which is that we are threatened by alien and hostile powers. "Evil is ter-

22. Thus advocacy of the abolition of the Devil goes against the thrust of the historical tradition. On the other hand worship of the Devil is in no way justified by historical tradition.

23. Clyde Nunn, "The Rising Credibility of the Devil in America," *Listening*, 9 (1974), 84–98.

Concentration camp victim, Europe, 1945. The truest picture of the Devil may be the effect of human cruelty and indifference. Courtesy Department of Defense, Washington.

ribly real for each and every individual," Jung said. "If you regard the principle of evil as a reality you can just as well call it the devil."[24]

I had better clarify immediately a difficulty in terminology. There is danger of identifying the Devil exclusively with the Judeo-Christian Satan. Conceptually, Satan is one manifestation of the Devil, not the Devil par essence. Similarly, the Judeo-Christian Yahweh is to be considered historically as one

24. Jung, "Good and Evil," p. 465. See also Jung, "Psychological Aspects of the Mother Archetype," in his *Four Archetypes* (Princeton, 1970), pp. 37, 39.

manifestation of the High God. To minimize this difficulty, I use the term "the God" for the High God—the divine principle—and "god" for the lesser gods. I avoid "God" owing to its inevitable associations with Yahweh. I use the term "the Devil," as opposed to Satan, to designate the personification of evil found in a variety of cultures. I also use the pronoun "he" for convenience in referring to both the God and the Devil, but this is not intended to restrict either to the male sex.

The Devil is the hypostasis, the apotheosis, the objectification of a hostile force or hostile forces perceived as external to our consciousness. These forces, over which we appear to have no conscious control, inspire the religious feelings of awe, dread, fear, and horror. The Devil is as much a manifestation of the religious sense as are the gods. Indeed, the emotions evoked by the experience of the Devil are at least as great as those evoked by the experience of a good god. "Evil is supremely the crucial experience of the sacred."[25] But unlike the Judeo-Christian God (as he has developed), the Devil personifies deliberate destructiveness. Sometimes such malice is ascribed to the High God or the other heavenly gods; sometimes it is ascribed to the lower, or chthonic deities; sometimes it is deemed the work of lesser spirits. The Fourth Lateran Council of 1215 referred to *diabolus et alii daemones:* the Devil and the other demons. These distinctions occasionally illuminate, but are not central to, the development of the personification of absolute evil.[26] I call this personification "the Devil,"

25. Paul Ricoeur, *The Symbolism of Evil* (New York, 1967), p. 9.
26. The terms "devil," "divine," and "demon" are totally unrelated etymologically. "Divine" comes from the Indo-European root *deiw*, meaning "sky," "heaven," or "god," a root that yields the *daevas* of Iran and the *devas* of India, and Latin *divus*. "Devil" derives, as do the cognates German *Teufel* and Dutch *duivel*, from the Latin *diabolus*, which also yields the Romance *diable*, *diablo*, and *diavolo*. The Latin is in turn derived from the late Greek *diabolos*, "slanderer," or "accuser," from *diaballein*, "to slander." The root meaning of *diaballein* is to "throw across," hence "to oppose," and its ultimate derivation is from the Indo-European root *gwel*, "to fly." "Demon" derives from the Greek *daimonion*, "evil spirit," from earlier *daimōn*, which in turn derives from *daiomai*, "to divide." Originally, in Greece a *daimōn* could be either benevolent or malevolent, and Homer uses the term *daimones* as the equivalent of "gods."

even though, in different times and societies, his name, gender, and number vary. I deal with the Devil in both of his fundamental roles, which, though related, are distinct: he is the font and origin of all evil; and he is the very essence of evil. As one sees how societies define evil and explain its origins, one also sees how they limn the portrait of the Devil.

The Devil, therefore, is no quaint or outmoded figure, but a phenomenon of enormous and perennial power in, or over, the human spirit. It may be that the growth of interest and belief in the Devil today marks a growing perception of the reality that is evil. "The profoundly religious outrage of some segments of the young against what they take to be the moral abuses of the adult society is based on the implicit assumption that there is not only evil in the world but sinfulness. Why else be angry at a man for doing evil unless you think he is responsible for his evil?"[27] The Devil is very much alive in the sufferings of the world today. And when these evils are past, there will be others, and then still others, each a wanton infliction of pain, each in itself an absolute, each demanding our attention. By understanding the principle behind these evils, by coming to know the Devil better, we can better understand—and combat—the evil that confronts each of us as individuals.

I have deliberately attempted to avoid the treacherous complexities of moral philosophy. Rationalizations are endless. Perhaps even the Devil has persuaded himself that he is doing the right thing.

27. Andrew M. Greeley, *Unsecular Man* (New York, 1972), p. 212.

2 In Search of the Devil

> But I have still not made the link between scientific hypothesis
> and the void which Jehovah lays before me.
> —Axel Lund, in Henrietta Buckmaster,
> *Wait Until Evening*

The Devil, then, is the personification of evil.[1] But what
does this mean? Who, or what, really is the Devil? An honest
response demands a clarification of intent and methodology.
Serious historical studies of the Devil have been very few, considering the importance of the topic. Gustav Roskoff's work is
good but over a century old; the only recent studies of great
value are Henry Ansgar Kelly, *The Devil, Demonology, and
Witchcraft*, Richard Woods, *The Devil*, and Herbert Haag, *Teufelsglaube*. My own account of the Devil is a work of history, not
of psychology, anthropology, or theology.

What, really, is the Devil? This is comparable to the question: What, really, is art? Absolute answers to such questions
are not obtainable. You can respond to the question"What is
art?" in a number of ways. You can refuse to define art at all.
You can define it in relative terms: art is to each person what
each person thinks it is. Or you can pursue a definition through
linguistic analysis. Rather, I choose the method of the history
of concepts, which is aimed at historical truth.

What is truth? Philosophers still carry on a hoary epis-
temological dispute as to whether we can have knowledge of

1. Generally, the Devil can be regarded as the personification of the origin
and essence of evil, but there are exceptions. In Thomistic theology, for example, evil has no ontological being and can therefore strictly speaking have
no essence.

things in themselves, of objective truth. The dispute may never be resolved. In the meantime, it is possible, and perhaps desirable, to emphasize understanding more than metaphysical truth. Understanding is not an accretion of external information but an assimilation or integration of knowledge into your experience as a human being. Know thyself—for if thou knowest not thyself, thou canst not know any thing. The Devil is understood, and ultimately confronted and defeated, as he is integrated into our experience as individuals.

Certainty cannot in this life be obtained on any level beyond the tautological. But we can obtain knowledge, if knowledge is perceived as integration and understanding, by means of a variety of angles of vision or thought structures. Each thought structure, or truth system, is an instrument through which the world can be understood and integrated. All truth systems are precarious, subject to judgment, change, or rejection. Perceptions of reality are multiple, and truth systems are multiple. Multiplicity produces a view of the world that is rich and broad.

This attitude toward truth means the rejection of all reductionism. There is not one system, but many. No one truth system can exhaust knowledge of a phenomenon. In the experience of humanity, a number of systems have laid claim to universality. All such claims, including the most current, scientism, are specious. No system is absolute. Indeed, every system develops and changes in time, as has recently been shown for science by Thomas Kuhn, Stephen Toulmin, and June Goodfield.[2] Among the systems that exist today are science, myth, poetry, mathematics, and history. They are multiple realities, subuniverses. To shutter oneself up in any one of them is to blind oneself to the disturbing but beautifully complex riot of reality.[3] And to the question which truth system is "best," there is

2. Thomas Kuhn, *The Structure of Scientific Revolutions* (Chicago, 1962); Stephen Toulmin and June Goodfield, *The Discovery of Time* (New York, 1965).
3. William James used the term "sub-universe;" Alfred Schutz "multiple realities." See also Philip Wheelwright, *The Burning Fountain* (Bloomington, Ind., 1954), esp. pp. 23–24, 56–72, 148. "To be conscious is not just to be; it is to mean, to intend, to point beyond ourself, to testify that some kind of

really no answer, unless it is that the best is the one most open and inclusive of most options. The approach I adopt is intended to embrace many approaches to the understanding of evil in terms of one valid truth system, the historical.

Just as a number of truth systems exist, a number of methods are appropriate to each. A method is a means of understanding within a truth system. There are, for example, a number of different methods of understanding history. Some methods are better than others in general; some are clearly better than others for solving particular problems.

History has these characteristics: (1) It strives for a sense of the individual reality of the person or event, a perception of the person or event as it was/is in life. History does not exclude—indeed it embraces and uses—studies of classes and movements, but its goal is always the understanding of the individual. In this way history is transcendent, almost religious. Through it we encounter individuals of the past much as we encounter individuals today, as living beings with their own hopes and fears, thoughts and feelings. And with their own open options. History does not treat a past action as if it were a dry brick designed for use in an eternally determined structure. It recognizes that the individual has a complex and ambivalent set of thoughts and feelings, and it attempts to feel with him how he made one choice and not others. History always is concerned with the living mind. (2) History does not design static systems, but dynamic ones. It deals with changes through time. Therefore narrative is the necessary and proper vehicle for the historian as opposed to the social scientist. The historian always explains condition C as having arisen from A through B.[4] (3)

---

beyond exists, and to be ever on the verge of entering into it although never in the state of having fully entered. The existential structure of human life is radically, irreducibly liminal. That is why there can be no science of man" (Wheelwright, p. 18). See also Rudolf Anthes, "Mythology in Ancient Egypt," in Samuel Noah Kramer, ed., *Mythologies of the Ancient World* (New York, 1961), p. 23. The truth of a symbol cannot possibly be judged by reason. A mythological concept is true if it makes something of the divine world conceivable in human terms.

4. See Arthur C. Danto, *The Analytical Philosophy of History*, 2d ed. (Cambridge, 1968).

Alchemical androgyne, Germany, fifteenth century. Some modern psychologists and mythographers see in the ideas of classical alchemy a deep and subtle understanding of the mind. This alchemical figure represents the coincidence of opposites, mental integration. The androgynous figure stands upon an ouroboros, symbol of the identity of end and beginning. Courtesy Germanisches Nationalmuseum, Nuremberg.

History is never impersonal but always humane, asking questions important to the human condition and to the historian himself. History is more than a game; it is the historian's life. Above all, it is aimed at integration of thought and feeling, of conscious and unconscious, of past and present, of disciplines and of modes of thought. Historical "understanding is not reconstruction, but integration. . . . The event of understanding alters what one was—which is to say, the interpreter genuinely *learns* something and does not remain inflexibly the same. . . . [Thus] the past can . . . have a truly persuasive power in the phenomenon of understanding."[5] (4) History is ironic: it puts a distance between the observer and the culture in which he lives, enabling him to broaden the spectrum of his options and to integrate the thoughts of the past into the present. (5) History is moral: it recognizes that our commitment to other men and women does not cease when they die. To the victims of Vietnam, of Dachau, even of Ashurnasirpal II, we have a duty that is not lessened at a distance of ten thousand miles or of three thousand years.

These are the general characteristics of historical thought as I understand it. Within these lines exist methodological options. The approach I adopt may be termed the history of concepts. I believe this method produces an understanding of the Devil that is coherent. Further, its value is greater than a number of other methods in that it encompasses and integrates the truths of myth, theology, literature, and art, and therefore transcends them. It looks at a concept "undergoing over long periods of time a necessary sequence of unfolding, self-realizing stages of development."[6]

The history of religions has been dominated lately by a number of nonhistorical approaches. It is frequently perceived in terms of comparative religions or typology, of Jungian arche-

---

5. David E. Linge, "Dilthey and Gadamer: Two Theories of Historical Understanding," *Journal of the American Academy of Religion*, 41 (1973), 536–553. The quotations are from Linge's interpretation of Gadamer, pp. 547–550.
6. Robert A. Nisbet, *Social Change and History* (London, 1969), p. 64.

types, of phenomenology, or of structuralism. Functionalism and, even more, the sociology of knowledge have begun to offer alternatives to these nonhistorical ideas currently in possession of history. The history of concepts, which I propose here, utilizes insights drawn from typology and sociology as well as from the older tradition of the history of ideas.[7] But it is in-

7. Functionalism is the effort to understand ideas in terms of the function they serve in a given society. Closely related is the historical sociology of knowledge, which also perceives ideas as arising out of social structure and which uses ideas to help understand the social structure. These methods supply valuable information to the historian of concepts but have for him the shortcoming that they do not ultimately take ideas seriously. Structuralism, made influential by Claude Lévi-Strauss and extended into historical thought by Michel Foucault and into the history of religions by Georges Dumézil, seeks to abstract from the diverse ways of doing a thing the *structure* of the ways of doing a thing. The structure is the reality and reveals the hidden meaning, the secret code, that underlies the apparent diversity of activity. Structuralism defines a totality—cooking, for example—and refuses to treat the elements individually. The meaning of cooking in a given society is the structure of relationship among the various customs, procedures, and tastes in cooking. Structuralism is deliberately a-individual, reducing the reality of the individual, and a-historical, because it analyzes structures in discontinuous succession and does not treat development through time. See the criticisms of Lévi-Strauss by G. S. Kirk, *Myth: Its Meaning and Functions in Ancient and Other Cultures* (Cambridge, 1970) and Peter Munz, *When the Golden Bough Breaks* (London, 1973), which help offset the foolish suggestion of an anonymous reviewer in *The Times Literary Supplement* that Lévi-Strauss's work constitutes a Copernican Revolution so that one is no longer entitled to interpret myth in other than a structuralist fashion. The point is that no truth system, however impressive, excludes other truth systems. Precisely the greatest value of structuralism is its ability to include a variety of systems.

Typology is used by comparatists—in comparative literature or comparative religion, for example. It categorizes concepts apart from their origin in time, place, or culture, and so is also explicitly nonhistorical. The history of ideas, a method constructed by Arthur O. Lovejoy and his followers, emphasized the development of intellectual constructs, sometimes apart from social conditions. For a critique of Lovejoy, see Philip P. Wiener, "Some Problems and Methods in the History of Ideas," *Journal of the History of Ideas*, 22 (1961), 531–548. The insights of Jungian psychology are especially helpful in understanding the history of concepts. "The aim of Jungian therapy is a restructuring of the self by the activating power of the symbolic, which leads to integration and 'individuation.' . . . The most critical phase of the process of transformation is what Jung calls the 'meeting' with the shadow; that is, a recognition in oneself of the instinctual, irrational, primitive, violent side of one's own nature. The integrative aim is not only to recognize this but to accept it,

dependent of, and different from, all of them. The history of concepts has a double purpose: to understand the process by which concepts develop; and to understand (even "define") the concepts themselves. This method assumes that concepts are real and important in themselves: as Epictetus observed, what disturbs men's minds is not events, but their judgments on events. The method is similar to the traditional history of ideas, but it differs in two ways. First, it draws upon social history, recognizing the truth of Mannheim's statement that knowledge is always held from a certain position. Concepts develop along lines partially determined by social conditions. Second and more important, it attempts to integrate the study of "high" thought with "low" thought, theology and philosophy with myth and art, the products of the unconscious with those of the conscious. It refuses, for example, to generalize about the idea of the Devil held in thirteenth-century France on the evidence of theologians alone, or on the evidence of popular legend alone. Rather, it takes the two together, recognizing the distinctions between them. A concept, then, is different from an idea in that (1) it is socially and culturally more broadly based, and (2) it includes psychological levels deeper than the rational.[8]

What is a concept? A concept is *not* a metaphysical, objective, substantial, Platonic idea. There may or may not be in objective reality a being corresponding to the concept of the Devil. If there is, knowledge of it is impossible to attain. Even if one reports a direct vision of the Devil—as Luther saw him lurking in the corner—the one perceiving assimilates that vision and transmits it to others in terms of his own psychological and social milieu. I intend to make no metaphysical statement about the Devil, no claim to what he may "really" be beyond human

neither suppressing [*sic*: read 'repressing'] it nor succumbing to it; it is thus transformed from a sinister and alien-seeming force into a helpful partner of psychic life": John Halverson, "Dynamics of Exorcism: the Sinhalese Sanniyakuma," *History of Religions*, 10 (1970), 334.

8. But it is hardly ever possible to obtain evidence of the thought of the illiterate (especially before the nineteenth century), except as filtered through the minds of the literate. The invention of oral records in the twentieth century has somewhat changed this situation.

perceptions of him. Often for the sake of simplicity and style I will speak of the Devil as changing or developing. Always what I mean is not the Devil *sub specie eternitatis* but the Devil as perceived by the human mind.

I assert the reality of the Devil, but by this I do not intend a judgment as to the metaphysical reality of such a being. "Reality is not a given fact, but a construction. . . . If men define their situations as real, they are real in their consequences."[9] In a moment I shall say that the Devil *is* the concept of the Devil. By that I do not mean to insist that the Devil is *no more than* his concept. He may or may not be. The only reality we can know is that of phenomena—mental constructs—and that knowledge is sure knowledge. The Devil is a real phenomenon; therefore, the Devil is real.

A concept, then, is what it has been thought to be. Art is what it has been thought to be. Democracy is what it has been thought to be. The Devil is what he has been thought to be. But if a concept is *all* that it has ever been thought to be, it is incoherent, chaotic, and unhelpful to understanding. Consequently this definition has to be refined. A concept consists of the *tradition* of the views of what it is. Eccentric positions that neither spring from, nor give rise to, general perceptions, that never receive any public validation, are of no consequence. If you describe a cat as a pachyderm with wings, your idea is not helpful in understanding cats. Only ideas that have achieved sufficient public validation, either at the time they were propounded or later, are significant. These ideas make up a tradition that, although it has many variants and encompasses many debates and oppositions, can be followed and discussed at least in its general outline. The Devil is what his concept is, and his concept is the tradition of human views about him.

Two fundamental questions about concepts remain: how are they described, and how are they formed? How is a concept described? A spectrum of concepts exists, ranging from the

9. Richard Woods, *The Devil* (Chicago, 1974), p. 55. See the similar position taken by Howard Kaminsky, "The Problem of Explanation," in Sylvia Thrupp, ed., *Millennial Dreams in Action* (The Hague, 1962).

most concrete and easily defined to the most abstract and least easily defined. On this spectrum we may place, as examples, cat, Panama, Devil, Democracy. *Cat* is a concrete concept about which reasonable men and women have been in general agreement. *Panama* is an abstraction, but it is specific enough to have commanded considerable agreement. *Devil* is a concept in part concrete and in part abstract. Opinions about the Devil have differed, and the concept is difficult, but still possible, to define historically. *Democracy* is an abstraction about which there has been great disagreement. It is a term with very fuzzy borders. I do not know whether it is possible to define the concept of democracy.

In terms of the history of concepts, then, the Devil exists (there is a concept "Devil"). "Cat" exists (there is a concept "cat"), but "cat" exists to a degree, or in a way, that "Devil" does not. The great majority of men and women have had direct perception of a cat, and the great majority of reasonable men and women have been and are in very close agreement as to what a cat is. But perceptions of the Devil have usually been more indirect than that of Luther with his inkwell. There is not and never has been close agreement among reasonable men and women as to what the Devil is. The cat therefore is accessible to more truth systems than is the Devil: there are more ways of skinning a cat than ways of skinning the Devil. Science, for example, can investigate cats, but it cannot investigate Devils.

It follows that there is a particular point in examining a difficult concept like the Devil historically. What a cat is can be determined in other and more satisfactory ways. But there is no better way of examining what the Devil is. The history of concepts integrates the theology, philosophy, mythology, art, literature, and popular legend of the Devil. It uses multiple angles of vision. Therefore the truth about the Devil discerned by the history of concepts is not merely valid within the limits of the method of history of concepts, but *transcends* it. The truth about the Devil established by the history of concepts is the best way to approach the understanding of the Devil. We can know, not the Devil himself, but only human perceptions of the Devil.

Head of Dionysos, Roman copy of Hellenistic original. The ambivalence of the deity is not merely a conjunction of cruelty and love. Here the god is androgynous, combining the most beautiful of masculine and feminine features. Courtesy Trustees of the British Museum.

This does not dilute the horror: "the Fiend in his own shape is less hideous than when he rages in the heart of man." [10]

To summarize the argument so far: (1) There is no objective definition of the Devil. (2) The Devil can be defined historically. (3) The Devil's historical definition can be obtained with reference to definitions of evil that are themselves existential. (4) The Devil is the personification of whatever is perceived in society as evil. (5) The concept of the Devil consists of the tradition(s) of perceptions of this personification.

But how is a concept formed? How does the concept of the Devil come to be? Each person is confronted in his own life with manifestations of powerful destructive forces both outside him and within him. He senses and refers them to his mind. This process may be called a perception. Each person inherits a highly differentiated brain whose structure is genetically determined. The brain imparts structures to the mind, which proceeds from the brain. These universal and inherited patterns constitute the structure of the unconscious. These structures are common to all people and to all peoples, although they are modified by individual experience and social environment, and thus the perception is expressed in symbols recognizable to others.

The work of Jung and Lévi-Strauss constitutes "an effort to elucidate the unconscious structure underlying conscious reality." [11] Jung called these structures archetypes. In his earlier

10. Nathaniel Hawthorne, "Young Goodman Brown." The position I take is similar to some varieties of phenomenology. Edmund Husserl distinguished between the *noesis*, the act of perceiving the sun, and the *noema*, the sun as seen. The phenomenon that we can and do know is neither of these, but rather the "reflected-on," the tension between noesis and noema, *the seeing of the sun as seen*. The synthesis of my perception of the Devil with the tradition of the Devil constitutes my knowledge of the Devil. I have been asked whether I would apply the same method in elucidating the concept of God. The answer of course is yes, though "God" is a more complicated concept than "Devil." I do not presume to know anything about God himself, but there is no reason why a history of God in the sense of a history of the concept of God cannot be written. Indeed, historians of religions have long been about such a program in one way or another.

11. John Raphael Staude, "Psyche and Society: Freud, Jung and Lévi-Strauss from Depth Psychology to Depth Sociology," *Theory and Society*, 3 (1976), 303.

work he conceived of archetypes in terms of images; later he thought of them more in terms of structures. Jung was more concerned with the *content* of the archetypes; Lévi-Strauss is more interested in the *form* of the structures. Here I am concerned with content more than with structures and so stand closer to the position of depth psychology than to that of structuralism.[12]

The basic building block of the concept, then, is the individual perception (P) of an individual event (e). That perception is rooted both in the external event and in the underlying structures of the mind (s). You hit me in the face—the external event—and my perception of (and reaction to) the blow is determined by the structures of my mind: $s + e = P$.

An individual will have many perceptions of evil in the course of his life. Each is rooted in the same interaction of event and structure, with the addition that each new P is in part formed by the previous bank of perceptions (P_n). Each new perception modifies or reinforces the bank of perceptions he already has. The perceptions of an individual combine over the years in a set or bank to create a general formulation (F) of evil in the mind, $P_n \longrightarrow F$. He formulates this general notion in terms acceptable to his personal psychology and his social environment—in myth, for example, in poetry, in painting, in moral theology, or in sociology.

Perceptions of evil often generate a sense that there is a pattern, or unity, in evil, and this may give rise to a personification of evil. Often, especially in modern empirical societies, a full personification of evil does not emerge. It does in most societies, for the reason that evil is felt as coming from without,

12. "Like Freud and Jung, Lévi-Strauss began from the conviction that cultural and mental phenomena obeyed an immanent and universal law. His task was to discern and describe this natural and universal order of the human mind, an order that transcended and cut across all class, generational, social, and cultural differences": Staude. It is possible that structuralism may end by providing the framework within which many truth systems can be fitted. The theory of the unconscious goes back beyond Freud, of course: see Henri Ellenberger, *The Discovery of the Unconscious* (New York, 1970). It was left to Freud, beginning with *The Interpretation of Dreams* in 1900, to present it in a highly developed and eventually persuasive form.

from outside the conscious mind. Personifications of evil arising spontaneously in the individual mind are usually rather vague; it is in the course of exchanging perceptions and formulations with other people that the personification becomes more explicit.

When you communicate your formulations and perceptions to other people, interactions occur, and gradually a constellation of formulations arises (C), an area of common agreement. $F_n \longrightarrow C$.

This process is not mechanical, and it is certainly not simple. New individual perceptions are constantly occurring, lending vitality to the constellation. The process $s + e = P$ is always going on, so that new perceptions are continually entering, and new or modified formulations are being made. Further, the interchange of ideas among individuals continually produces mutual modifications, and new constellations (C_n) gradually appear. If at any time the fundamental process $s + e = P$ ceases, so that no new perceptions occur, then the concept will freeze and die; it will cease to have any real meaning for the human situation. This withering of meaning has occurred, for instance, with "The Empire," a concept that had true reference to individual perceptions from the first into the nineteenth and even the early twentieth century but has now ceased to relate to living thought. (Historians will continue to discuss the meaning of "Empire," but it is only in this secondary sense that the term retains life.)

Over a period of time the constellations of formulations (C_n) form a tradition (T). $C_n \longrightarrow T$. Not every constellation becomes part of the tradition. In order to be incorporated, a constellation must be true to type; it must not negate, though it can expand and modify, the existing tradition. Traditions gradually develop boundaries that exclude the idiosyncratic and eccentric. So long as a constellation is true to the basic perception, it cannot be in itself invalid, but if it lies beyond the lines drawn by tradition, it may remain isolated and be forgotten. A tradition changes, develops, and expands in time; it is open-ended in the direction of understanding, but its sides, as it were, are limited by consistency.

The tradition is not to be interpreted too narrowly. Elements standing on its borders may stimulate its growth, as monophysitism and nestorianism stimulated the growth of Christian doctrine. A history of the concept of the Holy Spirit, for example, would have to include the unusual positions of certain mystics and heretics as well as more conventional expressions. Yet there are positions that must be excluded if the tradition is to be coherent. You may wish to believe, for example, that "Christianity" is defined as moral behavior without reference to doctrine, but this definition cannot be accepted unless the borders of the tradition are expanded so far as to make the concept meaningless. The destruction of the meaning of a word is a serious thing: Satan has been believed to set himself the task of destroying the truth (John 8:44).

The tradition of a concept has the following characteristics: (1) It remains true to type. The tradition of the Devil remains faithful to the basic perceptions of evil as the suffering of individuals. (2) The tradition develops in time. While remaining true to type, it will grow complex, often producing a marvelous variety and richness of texture. (3) At first the tradition will expand its borders, embracing a wide variety of ideas. (4) Later, its borders will constrict, and a focus will begin to emerge. In the period before the New Testament, the concept of the Devil enjoyed a wealth of mythological, theological, and iconographical expressions; later the hammer and chisel of rational theology pared and planed the tradition. The concept is still alive and may be approaching a focus. (5) Eventually the focus is reached in one of two ways: (a) the tradition ceases altogether to respond to living perceptions; it ceases to develop. In this event it may be said to be extinct, as with the concept of "empire." Or, (b) the tradition may reach a living focus of integration, a consensus, as with the concepts "sovereignty" and "epic poetry."

How then is a concept best understood in terms of this "tradition?" I propose that a concept is *not* best understood in light of its origins, but rather in light of the direction in which the tradition is moving. To take Christianity as a notorious example: I do not believe that the truth of Christianity will best be elucidated by a search for its *origins*, but rather by an obser-

vation of its development in tradition. This approach is a rever-
sal of the assumption that has dominated Christian and much
other religious scholarship for a very long time, an assumption
characterized by the genetic fallacy: that the true meaning of a
word—or of an idea—lies in its pristine state. To quote Louis
Dupré, "The great popularity of the evolutionary idea in the bi-
ology, sociology, and philosophy of the nineteenth century has
had a strange side effect in the study of religion. For several de-
cades it was assumed without question that the truth of a religion is to be found exclusively in its origin. Thus the search
for a definition took the form of a quest for the beginning, e.g.,
the 'quest for the historical Jesus.' " [13] Rather, Christianity, or
the Constitution, or the Devil, is understood best in terms of
the direction it takes through time, that is to say, its historical
development.

In studying any tradition that has not yet reached its focus
and is still alive, we cannot know, and should not assume, what
that focus will eventually be. Hence we cannot define a living
tradition in terms of its focus. Rather we must define it in terms
of the present state of its development. One can amuse oneself
by projecting what the focus may eventually be, but any con-
fidence in one's projection would be misplaced. The Christian
tradition of the Devil, for example, may yet have any one of a
number of fates, including the following: (1) the Devil may lose
his reality; that is to say that there will cease to be personal perceptions of personified evil; (2) the Devil may become so separate from the good God that absolute dualism will result; (3) the
Devil may be reunited with the good God in a process of integration (individuation).

The concept of the Devil is thus defined in terms of the tradition of perceptions of the Devil. There are a number of traditions of the Devil, for example, the Judeo-Christian and the
Hindu-Buddhist. It is impossible to follow historically the development of more than one tradition at the same time, for historical methodology insists upon explanation of movement from

13. Louis K. Dupré, *The Other Dimension* (New York, 1972), p. 72.

A to C through *B;* it cannot offer such explanation where there is insufficient reciprocal contact among societies. Because the personification of evil was most fully developed in Judeo-Christian thought, this book is limited to the Western tradition; it deals with non-Western ideas only briefly and for purposes of comparison.[14]

The history of concepts insists that the concept is important in and of itself, not merely in terms of its function in society. The method recognizes the importance of the social milieu in shaping concepts, but its stress is upon the concept itself rather than upon the society. The history of concepts differs from the history of ideas in its concern with mythopoeic as well as rational formulations of the concept. The value of myth has only recently been re-established—by Jung, Eliade, Lévi-Strauss, and others—as a consequence of the discovery of the unconscious. The publication in 1900 of Freud's *Interpretation of Dreams* made it possible to perceive in myths and in dreams the expression of unconscious thought. Jung's theory of archetypes and Lévi-Strauss' theory of preexisting structures of the unconscious explicitly argue the constant, unchanging nature of the unconscious. For Lévi-Strauss, there is a homology of structure between myth and mind. The particular expressions of the unconscious—individual dreams or myths—may vary, but if we understand the myths or dreams, we can penetrate to their inner meaning (Jung) or structure (Lévi-Strauss). Once understanding this, one can have an *Erlebnis* (lived experience) of a past civilization, of past concepts. No history is past; all history is lived presently, and there can be no doubt of its "relevance."

14. I recognize that this is something of a *petitio principii* in the question of diffusionism. It would be presumptuous either to deny or to affirm diffusionism, but as there are other answers as to why similar ideas occur in situations isolated from one another, and since the links between East and West in such matters have not been fully established or elucidated, it would be even more dangerous to proceed on the basis of connections that have not been established.

My method, history of concepts, bears resemblance to the method of "history of traditions" used by some Biblical critics. Cf. for example Delbert R. Hillers, *Covenant: the History of a Biblical Idea* (Baltimore, 1969).

Myths are products of the unconscious refined and modified by the conscious. Since the conscious is seldom if ever aware of all that the unconscious is expressing, the mythopoeic is a larger part of human experience than the rational. As Lévi-Strauss says, most human thought is not logical but analogical, and we understand human culture best when we understand through analogy. Henri Frankfort writes that myths "are products of imagination, but they are not mere fantasy. It is essential that true myth be distinguished from legend, saga, fable, and fairy tale. . . . True myth [speaks with] compelling authority. It perpetrates the revelation of a 'Thou.' . . . It is nothing less than a carefully chosen cloak for abstract thought."[15] Richard Woods makes the point in his discussion of the Devil: "Myth is the symbolic nature of the truth of human existence. . . . Thus, although myths are not literally or scientifically true at face value, they express a more profound truth at a deeper level of human consciousness. Such is the case, I believe, with the myth of the Devil."[16]

The ability of myth to transcend rational categories is of enormous value in understanding the Devil. In rational thought good and evil appear to be mutually exclusive. "Myth, on the other hand, tries to combine the two sides of the one, seeing light in dark, good in evil, order in disorder, and some sort of higher unity. The myth attempts to get the whole picture."[17] So long as we recognize that in bringing historical criticism to the study of myth we are translating symbolic modes of thought into cognitive modes, and that this brings with it all the problems inherent in translations, then we can say that myth, more than rational speculation, provides the material from which the concept of the Devil is ultimately constructed.

15. Henri Frankfort, "Myth and Reality," in Frankfort, ed., *The Intellectual Adventure of Ancient Man* (Chicago, 1946), p. 3. The objection to materialist interpretations of religion "is not the empirical adequacy of such analyses in particular instances, but rather the generalization of them as adequate for the understanding of the phenomenon of religion": Robert N. Bellah, *Beyond Belief: Essays on Religion in a Post-Traditional World* (New York, 1970), p. 7.

16. Woods, pp. 80–81.

17. Andrew Greeley, *Unsecular Man* (New York, 1972), p. 97.

Gustave Moreau, "Zeus and Semele," c. 1870. The mortal Semele, praying for union with her beloved Zeus, is slain by his greatness. This represents the myth of divine ambivalence par excellence: the very glory of the god is death to mortals. Courtesy Musée Gustave Moreau, Paris.

The common perception of almost all mythologies is the coincidence of opposites, the ambivalence of the deity. The God is understood as light and darkness, good and evil. The gods who manifest this divinity are themselves coincidences of opposites, each god or goddess ambivalent in itself, or expressing the ambivalence by being paired with a doublet of opposite nature. Mythology understands the principle of evil as the opposite side of the principle of good, as the shadow of the God.

The history of concepts can provide (1) the best available definition of the Devil; (2) a grasp of the concept of the Devil from the inside in a way that illumines human psychology; (3) a demonstration of the process by which thought develops; (4) an integration of the theological and philosophical with the mythopoeic, artistic, and poetic; (5) a connection with the historical sociology of knowledge, typology, depth psychology, phenomenology, and the traditional history of ideas; (6) a human and humane grip on the problem of pain.

This discussion has been couched in abstractions. Abstractions, themselves something of an evil, are necessary to establish history's ability to discover truth. But the perceptions of the Devil originated in the minds of individuals, people who were fully alive and who as persons demand our attention. Unless I understand the conquests of Alexander as a dying soldier's pain and thirst, unless I grasp the ideas of the Inquisition as the torn body of the heretic, unless I feel that these sufferings are my own, unless in other words I have charity, my ideas of evil are empty. The whole question of evil, however complex it sometimes becomes, remains essentially the question of Ivan Karamazov's little girl crying out to God in the darkness of her distress. As Hawthorne's minister said, "I look around me, and lo! on every visage a Black Veil."

3 The Devil East and West

Rem non modo visu foedam sed etiam auditu.

—Cicero, *Philippicae* ii 63

Personifications of evil in non-Western cultures provide a necessary perspective on Western concepts. Parallel formulations of the Devil in diverse and widely separated cultures may arise from universal human thought structures, or they may be the product of as yet unknown processes of cultural diffusion. In either event, they are striking. Because the cosmos is sometimes benign and sometimes hostile to humanity, and because human nature is also divided against itself, most societies that accept the idea of a divine principle consider the principle ambivalent. The God has two faces: he is a coincidence of opposites. The dual nature of the God can be expressed theologically, in rational terms, or mythologically, in terms of stories. In monotheism the God may be thought of as embodying two opposite tendencies in one person. In polytheism, where the God nature is expressed in terms of many gods, the individual deities may likewise have "two souls within their breasts" (Goethe: "Zwei Seelen wohnen—ach—in meiner Brust"). Or some of the gods may be considered good and others evil. The ambiguity of the God is clear in Hinduism. Brahma is called "'the creation and destruction of all people." He creates "the harmful or benign, gentle or cruel, full of *dharma* or *adharma*, truthful or false."[1]

1. Wendy D. O'Flaherty, *Hindu Myths* (Harmondsworth, 1975), pp. 42, 46.

The earliest Hindu texts often introduce evil as a given, without explanation. Later texts offer a variety of explanations for the origin of evil. The original ambivalence of the God appears in the explanation of the origin of evil in the Brahmanas: "The gods and demons both spoke truth, and they both spoke untruth. The gods relinquished untruth, and the demons relinquished truth."[2] Because these beings are all aspects of the God, he remains responsible for both good and evil. Sometimes evil spirits are blamed for the evil in the world; sometimes human error and blindness are said to be at fault. But everything is an aspect of the God, he is all, and he is ultimately responsible for all. "Evil is an integral part of God and stems from him."[3]

Why does the God do evil, or cause it to be done, or permit it to be done? Any attempt to answer this question is a theodicy, a justification of the God's ways with the world. It is in the nature of theodicies to be unsatisfying, and on a hot and thirsty day, "malt does more than Milton can to justify God's ways to man." Theodicies can be theological or mythological. Mythologically constructed theodicies often personify the malevolent aspects of the God and therefore produce gods or other beings comparable to the Devil.

Seldom in myth is anything seen as wholly evil, for myth is very close to the unconscious, and the unconscious is ambivalent. What comes from the unconscious is basically perception of self, and the self is perceived as both good and evil. Only the rational, intellectual conscious separates the natural ambivalence of good and evil into polarities, opposite absolutes.[4] Myth is complex and ambiguous. "As no symbol can possibly encompass the whole essence of what it stands for, an increase in the number of symbols [may well be] enlightening

2. Wendy D. O'Flaherty, "The Origin of Heresy in Hindu Mythology," *History of Religions*, 10 (1970), 288.

3. *Ibid.*, p. 298.

4. Making this distinction has in large part "destroyed [man's] capacity to respond to numinous symbols and ideas, [and so] has put him at the mercy of the psychic underworld": C. G. Jung, ed., *Man and His Symbols* (New York, 1964), p. 16.

Quetzalcoatl, Mexico, 900–1250 A.D. The benevolent and revered god of life and art is also god of death. The opposite sides of this freestanding sculpture show the two aspects of divinity. Courtesy the Brooklyn Museum, Henry L. Batterman and Frank Sherman Benson Funds.

rather than confusing. . . . A multitude of mythological concepts may exist for any single entity."[5]

The coincidence of opposites, of good and evil, in the God is frequently perceived as necessary. The basic postulate is that

5. Rudolf Anthes, "Mythology in Ancient Egypt," in Samuel Noah Kramer, ed., *Mythologies of the Ancient World* (New York, 1961), p. 22.

all things, good and evil alike, come from the God. But to the extent that people feel that the God is good and do not wish to ascribe evil to him, they postulate an opposition of forces within the godhead. The opposition gradually is externalized, and a twinning occurs.[6] The god principle is still the source of evil, but it is now twinned (literally or figuratively) into a principle of good and a principle of evil, the former usually being identified with the High God, the latter becoming the God's adversary. Such pairs are called "doublets."

The coincidence of opposites is sometimes expressed by the notion of the war in heaven. Often one set of gods, having been deposed by a younger generation of deities, is then considered evil. The Christians made demons of the gods of Greece and Rome, the Olympic gods transformed the Titans into evil spirits, and the Teutonic gods vanquished the giants. In its early development, Indo-Iranian religion had two sets of gods, the asuras (India: asuras; Iran: ahuras) and the devas or daevas.[7] In Iran, the ahuras defeated the daevas, the leader of the ahuras became the High God, Ahura Mazda, the god of light, and the Iranian daevas, consigned to the ranks of evil spirits, became minions of Ahriman, the lord of darkness. In India, the devas defeated the asuras. In one sense, the results in India were opposite from those in Iran; in a deeper sense, the process was very similar. One group of deities was vanquished by another and relegated to the status of generally evil spirits.

For the Kogi Indians of the Andes, "the good exists only because the evil is active; if the evil would disappear, the good would equally cease to be. The Kogi seek to bring all into Yúluka, a transcendent state of agreement."[8] In Western re-

6. Cf. ME *twynnen:* to split off, depart.

7. In spite of the similarity in appearance, there is no etymological connection between "Devil" and deva. "Devil" derives from Gr. *diabolos*, from the IE root *gwel*; *deva* from the IE root *deiw*, "sky" or "heaven."

8. Mircea Eliade, *The Quest: History and Meaning in Religion* (Chicago, 1969), p. 139. The concept of the coincidence of the opposition, characteristic of Taoism from the fourth century B.C. (yin and yang), was first discussed at length in the West by the fifteenth-century theologian Nicholas of Cusa. The idea has been revived in modern times and used extensively by Jung, Eliade, and Erich Neumann.

The asura Sumbha, Jaipur, eighteenth century. Vanquished by the devas, the asuras became demonic figures. Sumbha and his followers have horns, animal ears, and grotesque faces; one bears a trident. Courtesy R. Lakshmi, Bangalore.

ligions, the God and the Devil have moved into almost absolute opposition, yet the myths of many societies place them in close conjunction. The God and the Devil exist and work together from all eternity; or they are brothers; or the God creates the Devil; or, in an even closer relationship, the God begets him or produces him from his own essence.

The struggle between the polar opposites can be expressed in the ambivalence of traditional deities. The great gods of India, such as Kali, Shiva, and Durga, manifest both benevolence and malice, creativity and destructiveness.

Another expression of the two faces of the God is in myths of closely united yet adversary deities. Always the doublets are opposites; always on a deeper level they are the same being: "In

the agonized womb of consciousness these polar twins [are] continuously struggling," says Stevenson of his Jekyll and Hyde.
They are the good and the evil manifestations of one personality. Among the Winnebago, the sun has twins, Flesh, who is
passive, and Stump, who is rebellious. Among the Iroquois the
earth's daughter bears twin sons, who quarrel within her
womb. One twin is born in the normal way, but the second
twin is born through the armpit, killing his mother. The
younger son is called Flint, and his constant effort is to undo
the constructive work of his older brother.[9] The older son
creates animals; Flint tries to imitate him, fails, and in anger
kills the animals his brother has made. Flint creates cliffs and
mountains to frustrate the ease and harmony of communication
that his older brother wishes for men.[10] These doublets may be
understood as opposite parts of the divine self seeking integration, centering, and repose, or as cosmic principles (yin and
yang) that are both opposite and united.

The coincidence of opposites may be expressed sexually. The
androgyne or divine syzygy, the union of brother and sister in
one, is a symbol of perfection: the bearded Aphrodite, the original Hermaphrodite, the beautiful Dionysos, the Shiva who is
yoni and *lingam* conjoined, the Mayan Ometeotl, lord and lady,
light and shadow. The androgyne is the coincidence of opposite
sexes. But, as always when the opposites twin, split, and are
polarized, they are viewed as in conflict. Hence in myth the
male and female principles, the yin and the yang, may be in
contention, and the feminine principle, when in opposition to
the male, can appear inferior or even evil.[11] In herself, the

9. The story of the conscientious older brother and the feckless younger
brother was old before the Prodigal Son. It reappears frequently in literature,
in Thomas Mann's *Buddenbrooks*, for example (Tom vs. Christian).

10. The view that mountains are imperfections in the universe and impedi-
ments to man remained common into the eighteenth century. Cf. Marjorie
Hope Nicholson, *Mountain Gloom and Mountain Glory* (Ithaca, N.Y., 1959).
For the Iroquois story, see Eliade, *Quest*, p. 146. See also Eliade, *The Two and
the One* (London, 1965), esp. pp. 103–124.

11. Whether this is because men rather than women have made the myths
as well as written the theology is unclear. Some efforts have been made to
trace male domination over the female to a successful revenge of the male patri-

Shiva and his family, India, 1790. In this strange *déjeuner sur l'herbe*, the usually benign Shiva and his consort Parvati, Skanda on her lap, and the elephant-like Ganesha at his side, consume human flesh and string the heads of their victims. The divine principle is both loving and cruel: it gives and it takes away. Courtesy Victoria and Albert Museum.

female can have a positive character. She can be the fresh young maiden or the fostering mother. Or she can be the whore, the hag, the witch, the yawning mouth of the grave, the womb that has become the tomb. In Mexico, the cruelest deities were female: Tlacolteutl, goddess of sin and devourer of excrement, or Ciuacoatl, her face half red and half black, who goes through the night wailing and predicting misery and war. Kali fosters and destroys; Artemis is at once virgin, fertility goddess, and witch. Chicomecoatl, the savage snake-goddess, also bestows upon mankind both food and flowers. Coatlicue, the moon-bride of the sun, is both lovely and hideous, gentle and cruel, the west wind and the hurricane, love and death. Yet, although there are many evil female demons and witches, the principle of evil is infrequently perceived as female, and the Devil is seldom even provided with a consort. The reason for this may be the supposed inferiority of the female, which bars her from being either of the two opposite principles of the divine nature.

The underworld, the realm of the chthonic, is frequently associated with the principle of evil. On the one hand, the underworld symbolizes fertility, partly because of its association with the womb, but even more strongly because it is from beneath the earth that the crops and the green grass of spring push forth. It also yields gold, silver, and other desirable minerals. But on the other hand the underworld is associated with the tomb or grave.[12] It is there that the spirits of the dead

archy after the female gods of agriculture had replaced the male gods of the hunt. The sky god or High God deposes the Great Mother and rules in her place. All such explanations falter. References to struggles in the Paleolithic or Neolithic eras are based on little evidence, and in any event male dominance over the female is almost worldwide and so can scarcely be traced to any prehistoric arrangements made in Eurasia exclusively. On the ambivalence of the female, see especially Wolfgang Lederer, *The Fear of Women* (New York, 1968); Erich Neumann, *The Great Mother*, 2d ed. (New York, 1963); and Robert Briffault, *The Mothers*, 3 vols. (New York, 1927).

12. The very etymology of the word "hell" testifies to this constellation of meanings. The Indo-European root *kel* means "cover" or "concealment" and yields English "hole," "helmet" and German *hohl* (empty), *Höhle* (cave), *Halle* (hall, dwelling), and *Hölle* (hell).

Kali, India, eighteenth century. Kali, goddess of destruction and of life, dances on the body of her consort Shiva, and extends blessing and nourishment to animals. Courtesy Victoria and Albert Museum.

wander in a land of darkness or of shadow. The underworld of the Mexicans, like that of the Romans, was a place where the dead found repose more than punishment. The lord of the underworld (Pluto, for example) is god of both fertility and death, which helps account for the Western tradition that Satan is not only lord of evil and of death but is also associated with fertility and sexuality, a trait evident in the witches' orgy and in the horns that the Devil often wears.

Death itself is ambivalent. In India, one of the most evil asuras is Namuci, a powerful enemy of Indra. The god of lies, evil, and hatred, he is also the god of death and darkness, and his name signifies "he who never lets go." Yet, says St. Paul, unless a man die, he shall not live. Death is the prerequisite for resurrection and the entry into a new life, and the underworld is at least the part-time dwelling of the dying and rising deity such as Osiris or Persephone. In religions that have no resurrection, death can still be perceived as a transcendence of the world and an entry to a greater and higher reality, such as heaven. Among the Ural-Altaic and many African peoples, death is perceived as a going up, up into the hills, up a tree, or up a ladder, a journey to join the sky god in his eternal realm of glory. Thus the god of death is not necessarily a wholly fearsome being: he is terrible, but he can also be merciful. He can lead us out of a world of illusion and pain into a new world or a new life.

But although in principle the lord of the underworld can be benevolent or at least indifferent, he tends more often, because of his association with the torments of hell, to be malevolent: thus the historical association of the underworld and the Devil.[13] The reddish glow of hellfire and the reddish tint of land scorched by fire or an intemperate sun seem to have produced (together with blood) the association of redness with evil that persists in modern conceptions of the Devil's appearance.

Blackness and darkness are almost always associated with evil, in opposition to the association of whiteness and light with

13. See S. G. F. Brandon, *The Judgement of the Dead* (London, 1967), esp. pp. 175–181.

The wheel of becoming, Tibet, eighteenth century. Time creates and destroys. The cycle of life is grasped by a black, taloned monster who devours the wheel with his tusks.

good. This is true even in black Africa (though in Mozambique there is a demon called Muzungu Maya, "wicked white man"), so that negative perceptions of blackness are more causes of, than caused by, racism. When Shiva is black, the color represents the evil side of his nature; the color of Kali, the destroyer, is usually black. It is natural therefore that the Devil's most common color is black, though he is also frequently associated with red.[14]

Blackness possesses an immense range of negative and fearful associations. Basically black is the color of night, when your enemies can surprise you and when ghosts or nameless, shapeless beings can attack you unexpectedly. Cosmogonically, blackness is chaos; ontogenically it is the sign of death and the tomb, or of the ambivalent womb. Though pallor is associated with death and hence with evil—heretics and demons are often pallid in the Middle Ages—black indicates evil in places as disparate as Europe, Africa, Tibet, and Siberia, and recent experiments with American children seem to show a prejudice against the color black separate from racial attitudes.[15] Often black is associated with the direction west, because of the sunset. Ontologically it is nonbeing, the void; physically it connotes blindness; psychologically it signifies the fearful land of dreams and the unconscious. It is connected with mental depression, with intellectual stupidity, with religious despair, and with moral sin. It is associated with dirt and poison and plague. In ancient Mexico, it was associated with the obsidian weapons of war. A man running for mayor of a large city in the last decade learned how difficult it was to use the term black in a positive way. Addressing a large crowd of black voters, he assured them that though his skin was white, his heart was as black as theirs! In proudly asserting its blackness, a whole race has pitted itself against one of the most ancient and powerfully prejudiced symbols in the human psyche.

Like the underworld, the symbol of chaos has ambivalent as-

14. One of the few major exceptions to the perception of black as evil was in Ancient Egypt, the name of which (Chem) means the "black land," and where black was associated with the life-giving alluvial soil of the Nile Valley and contrasted to the evil burnt red color of the sterile desert. In European folklore, red frequently signified evil. The war-god Mars was red. Judas was portrayed as redheaded, the name of William "Rufus" was intended as an insult, and redheaded people were more often suspected of adhering to witch cults. The origin of red as symbolizing evil is unclear, though the association with blood is perhaps the most likely guess.

15. John E. Williams and John R. Stabler, "If White Means Good, Then Black . . . ," *Psychology Today*, July, 1973, pp. 51–54.

sociations with the Devil. Chaos, from the Greek *chaein*, to
yawn, appears in almost every mythology. Chaos is the formless, indeterminate, undifferentiated, inchoate state that exists
at (or before) the beginning of the world. It is often identified
with the primeval waters from which the earth was supposed to
have sprung. "At first," says the Rig Veda, "there was only
darkness wrapped in darkness. All this was only unillumined
matter." And Genesis says, "The earth was without form and
void, and darkness moved over the face of the abyss." This
yawning chaos, the *massa confusa* of the alchemists, is in one
sense good: it is the creative potency, the unleashed power,
without which nothing would be. But in another sense it is bad:
it must be transcended for the gods or men to exist. So chaos
may be perceived as a monster, a Leviathan or a Tiamat, that
must be overcome. The Nahuatl of Mexico said that primeval
chaos was a thing with countless mouths swimming in the
formless waters devouring all that she could seize (note that she
is female). She was vanquished by the gods Quetzalcoatl and
Tezcatlipoca and then torn in two so that the universe could be
differentiated. But she mourned her lost powers and roamed
the world demanding human sacrifice in order to feast upon
human hearts. Once the monster is vanquished, the cosmos can
emerge.[16] At the end of time, the cosmos may revert to chaos:
this in turn may be bad in that it represents the destruction of
the world, good in that it also represents a return or recreation
of that primeval power and creativity. When Shiva does the
Tandava dance, which expresses both joy and sorrow, the
dance annihilates the illusory world (*maya*) and integrates the
world with Brahman. Many rites and doctrines are aimed at the
recreation of chaos in order to release or regain creative force.
This is the fundamental meaning of the orgy and of festivals

16. Chaos is different from the flux of Herakleitos or the dharma of Buddhism, the endless and illusory shaping, separating, and reshaping of the
world, in that chaos is real, it has creative potency, and it yields, when overcome, true differentiation. Psychologically, chaos can represent the unconscious, which must be ordered and differentiated in the conscious; or it can
represent the parents (particularly the mother), who must be overcome so that
the ego may emerge.

such as the Roman Saturnalia and the medieval Feast of Fools.

Chaos rules at the beginning and the end of time.[17] Time is the creator of all things, but also their devourer. He is an old man, provided, like Death, with a sickle. Raging Kali is time (Kali being the feminine form of *kala*, "time"). In Tibet, the personified concept of impermanence is seen as a black monster embracing and devouring the wheel of life.

Chaos is often represented as a snake, serpent, or dragon. The Dayak of Borneo believe that the world is enclosed in a circle formed by the watersnake biting its tail. The primeval snake or serpent, the ouroboros, pursuing itself in an endless circle as do the yin and the yang, is a coincidence of opposites. The serpent can heal and help; the serpent can destroy. "The symbolism of the snake is somewhat confusing, but all the symbols are directed to the same central idea: it is immortal because it is continually reborn, and therefore it is a moon force, and as such can bestow fecundity, knowledge (that is, prophecy), and even immortality."[18] Deities wearing snakes as their emblems often bear them in the shape of the crescent moon, and through the moon the snake is associated with night, death, menstruation, and fertility (the phallic aspect adding to the serpent's fertility). The identification of the Devil with the serpent ties him again to these and to the monster that holds order and life captive and must be slain so that they may be released.

Horns, though commonly associated with the Devil in Western tradition, have a basically positive character. Commonly they signify fertility. Horns are identified with the crescent moon, which signifies fertility both in the basic idea of growth

17. It is curious that modern cosmogony recapitulates the perennial myth so closely: the universe is supposed to have been formed some ten billion years ago out of a chaotic mass of tremendously dense plasma; some astronomers believe that the universe will at some time cease expanding, collapse upon itself, and revert to chaos. See especially Mircea Eliade, *Cosmos and History* (New York, 1954).

18. Mircea Eliade, *Patterns in Comparative Religion* (New York, 1958), p. 164. See also *Patterns*, pp. 287–288; Eliade, *Myths, Dreams, and Mysteries* (New York, 1960), p. 219; Joseph Campbell, *The Masks of God: Primitive Mythology* (New York, 1959), pp. 384–391; Erich Neumann, *The Origins and History of Consciousness* (New York, 1954), pp. 5–38.

Ouroboros, palace of King Ghezo of Dahomey, nineteenth century. The primeval snake devouring its own tail is a mythological motif of ambivalence common to the most diverse cultures. The snake is male and female, beginning and end, alpha and omega, light and darkness, good and evil; it is the undifferentiated, chaotic state that pre-exists the cosmos and the cosmic separation and opposition of these qualities. Courtesy Musée de l'homme, Paris.

and through its association with menstruation.[19] They are associated with the phallic serpent and with the mighty procreative power of the "hillocky bull in the swelter of summer come in his great good time to the sultry, biding herds."[20] Shiva may take the form of both a bull and a *lingam;* bulls, the most appro-

19. The moon is also a symbol of purity. The combination purity/fertility in association with the moon is found in both the myths of Artemis/Diana and the iconography of the Virgin Mary.
20. Dylan Thomas, "Lament."

priate animal manifestation of the god, are branded with Shiva's sign, the trident. Vishnu and Krishna are also portrayed as bulls, and Poseidon is associated both with the horns of the bull and with the trident (the Hallowe'en demons we see today equipped with horns and "pitchforks" have an ancient origin). Powdered horn is considered an aphrodisiac, and a broken horn, from which the procreative power may flow out, is a cornucopia, a horn of plenty. The horns on stags or other wild animals signify a plentiful supply of game. Horns are also a sign of pure power and as such are identified with the rays of the sun: Moses after coming down from the mountain was supposed to have *qeren*, horns or rays of power emanating from his brow. A hat in the shape of horns, a medieval crown for example, the cap of Mithras, or a bishop's mitre, indicates the power of the wearer. Horn signs are made with the hand or affixed on walls or doors in order to obtain safety and protection (compare the traditional use of the horseshoe).

The horns of the Devil are thus basically a mark of his power, but they also have a specifically negative character. The moon is horned, but the moon signifies not only fertility but also night, darkness, death, and therefore the underworld. The horns of animals bring to mind the danger represented to men by some beasts, or the hostile war-animals that appear in many mythologies (for example, the devouring Minotaur), or the fundamental, mysterious, and frightening otherness of animals. The powder of a horn can be a poison as well as an alexipharmic or an aphrodisiac, and the wearing of horns may signify cuckoldry rather than fertility (though this use of the symbol seems to be restricted to the West in the Renaissance and afterwards). Horns appear not only on the Devil but on spirits (usually hostile ones) in a variety of mythologies. The horns of the Devil signify not only his power, but his associations with death and the underworld, and an uncontrolled, destructive sexuality.[21]

21. On horns, see Frederick T. Elworthy, *Horns of Honour* (London, 1900), and Jack Randolph Conrad, *The Horn and the Sword: the History of the Bull as Symbol of Power and Fertility* (New York, 1957).

The dancing sorcerer, Paleolithic, Cave of the Trois Frères, Ariège, France. This ancient picture of a man-beast, or a man dressed as a beast, was probably intended to help ensure plenitude of game. Horns, associated with the hunt, and through phallic and moon imagery, with agriculture, were a common symbol of potency and fertility. Courtesy Mrs. S. G. F. Brandon.

Goat or ram, Ur, third millennium B.C. This ancient Mesopotamian statue of gold shows the sense of the balefulness, mystery, and power of the beast that was to be so important in the iconography of the Devil. Courtesy Trustees of the British Museum.

In addition to the principle of evil, a legion of lesser spirits who personify specific evils, rather than evil itself, can be found in most societies. These spirits of extreme heat and cold, barrenness, disease or storms are sometimes considered ghosts, sometimes gods, sometimes manifestations of destructive natural forces. Seldom clearly distinguished from one another, they are wild and disruptive and have the strange and blurry quality that provokes the undirected terror the Greeks named "panic" after the god Pan. They possess the body, causing disease, or the mind, causing insanity. They appear as male incubi or female succubi seducing sleepers. They are usually ugly and often deformed, their deformity of appearance being an outward and visible sign of the deformity of their actions. Almost always they attack a person directly and crudely; seldom in non-Western cultures do they play the role of moral tempters assigned them in Christian tradition. Among the Arunta, "the evil spirits seize upon a particular individual who happens to be foot-loose and deprive him of his sense so that he runs about like one crazy and can rest neither by day or by night."[22] In Hinduism, the rakshasas are enemies of both men and gods. In Japan, the natural and supernatural worlds were closely intertwined, and, as well as people, animals, plants, and even inanimate objects had ghosts. These spirits were usually hostile, particularly the *oni*, who possessed great strength and ugliness. The *oni* usually had horns and frequently had three eyes; they might be either male or female.

A curious function of demons in both East and West is that they serve the God's justice by tormenting damned souls in hell. In Japan, twenty-four thousand demon servants of Emma-O were needed to drag the unfortunate souls before the god's tribunal. Frequently, as in the West, these beings have grotesque forms and use dreadful tools of torture. In China and Japan, as in the West, it is not always clear whether the demons are employees or inmates, whether they are damned and suffer-

22. Paul Radin, *Primitive Religion* (New York, 1937), p. 113. See also Radin, p. 245, and G. Van der Leeuw, *Religion in Essence and Manifestation* (London, 1938), pp. 134 ff.

ing themselves or whether they merely mete out suffering to others.

The Tempter, an evil spirit appearing in some sophisticated societies, is closer to the personification of evil. In Buddhist

Buddhist hell, sixteenth century. Emma-O, god and judge of the under-world, presides as a bureaucrat over the suffering of the damned, who are tormented by varicolored demons wielding instruments of torture.

mythology Mara ("death," or "thirst"), whose attributes are blindness, murkiness, death, and darkness, and whose daughters are Desire, Unrest, and Pleasure, attempts to obstruct Gautama's progress toward enlightenment by tempting him to return to a conventional Hindu life of virtue, but the Buddha, recognizing that the only true good lies in transcending the world, defeats him and drives him off.[23] The Toltecs believed that the man-god Quetzalcoatl was tempted by many demons who offered him wine and other enticements to lure him from the path of duty. Myths of a primeval fall from grace are worldwide, but the fall is usually the result of human or divine stupidity rather than the work of a Tempter.[24]

The curious figure of the Trickster, the spirit of disorder, the enemy of boundaries, is also related to the divine, but his functions are too ill defined to make it possible to equate him with the principle of evil. He is sensual, childish, foolish, sometimes ugly and cruel, but he is also lighthearted and funny. Sometimes his opposition to the gods entails a creative attempt to help man, as when Prometheus steals the gods' fire. The fundamental characteristic of the Trickster is the upsetting of order; and as in the myth of chaos, order upset can release creative energies as well as destroy established values.[25]

23. T. O. Ling, *Buddhism and the Mythology of Evil* (London, 1962), p. 61; R. C. Zaehner, *Concordant Discord* (Oxford, 1970), p. 173. See James W. Boyd, *Satan and Māra* (Leiden, 1975). Boyd argues that the Buddhists took the idea of the Devil less seriously and personally than did the Christians.

24. Brandon, p. 166; Charles H. Long, *Alpha* (New York, 1963), pp. 47 ff. Cf. the Mayan *Popul Vuh*, in which the gods atempted for a long while to create a being capable of serving them. First they created animals, then men of clay. They thought they had succeeded with men of wood, but these finally reverted to all fours and forgot the gods, who had to destroy them in a flood. After other trials, the gods at last created four splendid people, beautiful and wise. But they grew fearful that these paragons would become proud and forget them, and struck them down, introducing death and placing a barrier of unknowing between men and heaven, punishment for fault man was not even given time to commit. See also H. Abrahamson, *The Origin of Death* (Uppsala, 1951), and Geoffrey Parrinder, *African Mythology* (London, 1967).

25. Jung and others have seen in the Trickster the clearest manifestations in myth of the unconscious—ambivalent, sensual, disordered—and it is true that the myths of the Trickster bear a resemblance to dream material. On the Trickster, see Campbell, *Primitive Mythology*, pp. 269–273; Eliade, *Quest*, pp.

Buddhism [handwritten marginal note]

The cultures of Egypt, Mesopotamia, and Canaan stand directly behind those of the Greeks and Hebrews and so exercised at least an indirect influence upon the Judeo-Christian concept of the Devil. The gods of the Egyptians are all manifestations of the One God. This polytheistic monism is sometimes explicit, sometimes implicit. The God, and the gods, are ambivalent: evil and good, hurt and help all emanate from the one divine principle. In no way is Egyptian religion dualistic: there is no one principle of evil. The Egyptian cosmos is a coincidence of opposites, stable, a manifestation of divine order and harmony. The God wills the universe and creates it; but the universe is not merely the creation, but the manifestation of the God.

The universe is not a thing; it is alive; it pulses with godness. In a world where all things show forth the majesty of the God, the principle of evil cannot exist separately. It can exist only as part of the divine continuum, of the living cosmos. Death, disease, lying, deceit, all these are disruptions of the natural order and are evil, yet in the greater sense they are—as in Taoism—part of the order that transcends and includes both order and disorder. "I made every man like his fellow," says the God; "I did not command that they do evil, (but) it was in their hearts which violated what I had said."[26] Evil is the disruption of *ma'at*, the ordered, harmonious justice of the cosmos, by the individual. Only one Egyptian myth hints at a fall: the sun-god Re creates the world properly, but humanity plots evil, and Re is obliged to chastise them.[27] Evil is an isolated, individual act, and the individual is accountable in the Tuat for his life on earth. The location and nature of the Tuat is not certain, but it is generally understood to be the underworld. The soul of the dead person is weighed in the balance by the black, jackal-

153–158; and Roslyn Poignant, *Oceanic Mythology* (London, 1967). The standard work, dealing primarily with the North American Indians, is Paul Radin, *The Trickster* (London, 1955).

26. James B. Pritchard, *Ancient Near Eastern Texts Relating to the Old Testament*, 2d ed. (Princeton, 1955), p. 8. See also Henri Frankfort, *Ancient Egyptian Religion* (New York, 1948), p. 74.

27. Pritchard, pp. 10–11.

Seti I with Seth and Horus. Egypt, nineteenth dynasty. As his name sug-gests, Seti I founded a dynasty with special devotion to Seth. Here Seth cooperates with Horus the sky god, usually his mortal enemy, in pouring out life (symbolized by the stream of ankhs) on the pharaoh.

headed god Anpu (Anubis). Those found to be righteous live an eternal though shadowy existence, while the unrighteous who have violated *ma'at* are tormented and then consumed by the jaws of the demons or by the fire of Re, the fire that gives life to the world but scorches and burns the unjust as it does the bar-ren desert.[28] The "demons" who torment the souls of the dead are really spirits or gods themselves, and not thoroughly evil.

All Egyptian deities are manifestations of the whole cosmos,

28. Pharaoh, being a god, is exempt from judgment. He can do no wrong, and he lives eternally with the other gods. The fires of the Egyptian hell may have influenced the Jewish Gehenna and, through Gehenna, the Chris-tian hell. But note that the damned in India, China, and Japan were also frequently tormented by flames. Again, the question of diffusion versus spon-taneous generation has not been resolved. The trident as an instrument of tor-ture used by the demons upon the damned appears in Coptic texts of Chris-tian times, but nowhere in Egyptian hieroglyphic texts.

and so ambivalent: even Osiris the merciful is sometimes in early myth an enemy of Re, and a usually destructive deity such as Seth can be helpful to his own worshipers. The Pharaoh himself is morally divided, "That beneficent god, the fear of whom is throughout the countries like [the fear of] Sekhmet in a year of plague. . . . He fights without end, he spares not. . . . He is a master of graciousness, rich in sweetness, and he conquers by love."[29] No deity ever becomes the principle of evil, but in one god, Seth, the destructive and unharmonious element is more evident than in others.

The myth of Seth as the antagonist of the sky god Hor or Horus (hor = "face" or "sky") is as ancient as the Pyramid texts; the hostility between the two grows in time, and finally in the Hellenistic period Seth has become almost entirely evil. Some scholars interpret the origin of the myth as political: Horus is a god of lower Egypt, the north, and Seth is a god of upper Egypt, the south. Others insist that Seth and Horus (or Osiris in the myths) are deities of opposite ecologies, Seth representing the dry desert and Horus or Osiris the black earth or the fertilizng Nile. Egypt is one of the few cultures in which black is not the color of evil, but the color of the fertile, life-giving alluvial plains of the delta. Red was the evil color, the hostile hue of the scorching sands. Because of Seth's association with the desert, his color most commonly is red, and red-haired or ruddy people were considered in some special way his own. Plutarch and Herodotus comment that the Egyptians sacrificed redheaded people.[30] Seth is usually portrayed as a reddish animal whose species no one has been able to identify and which therefore is simply called the Seth-animal.

29. John A. Wilson, "Egypt: The Function of the State," in Henri Frankfort, ed., *The Intellectual Adventure of Ancient Man* (Chicago, 1946), p. 71.

30. For the political argument, see J. G. Griffiths, *The Conflict of Horus and Seth* (Liverpool, 1960). Black could on occasion be a threatening color even in Egypt. Anpu, the judge of the dead, was black, and even Seth sometimes took the form of a black pig. It is possible that the redness of Seth helped make red the second most common color, after black, of the Christian Devil. In the Middle Ages, ruddy people were considered proper sacrifices to the Devil.

The Dual Horus-Seth god, Egypt. Horus and Seth are a doublet, representing two sides of the divine principle. The followers of the two gods were
often antagonistic, but in some places Seth, who here looks toward our left,
and Horus were worshiped together as one god.

Whatever the political or geographical matrix of the conflict of Horus and Seth, "to the religious historian, the action in the foreground is not merely a reflection of the background."[31] One valuable interpretation of the conflict is psychological. It can be understood as the separation of a unity whose parts strive for reunification. Seth and Horus the Elder are brothers. In an alternative version, Seth and Osiris are brothers, and Horus the Younger, the son of Osiris and Isis, is Seth's nephew. Sibling deities in mythology are almost always to be taken as doublets of the same being, so that Seth is one half of a divine personality whose other half is variously represented as one or another of the Horuses or as Osiris. Seth and Horus were worshiped together in the early dynasties, and their twin natures sometimes represented in one two-headed deity. As Horus' alter ego, Seth defends the high gods against evil and is responsible for rescuing Re from the attack of the evil serpent Apep.

But the Seth/Horus doublet twins and comes into conflict. Being a violation of *ma'at*, this disharmony is evil and must be resolved. Horus the sky god and Osiris the dying and rising savior god were very popular and on the whole represent "good." That Seth is in conflict with his "good" doublet means that he himself has to be to some extent "evil." He therefore sets about to do the opposite of what is needed: rather than seeking union and harmony with Horus/Osiris, he seeks to destroy his adversary. Seth tricks Osiris into getting into a large chest, locks it up, and sinks it in the Nile, but Osiris' wife/sister Isis recovers the body and resurrects it. Osiris had to die that he might live and that his resurrection might give hope to mankind. Seth's killing of Osiris is thus a necessary act, but one which, as with Judas Iscariot later, is not imputed to him as a virtue.

While Osiris is dead, Isis bears a son, Horus the Younger, who is conceived without intercourse, or else begotten by

31. H. Te Velde, *Seth, God of Confusion* (Leiden, 1967), p. 78. Te Velde is a strong proponent of the psychological interpretation.

Isis. Egypt, nineteenth dynasty. Wearing the horns and moon of power and fertility, Isis holds the sistrum used in procession by her devotees. Horns became the most common sign of the Devil. Courtesy Roger Wood.

Osiris during his death. Horus the Younger now becomes the adversary of Seth—in other words, the other, "good," half of the divine Horus/Seth doublet. Seth tries unsuccessfully to murder Horus as a baby, and when Horus grows up he summons a great host to fight against his ancient enemy. In the end the two meet in a mortal combat, during which they mutilate each other. Horus castrates Seth, so depriving him of his power, but Seth in turn mutilates Horus: in the form of a black pig, he tears out Horus' eye and buries it.[32]

Both gods suffer from their bloody fray. That each loses a vital organ is a sign that their battle was a divine error. What is needed is not a struggle between the two parts of the divine nature but rather an effort at harmony, centering, union. Seth's attempt at union with Horus by sodomizing him fails because it is the wrong kind of effort—an effort at union by force and by transgression of *ma'at*. Only through peaceful centering, through a coincidence of opposites that again renders the divine nature whole and one, can the entity Horus/Seth (or Osiris/Seth) be restored. Unhappily, the myth does not relate the reconciliation.

The opposition of Horus and Seth was perceived as a series of opposites—heaven against earth, fertility against sterility, life against death, earth against the underworld—but never, at least not until the late period when the original myth had been altered, sheer good against sheer evil. Seth stands somewhere in the spectrum between Trickster and Devil.

The serpent in Egyptian mythology can be benevolent, but one serpent-deity, Apep, is an enemy both of Re and of mankind. The goddess Hathor is also ambivalent. She is the goddess of joy, the wife of Re, the loving mother and nurse of Horus the Elder, and, in the form of a divine cow, the giver of

32. Here the identification of Horus the Younger with Horus the sky god is strong. Originally, Horus the Elder lost one of his eyes. *Hor* means "face," and the sky is perceived as a face with two eyes, the sun and the moon. In combat the sky loses one of its orbs. The same myth is told in Scandinavia of the sky god Odin. Thus the mutilation of the sky god is transferred to his namesake (really himself) the younger Horus.

Hathor, Egypt, copy of a statue of the twenty-sixth dynasty, 572–525 B.C. Hathor, the benign mother goddess, wears horns of power and protects the Pharaoh Psammeticus under her chin. But her other manifestation was the raging lion-goddess Sekhmet.

milk and protection to the world. She later becomes associated with Isis, the mother of Horus the Younger; both Isis and Hathor are fertility goddesses and wear the crescent moon on their heads as a symbol. But Hathor can also take the form of

Sekhmet, "the powerful." This lion-headed goddess is the scorching eye of Re, the avenger of the gods on the wickedness of man. Re created mankind happy, good, and in harmony with its creator. But mankind has rebelled, plotted against him, and then fled in fear. "And the majesty of Re said: 'Behold, they are fled into the desert, their hearts being afraid because of what they have said.' " And Re's courtiers said to him, " 'Send forth thine eye, that it may slay them for thee——. Let it go down as Hathor.' Then went this goddess and slew mankind in the desert." Hathor/Sekhmet wades in human blood and exults in death. Sekhmet becomes the goddess of war, of battle, and of cruelty. "By thy life," she says to Re, "I have prevailed over men, and that is pleasant in mine heart." Sekhmet's blood lust then waxes so great as to distress Re, so that in order to prevent the extermination of every last vestige of the human race he has to resort to a ruse. He sends his servants out to fetch a red dye, which they mix into seven thousand jars of beer. They pour out the red beer in the path of Sekhmet, who mistakes it for blood, becomes drunk, and ceases her destruction. Here again is the story of the primeval sin and subsequent chastisement of man. Hathor/Sekhmet represent the avenging nature of the God.[33]

The civilizations of Mesopotamia and Syria helped shape the Western concept of the Devil more directly than did that of Egypt. Sumerian civilization stands directly behind that of Babylonia and Assyria, which directly influenced both the Hebrews and the Canaanites. Canaan in turn influenced both Israel and the Minoan civilization of Crete that preceded Mycenean and Hellenic culture. A common northwest Semitic (that is, Syrian) culture may have permeated the origins of both Greek and Jewish civilization; the extent of cultural diffusion is as yet unclear. The continuity between Sumero-Akkadian and Assyro-Babylonian religion, however, is such that it is possible to discuss them together. "The myths of the Akkadians (that is,

33. Adolf Erman, ed., *The Ancient Egyptians* (New York, 1966), pp. 47–49.

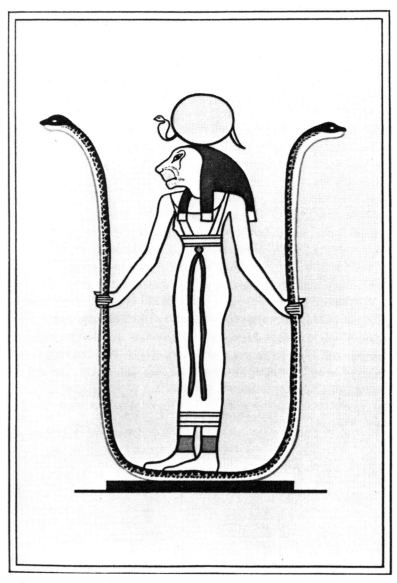

Sekhmet, Egypt. Sekhmet, the lion-headed goddess who is the destructive side of the kindly Hathor, was sent out by Re to punish humankind for their sins. Carried away, she destroyed nearly the whole human race before Re could check her frenzy.

of the Babylonians and Assyrians) derive largely from Sumerian prototypes."[34]

Mesopotamian religious thought differs from that of Egypt most strikingly in its fearfulness. The cosmos was always shattering, often without warning, and order had constantly to be regenerated and rebuilt. Human society was even more disordered than nature. Not for Mesopotamia was the idea that the king was a god presiding over an essentially unchanging universe. Mesopotamia attracted frequent migrations, mixing of peoples, invasions, and conquest, prompting a continual fear of war with its threat of annihilation, resettlement, or slavery. The Mesopotamians, especially the Assyrians, appear to have become fierce under fierce circumstances and to have added to the terrors of life by waging war constantly and in the most intimidating way. In pursuit of his imperialist policies Ashurnasirpal II (883–859) burned and pillaged any city that resisted him, along with many that did not, causing the hands and feet of the people to be cut off and their dead or dying bodies to be piled up in a vast heap to fester and rot in the sun. This was not wanton cruelty, of course—viciousness is often a matter of policy—for Ashurnasirpal conceived of his pile, no doubt correctly, as a deterrent to the resistance of other cities. And so the Aramaean city of Surah did not resist and opened its gates to the conqueror upon demand. The inhabitants were rewarded with leniency. Ashurnasirpal burned the city to the ground, carried off the people into slavery, ordered the legs cut off the Aramaean officers, and carried the governor off to Nineveh where he was publicly flayed alive.

In Mesopotamia, neither nature nor society was part of the divine cosmos, the universal order of things. The world was fundamentally alienated from the divine plan, and the inscrutable gods might help, abandon, or simply ignore a nation, a city, or an individual. A very early Sumerian poem raises the question of theodicy. In the poem, a suffering man complains that

---

34. Samuel N. Kramer, "Mythology of Sumer and Akkad," in Kramer, ed., *Mythologies of the Ancient World*, p. 120.

Deity, Assur-nasir-pal re-lief, Assyria, ninth century B.C. The Assyrian use of wings as the symbol of numinous power passed into the Judeo-Christian iconographic representation of angels and fallen angels. Courtesy Trustees of the British Museum.

he has worshiped the gods properly but has seen his enemies triumph over him. The gods respond by making everything come right again. A later, Babylonian, version, more similar to the Book of Job, consists of a dialogue between a sufferer and his friend. The sufferer inquires why those who worship the gods suffer and those who ignore them prosper. His friend en-treats him to submit to his lot and to be of good cheer, but he replies that nowhere do the gods seem to block the ways of demons. "How have I profited," he inquires, "that I have bowed down to my god?" Like Job, the sufferer receives no satisfactory reply.[35]

The Babylonian creation epic, the Enuma elish, expresses the fall of the gods and the primeval alienation among them in a story that resembles the tales of battles between elder and younger gods found in so many other religions. Here the motif is tightly interwoven with the victory of cosmos over chaos. Apsu and Tiamat, the primordial pair, dwell in the happy nothingness of the pristine abyss. But the younger gods they have engendered begin to trouble them:

> The divine brothers banded together,
> They disturbed Tiamat as they surged back and forth,
> Yea, they troubled the mood of Tiamat
> By their hilarity in the Abode of Heaven,
> Apsu could not lessen their clamor
> And Tiamat was speechless at their [ways]. . . .
> [Apsu said]: "Their ways are verily loathsome unto me.
> By day I find no relief, nor repose by night. . . ."
> [Apsu's] face grew radiant
> Because of the evil he planned against the gods, his sons.[36]

Tiamat, goddess of the primeval waters, or chaos, is reluctant to destroy her progeny, but Apsu is more concerned than his wife about losing sleep and, with the advice of Mummu, their son or vizier, he devises a plan to kill the younger gods. The young gods discover the plot and choose Ea to slay Apsu and imprison Mummu. Ea does his job and builds a peaceful house upon the body of Apsu, to which he invites the other gods, and in which he engenders his son, Marduk, god of Babylon. Thus far the younger gods have won a limited victory and have begun to build a cosmos (the peaceful house). But the physical universe has not yet been created, and raging Tiamat has not yet been destroyed.[37]

35. "The Babylonian Theodicy," in D. W. Thomas, ed., *Documents from Old Testament Times* (New York, 1958), pp. 97–104.

36. Pritchard, p. 61.

37. Some scholars interpret the text as saying that Ea built his house *in*

Tiamat now plans revenge against her offspring. She has engendered children other than the gods (another hint of Old Ones, like the Titans in Greece, opposed to the gods). The eldest of these Old Ones is Kingu, and Tiamat produces a vast horde of demons of horrid nature and appearance—scorpionmen and centaurs and other loathsome creatures—to serve under Kingu's command. Somehow Ea is not quite equal to this new challenge, and one of the younger gods, Anu, attempts to dissuade Tiamat from attacking, but he fails. Now his son (previously Ea's son) Marduk of Babylon is voted leader of the gods. Where Anu has attempted diplomacy, Marduk uses force, attacking his ancestress with flame, storm, and lightning. Tiamat opens her mouth to swallow him (chaos, the devouring female, attempts to destroy the principle of order by ingesting it, reabsorbing it, forcing it back into the primordial womb), but Marduk drives the storm-wind through her mouth into her belly and distends it painfully. While she is incapacitated, he shoots and kills her with an arrow. Water is the lifegiving stuff from which the cosmos is made, but it is also Tiamat, the chaos that must be overcome.[38]

Having disposed, without great difficulty, of Kingu and his host, Marduk splits Tiamat in two (that is, he differentiates the cosmos), placing half of her in the sky, and building a palace for himself and the other gods. Marduk now completes the organization of the universe, the creation of the cosmos and, having made the physical world, turns to the creation of man. He creates man for one purpose only, for the service of himself and

---

Apsu, or made the dead Apsu his house. In any event, by triumphing over his ancient ancestor, Ea (Sum. Enki) in a sense *becomes* Apsu, for as Apsu was the god of the sweet waters when they mingled undifferentiated with the salt, Ea is now the god of the differentiated waters.

38. In Sumerian myth there is a similar conflict between the God, as Ninurta, Enki, or Inanna, and a dragon named Kur or Ashag, who in most versions is lord of the great underworld (Kur) beneath the earth and above the abyss. Kur is the underworld, and he is also sickness and death. The God slays Kur, but his death causes the primeval waters under the earth to burst forth flooding everything with their deadly darkness. This flood is checked when Ninurta piles stones upon the body of Kur, thus damming up the waters.

the other gods: man's chief responsibility therefore is to sacrifice to the gods and to work in the temples (could anyone other than a priest have composed the Enuma elish?). The curious thing is that Marduk fashions mankind out of the blood of Kingu. The implications are not drawn, but it might have been said that man's fallen nature derives from his descent from this demonic prince, the son of Tiamat.

The deities of the Babylonian underworld manifest qualities that are at best dubious. The "queen of darkness" is Ereshkigal, originally a sky goddess carried off by force to the underworld by the dragon Kur and there enthroned as its lady. She shares her throne with Nergal, the son of Enlil and originally a sun deity. Nergal forces his way into the underworld using heat and lightning as weapons and threatens to destroy Ereshkigal, who averts ruin only by agreeing to marry him. These dark deities are gods of destruction, plague, war, and death, yet they show their ambivalence both in their functions (Nergal is also a god of healing) and in their origins as sky gods who have fallen to their present chthonic state. As sister of the star goddess Ishtar (Sumerian Inanna), Ereshkigal is her doublet, and the famous myth of Ishtar's descent into hell confirms the relationship. Ishtar descends into the underworld for reasons that are unclear—probably she wishes to rule it herself. Understandably, she fears that her sister Ereshkigal will resent her temerity and put her to death. She must pass through seven gates, at each of which she is met by a demon who strips her of one article of clothing until at last "She is brought stark naked and on bended knees before Ereshkigal and the Anunnaki, the seven dreaded judges of the Nether World. They fasten upon her their eyes of death, and she is turned into a corpse, which is then hung from a stake.[39] While Ishtar is dead, all the earth above turns sterile. With the help of Enki, she is revived, but the rule of the underworld is that no one can return to life unless she provides a substitute victim. When Ishtar returns above, she goes to Kullab, where her husband, the shepherd

39. Kramer, p. 108.

Pazuzu, Mesopotamia, second millennium B.C. Horned, taloned, winged, with a saturnine face, the Mesopotamian demon Pazuzu was lord of the scorching north wind, a destructive manifestation of the God's power. Courtesy Musée du Louvre.

Tammuz (Sumerian Dumuzi) is, far from mourning her, enjoying himself on the throne in her absence. Ishtar looks upon him with the "eye of death" and hands him over to the demons of the underworld, from which he never returns.[40] Hell is here not only a region of death but a power that, when it imprisons the goddess of love and fertility, can cause blight and sterility on the earth.

The demonology of Mesopotamia had enormous influence on Hebrew and Christian ideas of demons and the Devil. The demons of Mesopotamia were generally hostile spirits of lesser dignity and power than gods. They were sometimes considered the offspring of Tiamat, but more often they were thought to be children of the high god Anu. The terrible *anunnaki* were the jailers of the dead in hell. The *etimmu* were ghosts of those who have died unhappy. The *utukku* lived in desert places or graveyards. Other evil spirits were demons of plagues, demons of nightmares, demons of headaches, demons of the windstorm (such as Pazuzu), and demons for every human ill. Among the most terrible was Lilitu or Ardat Lili, the ancestral prototype of the biblical Lilith (Isaiah 34). Lilitu was a frigid, barren, husbandless "maid of desolation" who roamed the night attacking men as a succubus or drinking their blood. Labartu, carrying a serpent in each hand and often accompanied by a dog or a pig, attacked children, mothers, and nurses. Usually the demons were grotesque, appearing as ugly animals or as misshapen humans with partly animal forms. To protect oneself against them one resorted to the use of amulets, incantations, exorcisms, or other magic, but particularly to the careful worship and cultivation of one's tutelary deity. "The man who hath not god as he walketh in the street, the demon covers him as a garment."[41]

40. This myth was misunderstood by Frazer. Dumuzi/Tammuz is not a dying/rising god, for once dead he never rises. It is his spouse Inanna/Ishtar who dies and rises again.

41. Georges Contenau, *Everyday Life in Babylonia and Assyria* (London, 1959), p. 255.

Lilitu, Sumer, second millennium B.C. The prototype of the Hebrew Lilith, Lilitu roams the world at night seducing sleeping men and slaying children. Winged and taloned, she is surrounded by owls and jackals, baleful hunters of the night. Courtesy Mrs. S. G. F. Brandon.

The term Canaan is used sometimes in its narrow, biblical sense and sometimes in the broader sense applying to the whole coast of what is now Syria, Lebanon, and Israel. The distinctive culture of the Canaanites had a great influence upon that of the Hebrews. The high God of Canaan was El, whose name was adopted by Yahweh (*el shaddai*, Elohim), the god of the sky and of the sun, often portrayed as a bull. His son was Baal ("the lord"), equated with Hadad, a god of lightning and thunder who became an agricultural deity when the Amorites settled down from roaming to a peaceful life in Canaan. Other deities of the Canaanites were Dagon, deity of vegetation, especially grain; Reshef, god of the desert, of war, and of plague; and three goddesses whose attributes and functions were often indistinguishable: the sea goddess Asherah, Astarte, and Anath, the maiden sister of Baal.[42] At the center of Canaanite religion was a fertility cult, the chief figures of which were Baal, Anath, and their enemy Mot, the lord of death and sterility. For centuries our only real knowledge of the Canaanites came from the Bible, whose Jewish authors perceived Baal as evil; but for the Canaanites themselves he was the savior god, the lord of life and fertility, whose symbols, like those of his father the high God El, were the bull and the crescent horns.

According to Canaanite myth, when Mot (cf. Hebrew *mot*, "death") is ravaging the world, Baal goes out to fight him. After a long struggle, Mot defeats Baal, and the lord bows and humiliates himself before his fierce foe, promising to be his slave. Mot kills him, or swallows him, or sends him to the underworld (all variants of the same act). Baal is gone from the face of the earth for seven years, during which the crops wither and the world is barren.[43] Death would rule forever, did not

---

42. The Hebrews distorted the name of Astarte to Ashtoreth in order to make it sound like *boshet*, "shame." In the western Mediterranean, the Phoenician colonists called Astarte Tanit. Her most common symbol was the crescent moon (or horns). In one of his forms, Baal-Qarnaïm, Baal possessed two horns and a tail. See Mitchell Dahood, "Three Parallel Pairs in Ecclesiastes 10:18," *Jewish Quarterly Review*, 62(1971), 84–85.

43. There is a dispute as to whether Baal's death is a yearly event or occurs in cycles of a number of years; it may be seven years, but in Semitic lan-

Baal's sister Anath, the terrible maiden goddess of love and of war, wander over the earth seeking her dead brother. At last she finds his body and gives it proper burial. Then in revenge she seeks out Mot, and "Death, thou shalt die." She seizes Mot, and "with sword she doth cleave him. With fan she doth winnow him—with fire she doth burn him. With hand-mill she grinds him—in the field she doth sow him."[44] The killing of Mot is at the same time an act of fertility designed to make the grain grow, and indeed the death of death revives Baal. He returns from the world below, and the earth blooms. But Mot too revives, and the two gods fight again. One version of the myth indicates that a kind of reconciliation is at last achieved, but the main tradition is that Baal and Mot, life and death, are locked in eternal combat. Mot, like Seth in Egypt, is the closest thing to a principle of evil in Canaan. Yet the fact that Mot is locked with Baal in unceasing combat also (with the additional evidence of the reconciliation story) makes a doublet of Mot and Baal. Mot and Baal, death and life, are the God and the work of the God, his rule and his constitution of the universe.

Anath and Baal are themselves twins, a doublet, a coincidence of opposites. Not only are they brother and sister, but Baal the bull mates with Anath in the form of a cow. And their functions are sometimes identical. Baal and Anath each fight with Mot, and they each (in different versions of the myth) struggle with an evil dragon named Yam. But the violence of the virgin Anath is not always directed in a way helpful to mankind. In one myth, Anath is confronted, for unstated reasons, with a hostile army of men:

> And lo Anath fights violently
> She slays the sons of the two cities
> She fights the people of the seashore
> Annihilates mankind of the sunrise. . . .

guages "seven" can mean an indefinite number. All interpretations of Canaanite religion are open to question because of the difficulties of the texts.

44. Translated by H. L. Ginsberg in James B. Pritchard, *The Ancient Near East* (Princeton, 1958), p. 113.

Anath, Ugarit, about 1400–1200 B.C. The maiden sister of the benign fertility god Baal, Anath helped defend her brother against the assaults of the god of sterility, Mot. But, as with Hathor/Sekhmet in Egypt, Anath's wrath could turn into a killing frenzy capable of destroying the world of mankind. Courtesy the Bialik Institute, Jerusalem.

> She plunges knee-deep in the blood of heroes
> Neck-high in the gore of troops. . . .[45]

Cyrus Gordon argues that the destruction of the people of the seashore (west) and sunrise (east) represents worldwide destruction. If this is true, the rampage of the maidenly Anath is the equivalent of that of the Egyptian Sekhmet. The motif, also found in Egypt, Mesopotamia, and Israel, is that the God plans the destruction of mankind but holds his hand to spare a remnant from the slaughter. Anath's rage represents the destructive power of the deity.

Hittite religion, a complicated mixture of native Anatolian, Indo-European, Canaanite, and Mesopotamian elements, offers relatively little discernibly related to the development of the principle of evil, but there is a Hittite version of the generational struggle among the gods. Alalu, the king of heaven, is deposed by his son Anu, who casts down his father "into the dark earth." Anu's own son Kumarbi now rises up against his father. A mighty struggle ensues during which Kumarbi bites off his father's penis (cf. Chronos' castration of Ouranos). But Anu has his revenge: his penis, working inside Kumarbi, impregnates him with a number of deities, including the storm god Teshub. Teshub becomes the most important deity of Hittite mythology. In one myth he struggles with a dragon named Illuyankas in a battle reminiscent of that of other gods with Kur, Tiamat, Yam, or Leviathan. Kumarbi, the deposed father of the storm god, continues to nurse hopes of revenge, and he begets an evil son Ullikummis (evil in the sense of his opposition to the storm god). Ullikummis is of enormous size, a giant whose form reaches to high heaven. He threatens the storm god and at the same time does baneful deeds to mankind, but he is finally vanquished. In yet another story, the Telpinu myth, the storm god is angry and in his wrath parches all the fields, causing men and animals to die. The storm god's father goes to the

45. Translated by Cyrus Gordon, "Canaanite Mythology," in Kramer, pp. 197–199.

storm god's grandfather and asks: "Who sinned [so that] the seed perished and everything dried up?" But Anu, understandably vexed with his son Kumarbi, replied, "No one sinned, but you alone sinned!" Kumarbi and his titanic son Ullikummis come closest to being the malign deities of the Hittite pantheon, but they do not in any clear fashion represent or personify the principle of evil.[46]

A revolution in the history of concepts occurred in Iran shortly before 600 B.C. with the teachings of the prophet Zarathushtra, who laid the basis for the first thoroughly dualist religion. Zarathushtra's revelation was that evil is not a manifestation of the divine at all; rather it proceeds from a wholly separate principle. While thus moving from monism to dualism, Zarathushtra also moved from polytheism in the direction of monotheism. The latter was not a necessary consequence of his discovery of dualism, for it is possible to posit a pantheon of good deities emanating from one principle and a pantheon of evil gods arising from the other. Indeed, the later Zoroastrians took this position. But although Zarathushtra was certainly monolatrous, insisting that worship could be offered only to Mazda, his monotheism seems to have been shaky. Monotheism is not incompatible with a modified form of dualism that posits a spiritual ruler of evil who is inferior to the spirit of good—such is the Christian tradition.[47] Yet Zarathushtra's spirit of evil, however inferior, has many of the characteristics of a god.

Whether or not Zarathushtra was a monotheist, he was a dualist. Religious dualism posits the existence of two principles. These two principles are not necessarily both divine, or equally divine, or equal in anything. They need not be (though they usually are) antipathetic. They *do* have to be entirely independent and are usually of separate origin (or of no determinable

46. Hans Güterbock, "Hittite Mythology," in Kramer, p. 145. There is an analogy to the Kumarbi myth in Gen. 6:1–4.

47. Another alternative to monism is pluralism, where there are not one or two absolute principles, but many. The complications of this position are such that it has seldom been embraced in religions.

origin). Thus not everything that exists is created or caused by one principle (what we are accustomed to call the God). Some things are derived from another principle. Each of the principles is absolute in itself, but neither has absolute or omnipotent power.

Dualistic religions form a spectrum from the extreme and absolute of Zoroastrianism, becoming more and more attenuated through the Zoroastrian heresy Zervanism, Gnosticism, and Manicheism to Christianity, Judaism, and Islam, where dualism almost ceases to exist.[48] All these religions, however different from one another, stand together in their distance from monism. All posit a God who is independent, powerful, and good, but whose power is to a degree limited by another principle, force, or void. The dualism of Zoroastrianism or of Manicheism is overt; that of Judaism and Christianity is much more covert, but it exists, and it exists at least in large part owing to Iranian influence. The dualism of Christianity and that of Iran differ in one essential respect. The latter is a division between two spiritual principles, one good and the other evil; Christianity borrowed from the Greeks the idea that spirit itself is considered good, as opposed to matter, which is considered evil. But the dualism introduced by Zarathushtra was a revolutionary step in the development of the Devil, for it posited, for the first time, an absolute principle of evil, whose personification, Angra Mainyu or Ahriman, is the first clearly defined Devil.

Dualism wrenches from the unity of the God a portion of his power in order to preserve his perfect goodness. Zarathushtra's teaching was a radically new theodicy, and one that is still arguable. As to whether dualism was or is preferable to monism there can be two opinions. On the one hand, if the unity of the God, and therefore of the cosmos and of the psyche, is broken,

---

48. Orthodox Islamic teaching is so monotheistic that it is almost a distortion to place Islam in this category. Islam found Zoroastrianism and Manicheism wholly incompatible with the teachings of Mohammed. Nonetheless, the ideas of Iblis or Shaitan exist in popular Muslim thought, and Islam is clearly remote from the monism of Hinduism or of Egyptian religion.

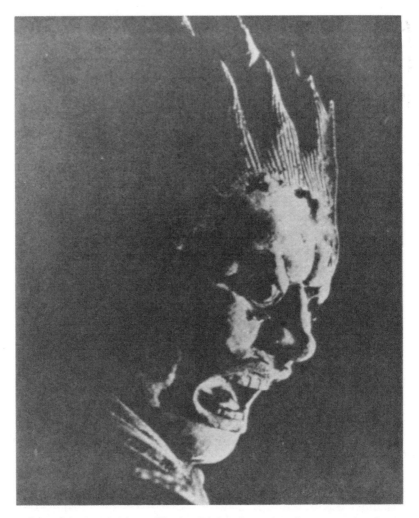

One of the jyuni shin-so (Twelve Divine Generals) who surround and pro-tect a Buddhist deity, Japan, eighth century. The flaming hair and fierce countenance represent anger against evil. Similar hair appeared on the heads of French demons in the twelfth century. Courtesy Asuka-En, Nara, Japan.

it becomes more difficult for nature, and for the psyche, to come to terms with itself. By insisting upon the struggle of two hostile principles warring for the mind, and by calling for war upon the evil principle, dualism abets repression, rather than healthy acceptance and conscious suppression of violence. This encourages the growth of the psychic shadow, the projection of hostilities, and the increase of destructive behavior. Dualism may arise from, or at least reinforce, a paranoid schizophrenic experience of the world as divided into good guys (or spirits) and bad guys (or spirits). On the other hand, it offers some advantages. Christianity has always found it difficult to reconcile the God's goodness with his omnipotence; Zoroastrianism preserves the absolute goodness of the God by sacrificing his omnipotence. In addition, dualism does seem to offer an explanation of the world as we really observe it, a world in which the mixing of impulses to good and impulses to evil is not readily explicable. Much would in fact become understandable if there were a force drawing us to evil as well as one beckoning us to good. Finally, some have argued that the idea in monistic religions of transcending good and evil is both fallacious and immoral. The evils of the world are so many, so great, and so piercingly immediate that they demand not mystical acceptance, but the will to take arms against them.

But does dualistic theodicy really work? The question cannot readily be answered. Some dualists (the Zervanites) argued that the two principles proceeded from one ur-principle, itself imperfect. But how can an ur-principle, absolute as by definition it must be, really be imperfect? The orthodox Zoroastrians claimed that the two principles are totally independent, yet they meet and clash, and the good one will inevitably prevail over the evil one. But if it is certain that the good spirit will prevail over the evil, why does he require the motion of time? If in eternity the power of one spirit wills, and is capable of, the destruction of the other, why does he not defeat him in that eternal, timeless moment? Indeed, why does he tolerate his emergence at all?

In any event, dualism insists upon the existence of an absolute and radical evil. Not only does this in part respond to our perceptions of the world, but it for the first time limns a figure clearly recognizable as diabolical.

The Iranians, an Indo-European people, originally arrived in

Iran as nomads in the second half of the second millennium B.C. Gradually agricultural and pastoral occupations supplanted the nomadic life. The struggle between sedentary and nomadic peoples still raged in Zarathushtra's time, however, and his patron, the Chorasmian king Vishtaspa, was frequently at war with the nomads. It has been suggested that this struggle provides the background of Zarathushtra's dualism, and the importance of the ox in the Gathas and Zarathushtra's reference in the Gathas to the nomads as people of the lie (Druj) indicate his commitment to Vishtaspa's side of the struggle.

The sources for the history of ancient Iran are fragmentary. Three quarters of the great book of Zoroastrianism, the Avesta, is lost. The paucity of sources has occasioned great differences of opinion among Iranists, and what follows can be based only upon what seems the best opinion among them. The religion of Iran before Zarathushtra was similar to the Vedic religion of India. The original pantheon was ruled by the sky god Dyaosh (cf. Sanskrit Dyaus, Greek Zeus), who was also called Mazda. Mazda and Mithra were both originally gods of the heavens. There was a conflict between Druj (the lie) and Asha or Asha-rita, truth and order (cf. *ma'at*). Asha-rita is comparable to the Vedic *rita*, right order, and the Rig Veda alludes to, but does not expatiate on, a conflict between *rita* and the lie (*an-rita*). This conflict between truth and the lie was one of the main sources of Zarathushtra's dualism: the prophet perceived Angra Mainyu, the lord of evil, as the personification of the lie. For Zoroastrians (as for the Egyptians), the lie was the essence of evil. This is a position some modern theologians have respected. C. S. Lewis suggested that the lie is the worst of sins because it attacks the structure of meaning itself and renders the cosmos unintelligible and unlovable. Martin Buber observed that a lie was possible "only after a creature, man, was capable of conceiving the being of truth. . . . In a lie the spirit practices treason against itself."[49] Later Mazdaists considered Druj a female demon-general of the whole host of evil spirits.

49. Martin Buber, *Good and Evil* (New York, 1953), p. 7.

Parthian goddess, Persia, first or second century A.D. This representation of a Near Eastern fertility deity wears the horns of power and fecundity. Courtesy Photographie Giraudon, Paris.

Zarathushtra's dualism was also based upon the conflict between the ahuras and the daevas. In India, the elder gods, the asuras, were defeated and overthrown by the devas, who became "the gods" and relegated their ancient enemies the asuras to the level of demons. But in Iran, the ahuras defeated the daevas, and apparently Zarathushtra was himself partly responsible for their victory.

Zarathushtra may have been the first theologian, the first individual to create a rational system of religion. He may have been a member of the priestly caste, but it is clear that he viewed himself as a prophet, a man whose direct revelation from the God impelled him to challenge the assumptions of the religion in which he had been brought up. His ideas, like those of other great leaders, underwent considerable change, and one must distinguish between the doctrine of Zarathushtra himself and Zoroastrianism (or Mazdaism), the religion of his followers.[50]

There are at least four major strands in Zoroastrianism: (1) the teachings of Zarathushtra himself; (2) those of Mazdaism; (3) those of Zervanism, a heretical offshoot of Mazdaism; (4) those of the Magi, whose teachings gradually diverged from orthodoxy and eventually helped produce the Mithraism of the Hellenistic period.

Zarathushtra was largely responsible for the relegation of the daevas to the ranks of the demons by elevating one of the ahuras, Ahura Mazda, to the position of the one God. The daevas then logically had to be categorized as enemies of the God. Zarathushtra explained that the daevas became evil by their own free will and choice: "Between the two [spirits] the false gods (daevas) also did not choose rightly, / For while they

50. Zoroaster is the Western form of Zarathushtra. I shall use "Zarathushtra" when referring to the prophet himself, and "Zoroaster" and "Zoroastrianism" or "Mazdaism" when referring to the ideas of his later followers. When I do not specify the origins of doctrines, they are Mazdaist rather than emanating from Zarathushtra himself, about whom relatively little is known. When referring to the doctrines of Zarathushtra himself, I call the two spirits Ahura Mazda and Angra Mainyu. When referring to the beliefs of Mazdaism, I use the later terms Ohrmazd and Ahriman.

pondered they were beset by error, / So that they chose the Worst Mind."[51] Later Mazdaism would make Ahriman the creator, as well as the leader, of the daevas.

In Zarathushtra's theology, the gods are no longer manifestations of the One, as they were in India and Egypt. The One rules alone, sufficient to himself. The other gods, divorced from the One and having thereby lost their divinity, do not cease to exist, but rather become spirits inferior to the God. If their nature is identified as primarily good, they become what we call angels; if evil, they become what we call demons. Angels and demons thus occupy a middle ground between polytheistic monism and an extreme monotheism that denies the existence of more than one god. Zarathushtra argued that the daevas were evil spirits whose influence must be resisted. Yet he was not entirely successful in his war against these beings, for they retained their worshipers, who considered them beneficent.

After the death of Zarathushtra his teachings were modified by the Magi, the old hereditary priestly caste, who reintroduced much of the old religion and diluted the prophet's monotheism. For five centuries after the conquest by Alexander in 330 B.C., the state of Zoroastrianism is unclear, but with the foundation of the Sassanian monarchy in 226 A.D. it was restored to favor, and the second great period of the religion began. The complicated and sometimes confused theology of the Sassanian period is found primarily in the Pahlavi books (third to eighth century A.D.), of which the most important are the Bundahishn and the Denkart. The Sassanian period also produced a number of heresies, such as Zervanism, Manicheism, and Mazdakism; the Sassanian monarchs and their priests used capital punishment in repressing the heresies, for Mazdaism became a legalistic public cult of the Sassanian state.[52]

51. Gatha-Yasna 30:6, in Jacques Duchesne-Guillemin, ed., *The Hymns of Zarathustra* (London, 1952), p. 105.
52. Some Iranists, notably Duchesne-Guillemin, argue that Zervanism is an ancient doctrine rather than an innovation of the Sassanian period. A non-

Ahura Mazda, Persepolis, late sixth or fifth century B.C. Ahura Mazda, or Ohrmazd, the principle of light and eternal enemy of Ahriman, the lord of darkness, is here shown with the sun, symbol of light, and wings, symbol of divine power. The use of wings as a sign of power passed into the iconography of the Devil. Courtesy Antonello Perissinotto, Padua.

Zarathushtra argued that two spiritual principles exist. One is Ahura Mazda, the God, lord of goodness and of light. The other is Angra Mainyu ("Destructive or Tormenting Spirit"), lord of evil and darkness. Ahura Mazda has in his complete freedom of will chosen the good, and Angra Mainyu in his complete freedom has chosen the evil. "Now at the beginning the twin spirits have declared their nature, the better and the evil. In thought and word and deed. . . . Of these two spirits, the evil one chose to do the worst things; But the Most Holy Spirit, clothed in the most steadfast heavens, joined himself

Iranist can only judge by the balance of opinion, which weighs heavily in favor of the Sassanian origin of the heresy, though the worship of a god named Zurvan was much older.

unto Righteousness." [53] The two spirits are opposites, then, but they are also twins, a coincidence of opposites. The difference between Zarathushtra's doublets and those of the Egyptians is that rather than the opposites being manifestations of the One being, they are dissociated, independent principles.

Or almost independent. Zarathushtra's thought is more ambivalent—transitional, perhaps—than that. The Gatha quoted above refers to a being called the Most Holy Spirit. The Gathas seem to imply One God, Ahura Mazda, who generates twins, Angra Mainyu, the evil spirit, and Spenta Mainyu, the holy spirit. This notion is a coincidence of opposites resolved in the One, but a modification occurred shortly after the death of Zarathushtra. Spenta Mainyu came to be identified with Ahura Mazda, the son with the father, and hence Ahura Mazda himself became the twin brother of Angra Mainyu. This idea, in which Ahura Mazda's fatherhood is blurred and finally lost sight of, leaves two wholly independent principles. This is an absolute dualism. But the original position of Zarathushtra, in which the good and the evil spirit are both parts of the divine nature, was revived in a different form by the Zervanite heretics. To summarize, Zarathushtra himself took a position midway between monism and dualism; Mazdaism moved decidedly toward dualism; Zervanism made a partial return in the direction of monism. In all three, the evil spirit opposes the good spirit, but the opposition is most clear-cut in orthodox Mazdaism.

The orthodox Mazdaist position is most completely articulated in one of the Pahlavi books, the Greater Bundahishn. [54] In the beginning there were two spirits, Ohrmazd (the later version of Ahura Mazda) and Ahriman (the later version of Angra Mainyu), and they were separated by the void. Ohrmazd is good, light, and unlimited in time (eternal), though limited in space by the void and by Ahriman, who lies on the other side of the void. Only by defeating Ahriman can Ohrmazd free

53. Gatha-Yasna 30, in Duchesne-Guillemin, p. 105.
54. There is a longer and a shorter version of the Bundahishn; the shorter version may have been written as late as the ninth century.

himself from his limitation in space and become infinite as well
as eternal. Yet the good Ohrmazd initiates no struggle with
Ahriman.

Ahriman is dark and evil. He is limited in space by the void
and by Ohrmazd, who lies beyond the void, and he is limited
in time by the certainty of his eventual ruin at the hands of
Ohrmazd. The precariousness of his existence is indicated by
certain texts that speak of his nonbeing: Ahriman "is not," or he
"once was not and again will not be," or he "was and is, yet
will not be." The nonbeing of Ahriman is meant to indicate his
non-Ohrmazdness, Ohrmazd being equated with absolute
being. There is no doubt that Ahriman exists, vexing Ohrmazd
and his creation, but his being is contingent, not absolute. This
ambiguousness regarding the existence of evil indirectly influenced Christianity, in which it became one of the classical questions of theology and still causes misunderstandings.[55] Ahriman
is also the essence of destruction and so at the perfect center of
our definition of evil. He is "The Destroyer . . . , the accursed destructive Spirit who is all wickedness and full of
death, a liar and a deceiver."[56] In this theology, Ohrmazd and
Ahriman are good and evil by their own choice, but also ontologically, eternally bound by their natures. The God has been
freed from all taint of evil: he is not evil himself, he does not
create evil, and he does not willingly tolerate evil; indeed he
wars against it incessantly. One of Ohrmazd's first acts is to
limit time, to remove it from the infinite by setting a term to it,
for he knows that only in time can he struggle with Ahriman
and so destroy him.[57] The time he creates endures twelve thousand years (a figure probably derived from the zodiac).

In the beginning, Ohrmazd knows of the existence of Ahriman, but Ahriman, in his dark ignorance on the other side of

55. Cf. Antonio Moreno, *Jung, Gods, and Modern Man* (Notre Dame, 1970).

56. "Selected Counsels of the Ancient Sages," in R. C. Zaehner, *The Teachings of the Magi* (New York, 1956), p. 23.

57. Note that this limitation of time, and the conception of time as meaningful, progressive, and necessary for the eventual triumph of the God, appears again in the thought of the Christian fathers, especially Augustine, and
becomes the basis of historical thought in the West.

Birth of Ohrmazd and Ahriman, Luristan, eighth century B.C. The large central figure is Zurvan; emerging from him are his twin sons, the doublet Ohrmazd and Ahriman, the light and dark sides of the divine principle. Courtesy Photographie Giraudon, Paris.

the void, knows Ohrmazd not. But in the course of the first three thousand years, Ahriman discerns across the void a point of light and, seeing that light, covets it, longs for it, lusts for it, and determines to possess it. Ohrmazd now creates the good things, and Ahriman creates evil things, such as scorpions and toads. In his envy and lust, Ahriman attacks the work of Ohrmazd with his weapons of darkness, concupiscence, and disorder. Ohrmazd, though he knows that his enemy must be destroyed, in his goodness attempts to avert the struggle. In the spirit of love and mercy he offers Ahriman peace if Ahriman will agree to praise the good creation. But Ahriman, limited by his evil nature, believes that Ohrmazd's gesture is a sign of weakness, and he refuses the offer. Ohrmazd shows him what his inevitable fate must be, and Ahriman, stunned by this terrible revelation of his ruin, falls into the outer darkness (the void?), where he lies unconscious for three thousand years. After that period, he revives and engages Ohrmazd in a war that for three thousand years is equally balanced. The final

Zurvan, Hellenistic, heavily restored. The Zervanite heresy of Mazdaism regarded Zurvan, the god of time, as the father of both light and darkness, of both Ohrmazd and Ahriman. Courtesy Mansell Collection, London.

three thousand years end with the destruction of the evil one.

The Zervanites of the Sassanian period returned to the more transitional position that Zarathushtra and his immediate followers may have taken, though they expressed it in different terms. For the Zervanites there is one ur-principle, Zurvan, infinite time. Zurvan is the One, the All, a coincidence of opposites containing within himself the good and the evil, the male and the female, light and darkness, bliss and misery, order and disorder. Zurvan is eternal and lives by himself. But he wishes a son. For a thousand years he sacrifices (this apparently means "exercises his creative powers") without success, so he doubts the efficacy of his sacrifices. At the end of a thousand years, his wife (really the female half of his androgynous nature) gives birth not to one son but to two, the one the product of his love and his desire, the other the result of his moment of doubt. The doubt of Zurvan constitutes a kind of fall on the part of the deity, and henceforth the sacrifice and honor previously paid him is offered instead to the son of his desire.

The son of Zurvan's desire is Ohrmazd, warm and moist, the god of goodness, light, and life. The son of his doubt is Ahriman, cold and dry, lord of darkness and evil. To Ahriman Zurvan had planned to give nothing, for his intent was to bestow the rule of the world upon the son he loved. But Ahriman thrusts himself first out of the womb and claims the rule, to the horror of his father, who exclaims, "My son is light and fragrant, but thou art dark and stinking." And so for a time Ahriman obtains lordship in this world, though the moment of his destruction and the triumph of Ohrmazd is set. The story of Jacob and Esau comes quickly to mind, and indeed what we have here is another set of doublets. Ohrmazd and Ahriman are the two halves of Zurvan that have been separated by the act of generation. However, the difference between the Zoroastrian/Zervanite position and that of the other religions we have observed is again remarkable. The solution to this twinning in the nature of the One is not the eventual reconstitution of the divine (or psychic) whole, but rather the elimination of one of the two by cosmic battle (psychic repression), a solution very similar to that adopted by late Judaism, Christianity, and Islam. The Devil has become a totally alien force, not to be assimilated but to be destroyed. We are not to recognize the evil in ourselves and consciously suppress it; rather, we are to deny that it is in us, insist that it lies somewhere outside us, and therefore strive for the perfection that will come when we have driven off its assaults. Whatever the merits of this theodicy, its psychological difficulties are manifest.

Having imprisoned Ahriman in the darkness, the God now

creates the cosmos by thinking it. Zarathushtra says that Ahura
Mazda creates light and darkness and all things visible and in-
visible. Later Mazdaists ascribed only the creation of the light
and of good things to Ohrmazd, assigning to Ahriman the creation of darkness and of evil things. Some material things may
have been made by Ahriman, and Ahriman's assaults upon the
world have corrupted much of what was originally created
good. But basically the material universe is real (though less
real than the spirit), and it is a good. The dualism of Mazdaism
is never a dualism like that of the Manicheans later, which sets
the material world against the spiritual world, and in no way is
Ahriman the god of matter or even, as in Christianity, the "lord
of this world."

In addition to the material world, Ahura Mazda created the
six *amesh spentas* (Pahlavi: *amahraspands*), Good Mind, Truth,
Rightmindedness, The Kingdom, Wholeness, and Immortality.
These spirits, with Spenta Mainyu, form a council of seven
around Ahura Mazda.[58] These seven are an example of the
middle ground between polytheism and monotheism. It is not
clear whether the *amesh spentas* are created by Ahura Mazda or
are in some way emanations of the God. They may thus be
considered either gods or angels.

Ohrmazd now creates life in the material world, placing in
the universe four manifestations of life: vegetation, fire, the
primal bull (or ox), and the ideal man. This man, Gayomart, is
shining, complete, in all ways a perfect microcosm. And Ohrmazd is well pleased with what he has done.

But Ahriman, who has for three thousand years been lying in
the outer darkness, is revived from his slumbers by the minis-
trations of the Whore, Jeh, and renews his assault upon Ohrmazd and his works. So the third three-thousand-year period
begins, the period of almost evenly matched war in the cosmos.
Despairing, yet still possessed of enormous power, Ahriman
bursts forth from the outer darkness and attacks the sky, rend-

58. There is no proof that the number seven is an indication of Babylonian
influence, but it seems probable that, whether or not of Mesopotamian origin,
the number is derived from the seven planets.

ing it apart, and plunging through the atmosphere toward the earth. Reaching the earth in his plummeting descent he tunnels a vast hole through it and, emerging on the other side, enters the primal waters under the earth. Having now for the first time introduced violence and disorder into the cosmos, he causes darkness to fall: "At midday did he trample on all the world and make it as dark as the darkest night."[59] He creates all loathsome things, such as scorpions, toads, and vipers; he creates ugliness, and he unleashes all destructive forces, storms, drought, disease, and death. He creates the whole host of demons, beginning with seven archfiends commissioned to thwart and attack the seven amahraspands. And turning the fury of his destructive force upon the jewel of Ohrmazd's creation, he destroys life, killing the fire, the plants, the primal ox, and Gayomart, the perfect man. Ahriman has triumphed. Of the orderly and benevolent cosmos he has made a disorderly and noxious ruin. And the spirit of destruction is well pleased with what he has done.

Now Ahriman prepares to return to the outer darkness to gloat over his victory. But Ohrmazd creates the *fravashis*, the souls of men yet to be born. The *fravashis*, choosing freely to help Ohrmazd against his ancient foe, prevent Ahriman from leaving the cosmos. They bind him within the cosmos and within time, so that Ohrmazd may have the time to repair his shattered world and in the end vanquish and destroy the destructive one. Ohrmazd now brings about the resurrection. The corpse of the great ox fertilizes the sterile land, and Ohrmazd causes a rain to wet the dry earth, so that plants again may grow and green the world. The fire is rekindled. The seed of the dead Gayomart enters the womb of Spandarmat (the earth), and from that union spring the ancestors of all humankind, Mashye and his wife Mashyane. The first couple have free will, and initially they choose to love and serve Ohrmazd. But Ahriman tempts them with the worst of all sins, the essence of sin itself; he tells them a lie. They believe it, and they repeat it.

59. R. C. Zaehner, *The Dawn and Twilight of Zoroastrianism* (London, 1961), p. 262.

Choosing the lie over the truth, Mashye and Mashyane say that Ahriman, not Ohrmazd, has created the material world, "water, the earth, plants, cattle, sun, moon, and stars, and . . . all fertile things."[60] This lie is accompanied by another sin: the first couple offer an ox in sacrifice. To Zarathushtra and his followers, cattle were holy, as they were in India, witness the initial creation of the primal ox with the primal Gayomart. Mashye and Mashyane, tempted by Ahriman but sinning of their own free will, fall from grace. The result is, as it was to be in Christianity, ambivalent: on the one hand, the couple gain knowledge and understanding of the arts of civilization. They learn to make clothing, to cook, to work with wood and metal. But chiefly they learn suffering. Into a world hitherto perfect now intrude strife, hatred, disease, poverty, and death. Mashye and Mashyane can no longer function according to their nature. Though Ohrmazd wishes them to be fruitful and multiply, they abstain from intercourse for fifty years, and when at last they again come together and engender twins, they eat them. Following this manifestation of the utter corruption of their nature, Ohrmazd causes them to be fertile again; more children are born and, their parents having tamed their most ferocious urges, survive to become the ancestors of the human race.[61]

But the effects of the fall remain with us. Humankind lives in a world rendered imperfect by Ahriman and further corrupted

60. Zaehner, *Dawn*, p. 267.

61. Thus the perfection of the world was twice disrupted. According to the insights of structuralism, we can see the two myths, the ruin of Gayomart and the fall of Mashye, as representing one fact: the alienation of mankind from the cosmos. Yet there is an important difference between the myths. Gayomart's ruin was in no way his fault, but purely the result of Ahriman's direct and malicious intervention; whereas Mashye fell of his own free will. The first myth emphasizes the responsibility of Ahriman for evil; the second the responsibility of mankind itself. The analogy to Christian thought is very close: sin is the work both of the Devil and of the humans who yield to temptation. Evil results from both the free choice of Satan and the free choice of humankind. Note: these myths are both later Zoroastrian myths. Zarathushtra himself followed the old Indo-Iranian tradition that made Yima (Hindu Yama) the first man. Yima fell, Zarathushtra said, because he improperly distributed sacrificial meat to the people.

by the defection of our first parents. Human nature is henceforth threefold. It is demonic as well as animal and divine. Yet in no way does the sin of Mashye and Mashyane bind us to sin. We retain our free will and our free choice. The original sin of our first parents warped the conditions of our lives, but it did not bend our will toward Ahriman. If, then, we live lives of moderation and of respect for the God, and if we avoid the temptations placed in our path by Ahriman, we do the God's will. The world that Ohrmazd has created is good, and we are to enjoy its fruits. After the obligation always to fight the lie, moderation is the chief duty of the Mazdaist.[62]

The world in which we live is thus disfigured both by our own fall and by the malice of Ahriman, who has in the service of further destructiveness populated it with demons. Ahriman, the lie, the destroyer, is himself the chief of all the demons, a vast host composed in part of the vanquished daevas and in part of personifications of destructive forces or of sins. Seven chief demons, seven archfiends, aid Ahriman in his struggle against the forces of light. The seven archfiends, led by Aeshma (wrath), are Wrongmindedness, Heresy or Apostasy, Anarchy or Misgovernment, Discord, Presumption, Hunger, and Thirst. Under the command of these archdemons are hosts of other evil spirits, some of whom figure prominently in the development of the concept of the Devil. In Iranian thought, as in Christianity, the lesser demons are theoretically distinct from the Prince of Darkness, but in fact their attributes are often

62. The sins postulated by the Zoroastrians are for the most part comparable to those of other religions—sins of violence: anger, murder, rape, and abortion; sins of immoderation: gluttony, drunkenness, boasting; sins against society: dishonoring parents, parsimony, ill humor. Adultery was a sin, but fornication was not. Indeed, celibacy was regarded as a sin (as was any asceticism), a vice of immoderation, a refusal to use the things of this world for the purposes that the God intended. There was also a wide variety of sins involving the violation of ritual tabus: eating cattle or other domestic animals, doubting Ohrmazd, performing religious rites improperly, bringing excrement into contact with water, and so on. The chief sin, the essence of sin itself, remained the lie. More than anything else, the lie was thought to disrupt the cosmic order willed by Ohrmazd. That is why the lie and destruction are so closely linked in the character of Ahriman.

muddled. The god Vayu, lord of the air, was also a god of battle. Sometimes he supported Ohrmazd in war, sometimes Ahriman. Gradually his association with the destructive side of war became the more pronounced side of his character, and he became a god or demon of death. The primal ambivalence of Zurvan has already been noted, and insofar as he represented time in its consuming or destroying aspects he may have been considered evil. There were vast numbers of minor evil spirits, such as Zahhak (Azhi Dahaka), from whose shoulders sprouted two demonic serpents. Zahhak was also portrayed as a dragon with three heads and a body full of lizards and scorpions. The Zervanites appear to have considered the planets evil spirits because these heavenly bodies described irregular courses in the heavens, any irregularity being perceived as a disruption of the proper order of the cosmos. Associated with Ahriman and his demons were the unclean creatures that Ahriman had made, such as rats, frogs, cats, and snakes. The demons could change their forms, and Ahriman could take on the appearance of a lion, a snake, a lizard, or even a handsome youth. Some Zoroastrian theologians argued that Ahriman did not have a proper material body at all, matter being the creation of the good God. The evil one might thus adopt any material form he saw fit, since his numerous disguises were another sign of his inner nature of liar and deceiver. The demons lived in the unclean creatures, or they roamed through the air, and they could enter into the bodies of human beings, possessing them and causing disease, insanity, or death.

Some demons were associated primarily with the female. The female principle is ambivalent in Mazdaism as elsewhere, but it appears more often in a negative than in a positive manifestation: some texts report Ohrmazd's dissatisfaction with having to create a female in order to propagate the human race. Though Spandarmat, the good earth, is a positive Great Mother figure, there are more frequent manifestations of the negative Terrible Mother. Druj, originally the abstraction of the lie, becomes in the Pahlavi period a female leader of the host of demons. Az, the spirit of concupiscence, deception, and disorder, is masculine in the Avesta, but in Manicheism and possibly in Zervanism Az is a feminine spirit of greed, lust, avarice, and error. Jeh (Jahi), the Great Whore, is a female demon of debauchery and lust, but she is more than that: she is one of Ahriman's chief helpers, a force that from the beginning aids him in destroying the cosmos and is responsible for reviving him from the unconscious state in which he lies after Ohrmazd has revealed to him the eventual ruin into which he will fall. One myth presents Jeh as the mistress of Ahriman. Having had intercourse with the Prince of Darkness, she then pollutes Gayomart, the perfect man. Woman the vile seducer is more prominent in Zoroastrianism than woman the fostering mother. The lord of darkness himself was always uncompromisingly masculine, but then so was the god of light. Masculinity seems to have been reserved to the two principles simply because they were ontologically superior to other beings.

Mazdaist eschatology, like Christian, takes two forms, one personal, the other cosmic. The death of each person is a little end, the dissolution of the small cosmos that is a human being. Upon death, the soul proceeds to the Chinvat Bridge, where he is judged by the three just but terrible judges, Mihr, Srosh, and Rashnu. His good deeds are weighed against his bad while demons crowd around seeking to tip the balance against him. The judges see that justice is done, and after the trial, the soul is allowed to continue on the Chinvat Bridge. If his good deeds have proved the better balance, he is met by a beautiful maiden personifying the goodness of his soul (cf. Beatrice), who leads him across the bridge and into Paradise. If the bad deeds outweigh the good, the bridge turns beneath him, presenting a razor-sharp edge to his feet, and he topples uncontrollably into the abyss, where Vizaresh, Vayu, and other fearsome demons carry him off into hell.[63] As in Christianity, neither the God

63. Note that here Vayu is at the most hostile extreme of his mixed character. The passage of the Chinvat Bridge is very similar to a motif of Christian mythology, the ladder to heaven. The soul's pilgrimage to heaven is perceived as an effort to scale a high ladder. Some succeed in making the ascent, but others slip from the rungs and fall into hell.

The Chinvat Bridge, India, sixteenth century, showing the mechanics of judgment in Mazdaism. The souls of the saved pass over the bridge to Paradise; those who are found wanting are flung off into the pit below. Courtesy Photo. Bibl. Nat. Paris.

nor the judges will us to go to hell, nor does the spirit of darkness force us to go there, though at the judgment his minions display their eagerness to carry off our souls. If the bridge turns under us and sends us hurtling to hell, it is because we have freely chosen the darkness over the light.

Hell is located in the middle of the earth, in the cavity created when Ahriman plunged from the heavens and bored a tunnel through the quaking earth. Hell is infested by hostile demons, who are the only companions of the damned soul, and who torment it by gnawing it, swallowing it, or piercing it with spears. The soul must also suffer terrible heat and biting cold, nauseating filth and stench, and it must consume the most loathsome and putrid food. As in other hells, torments are adapted to the crime, so that, for example, an adulteress is suspended by her breasts while vermin gnaw at her viscera. Those whose lives have been neither clearly good nor wholly bad are spared the pains of hell but denied the joys of Paradise. They merit spending the rest of recorded time in Hamestagan, where they suffer a dull and shadowy life oppressed by extremities of heat and cold. Hamestagan has been compared to the Christian purgatory; it is perhaps more comparable to Dante's circle of trimmers. Neither Hamestagan nor Mazdaist hell is eternal; when time at last comes to an end, all souls will be saved. For the Mazdaists, the final triumph of Ohrmazd over Ahriman necessarily implied the restoration of the entire cosmos, and it was illogical that the God should allow souls to remain in hell. At the *Frashkart*, the great renewal of the world, all creatures, including the damned souls, will enjoy bliss.

The *Frashkart* is the great end, the *eschata* or last things of the macrocosmos. After three thousand years of warfare, Ohrmazd presses Ahriman on every side, and, sensing their imminent defeat, the forces of evil turn their destructive powers against one another, causing disruption and ruin in their own ranks. All the more frenzied by their sense of impending doom, they exert themselves more than ever before, and the entire cosmos is shaken by wars and rumors of wars, by giant battles, by plagues and other disasters. The sun and the moon pale in the heavens, and the stars fall from the sky. But at last the Prince of Darkness and his minions are exhausted, Ohrmazd presses the final attack, and Ahriman falls, this time utterly and finally. Orthodox opinion varied as to whether Ohrmazd destroys Ahriman or whether he renders him forever a helpless prisoner; the Zervanites held that Ohrmazd, exploiting the destructive hatred that the forces of evil turned against one another, allows the demon Az to devour the lord of evil and then destroys Az, eliminating all traces of the evil. In either event, evil, and the threat of evil, are forever removed, and Ohrmazd is now infinite, eternal, and omnipotent.

The world does not end with the end of the evil eon, however; rather, it is restored to the perfection it enjoyed in the days of Gayomart and the great ox. Moreover, this is not merely a restoration of the golden age but an improvement, a *renovatio in melius*, for no longer does Ahriman have the potential for spoiling the shining new world. A "savior" named Soshyans, the last of three beneficent beings born in the latter days to virgins impregnated with the seed of Zoroaster, appears and harrows hell, reconstituting decomposed bodies and reuniting them with their souls. After a brief period of suffering, all are admitted to eternal bliss. Thus the principle of evil, though it may have no origin, no beginning, does have an end, and in the end all hopes, both for the cosmos and for the small cosmos that is the individual, will be fulfilled.

The radical ideas of Zarathushtra and his followers constituted a revolution in the concept of the Devil. But it is difficult, given the religious confusion of the Hellenistic period, to define precisely the extent of Iranian influence in the eastern Mediterranean world of the Greeks and the Jews. Both Zervanism and, later, Manicheism were heresies of Zoroastrianism or at least deeply rooted in it. Very different is Mithraism, the religion that in the Roman Empire enjoyed such popularity as to be a serious rival of Christianity. Mithras was originally an Indo-Iranian solar deity. In his effort to move toward monotheism, Zarathushtra emphasized the power of Ahura Mazda to the point of ignoring Ahura Mithra, and we have no idea what the prophet thought of this deity. His followers restored Mithras to power, assimilating him to Mazda and worshiping him as a manifestation of the god of light. But apparently the unregenerate daeva-worshipers untouched by Zarathushtra's reforms also continued to worship Mithras, and some of the later Magi may have been drawn in this direction. Hellenistic Mithraism descends directly from this tradition, rather than from Mazdaism, and it is best understood in the Hellenistic, rather than in the Iranian, context. Nowhere is this more clearly suggested than in the central rite of Mithraism, which imitated the great, eternal act of the god Mithras, the taurobolium or sacrifice of the bull. Now, Zarathushtra specifically and deeply honored the sanctity of cattle and condemned their sacrifice, and later Mazdaist tradition had it that the great ox or bull was, with Gayomart, one of the first creatures in the pristine cosmos. One of Mashye's original sins was the sacrifice of an ox or a bull, and it was Ahriman who, when he burst in fury upon the cosmos, slew the great ox. To a Mazdaist, the sacrifice of a bull or an ox is an imitation of Ahriman and a great blasphemy. It is therefore difficult to understand how Mithraism could have sprung directly from Mazdaism, though both were rooted in the same Iranian milieu.

Mazdaism undeniably influenced Jewish and Christian thought, but the degree of the influence is uncertain. For one thing, the greatest period of Zoroastrian theology was the Sassanian period, which began two hundred years after Christ. Of course Mazdaist ideas had been current for centuries before, but it is difficult to establish the extent to which they might have been known to Christians. The many similarities in the Iranian and Judeo-Christian notions of the evil one, of hell, and of resurrection probably indicate a high degree of cultural diffusion. Iranian influence seems undeniable upon the Essenes (especially in the Manual of Discipline) and upon the Gnostics (Ialdabaoth's similarities to Ahriman are striking). The vectors established in Iranian religion move the concept of the Devil strongly away from the more ambiguous realms of monism into the sharp distinctions of the dualist opposition of good and evil.

4 Evil in the Classical World

Πόθεν τὸ κακόν; Whence does evil come?

It was the Greeks who first posed the question of the origin and nature of evil in strictly philosophical terms. But the Greeks and their predecessors, the Myceneans, Minoans, and Pelasgians, also had a treasury of folklore, myth, and legend upon which they drew. The extent to which the Greek traditions were influenced by those of the Ancient Near East and Iran are still being investigated by historians and archaeologists, but with each passing decade those influences appear a bit stronger. Linear A, the earliest written language of Minoan Crete, may be Semitic, only later replaced by the Greek Linear B. Certain structural similarities between Homer and the Hebrew "Elohist" writer are evident, and the flourishing trade between Egypt and Crete in the Minoan period has long been recognized.[1] The influence of Minoan Crete, powerful in the period between 2200 and 1400, came to an end in the period of the Achaean invasions; Minoan culture was transplanted to the mainland and modified in the Mycenean civilization that flourished from 1600 to 1100. These civilizations, and the culture of the Pelasgians, who inhabited the mainland before Greek invaders began to arrive about 1300, lie in the background of the Greek or Hellenic civilization that was already established at the time of the Trojan War (1200–1180). The

1. Erich Auerbach, "Odysseus' Scar," in his *Mimesis* (Princeton, 1953), pp. 3–27.

myths and legends of the Hellenes are therefore partly their own, and partly derived from their predecessors and the Ancient Near Eastern cultures beyond. The influence of Iranian dualism may have made itself felt in Greece as early as the sixth century B.C.

The gods of the Greeks, like those of Egypt and Mesopotamia, were ambivalent manifestations of the one God. The apparently contradictory ethical and ontological qualities of the gods indicate confusion less than they do the coincidence of opposites. In Homer, little distinction is made between *theos* and *daimōn*, and the characteristics of both are ambiguous. But although gods or demons have baleful or destructive elements, there is no one principle of evil. Both good and evil are seen to proceed from the one God, of whom the individual gods are manifestations. Thus the gods as a class, and each god or goddess independently, possess both good and evil qualities. This ethical ambivalence is underscored by another. Almost every god shows signs of both an ouranic (heavenly) and a chthonic (underworld) character, the chthonic being more often assimilated to the concept of evil. All these ambiguities result in part from the fact that the figure of each god as known in the classical period is a synthesis of many diverse elements derived from local cults, some as old as the Minoan period and some even derived from Near Eastern origins.

The king of the gods was Zeus Patēr, the Dyauspitr of India and the Jupiter of Rome, his ancient Indo-European name meaning "sky father." But as sky father, Zeus could bring lightning, hail, and roaring winds as well as kindly light and fertile rains: hence his name *maimaktēs*, the wrathful one. In some localities, notably in ancient Crete, where he was Zeus Kuros, the characteristics of the king of the gods were decidedly chthonic: it was only the authority of Homer that fixed him permanently in the classical consciousness as an ouranic deity. The consort of Zeus, Hera, queen of the gods, was originally a Mycenean goddess from Argos, assimilated into Greek religion during the Hellenic invasion of the peninsula. As wife of Zeus, she became a sky goddess bringing both warm weather for crops and destructive storms. She was also a chthonic goddess, identified with the primeval earth deity Gaia or Gē as a goddess of fertility and childbearing. The primal fertility goddess was lady of snakes and monsters such as Typhoeus and the Lernaean Hydra, the many-headed serpent. The ethical ambivalence of the king and queen of the gods is reflected in their sexual ambiguity, for in a sense Hera was the female principle of Zeus, as Artemis was of Apollo, and Persephone of Plouton.

Some of the offspring of this royal couple possessed terrifying natures. One son, Hephaistos, was god of volcanic explosions and consorted with the spirits of caves and of mountains. Another, Ares, was god of storms, cruelty, and unrestrained warfare, a mad killer. Yet he was worshiped by warriors who honored martial valor, and his savage nature seems to have been at least somewhat mitigated by his affair with Aphrodite, the goddess of love. Aphrodite, like love itself, could be gentle or frenzied, her influence soothing or enraging.

Athene, another Mycenean goddess adopted by the Greeks, was more often benevolent: she presided over calm skies and, by analogy, over art and wisdom. Yet her skies also could darken, and she then brought clouds and lightning and their human analogy of war. Athene is most often portrayed in classical times as a goddess of war, but of disciplined, restrained war as opposed to the brutal slaughter preferred by Ares. She was also sexually ambiguous—indeed, almost androgynous. She was Pallas Athene, *pallas* being perhaps close in meaning to *parthenos*, virgin, and her statues often portray her striding off to war like a Balkan athlete. Poseidon, the god of the seas, was numbered among the heavenly gods, but the sea is dark, fearsome, and chthonic. Through water Poseidon was also associated with fertility. His ambivalence is clear, for he ruled over a sea that can be shining and calm or else grey, cold, and stirred by savage winds. Of all the ouranic gods Hermes was closest to the chthonic. In myth he wings his way through the skies as messenger of the heavenly court, but his cult was chthonic, his preferred symbol the phallus, and as Hermes Psycho-

Pan, sixth century Coptic ivory preserved in the ambo of Henry II, Aachen. The iconography of Pan and the Devil here coalesce: cloven hooves, goat's legs, horns, beast's ears, saturnine face, and goatee. Other than the carving's context, only the pan pipes identify this figure as Pan rather than Satan. Courtesy Schwann Pädagogischer Verlag, Düsseldorf.

pompos he was the god who led the dead to the underworld. Hermes preserved the primitive characteristics of the Trickster, as in the famous prank where he stole the cattle of the sun from Apollo. It is from Hermes Psychopompos, who had wings on his legs symbolizing his position as messenger of the gods, that the medieval tradition of portraying the Devil with leg wings arose.

The son of Hermes was Pan, who was born hairy and goat-like, with horns and cloven hooves. A phallic deity like his father, he represented sexual desire, which can be both creative and destructive. The iconographic influence of Pan upon the Devil is enormous. What in the tradition made it possible for the image of Pan to be joined with that of Satan? Medieval tradition frequently speaks of the hairiness of the Devil, sometimes of his horns, and occasionally of his cloven feet. The Devil is frequently described as taking animal forms, most commonly that of the goat.[2] The root of the similarity is the association of the Devil with the chthonic fertility deities, who were rejected by the Christians as demons along with the other pagan gods and who were particularly feared because of their association with the wilderness and with sexual frenzy. Sexual passion, which suspends reason and easily leads to excess, was alien both to the rationalism of the Greeks and to the asceticism of the Christians; a god of sexuality could easily be assimilated to the principle of evil. The association of the chthonic with both sex and the underworld, and hence with death, sealed the union.

The god generally recognized as ruler of the underworld was Hades, who presided over the dark and dreadful kingdom of dead souls and brought death to crops, animals, and mankind.

---

2. Besides the goat, the ass, pig, wolf, dog, cock, hare, cat, bull, and horse are frequently symbols of fertility in world religion. They also appear frequently in Christian tradition as forms of the Devil. The snake, curiously, appears only infrequently. The Green Man, another common fertility symbol of Western Europe, also is assimilated to the image of the Devil. For a modern rendition of this connection, see Kingsley Amis, *The Green Man* (New York, 1970).

Yet his other name was Plouton, god of wealth, for the underground not only consumes the dead, receiving their souls as well as their corpses, but it also pushes up the tender crops in the spring and therefore promises renewed life. The ambivalence of Hades was reflected in that of his spouse, the gentle Persephone, lady of springtime, whose cruel husband ravished her from the face of the earth. It was she who in the spring, emerging from her underground prison, caused the earth to green; but it was she also who emerged to lead the Erinyes, the terrible spirits of revenge, in their pitiless search for vengeance. Thus the deities of the underworld, in Greece as elsewhere, brought both fear and hope.

Artemis and Apollo were the twin children of Zeus and Leda. Apollo, the most beautiful of the gods, was associated with the sun, and along with sunlight, with purity, reason, and art. But he also brought disease, destructive natural forces, and sudden death. Even the origin of his name is disputed. Aeschylus, Euripides, and Plato all derived it from *apollumi*, "to destroy." Nor is Apollo's sister Artemis less a puzzle. Her name may derive from *artemes*, "pure," "safe," or from *artamos*, "butcher," "destroyer," and her characteristics are likewise ambivalent. The most virginal and pure of the heavenly goddesses, she could also appear as the many-breasted Artemis of the Ephesians, a fertility goddess closely associated with Cybele, Ma, and the Great Mother of the Gods. As goddess of the moon, she was associated with fertility through the monthly periods of women and through the crescent, growing stage of the moon. As Lucina, her Roman counterpart Diana presided over childbirth. Artemis was the protectress of wild beasts and also their huntress; as bow-bearer she brought death to both animals and men. When annoyed, she might, as she did to Acteon, cause a man to be torn to pieces by his own hounds. Nowhere was her dark side more pronounced than in her identification with Hecate, the daughter of Night and of Tartarus, and the mother of Scylla. Lady of the underworld, of chthonic rites, and of black magic, Hecate had three faces symbolizing her power over underworld, earth, and air. This threefold power of Hecate is

Left, Artemis the huntress, Greece, fourth century B.C. (courtesy Mansell Collection, London). Right, Artemis of the Ephesians, Ephesus, first century B.C. or A.D. (courtesy Alinari Baglioni, Florence). Sister of the sun god Apollo, cheerful maiden huntress and protector of wild animals, Artemis is also a fertility goddess, symbolized by her power over the moon. In an extreme manifestation of her fertility cult, she was worshiped at Ephesus as a black and many-breasted figure closer to the fertility goddesses of the Middle East than to the airy deities of Olympus.

comparable to the triple lordship over sea, earth, and sky exercised by Poseidon, whose trident, which symbolizes this lordship, passed into the iconography of the Devil as the modern "pitchfork."

As long as Greek religion was a living religion, not too much standardized and refined by literary traditions, each god was perceived as a manifestation of both the kindly and the destructive aspects of divinity. The ambivalence of the God appears throughout Greek literature, myth, and philosophy in the classical period. Homer's work contains no clear separation of good and evil and certainly no hypostatization of either.[3] The will of the God is not known. Beyond men and beyond gods there exists a remote, impersonal force called *moira* that assigns to each god and each man his proper function. *Moira* is completely without personality or even conscious will; it is a shorthand concept that "states a truth about the disposition of Nature," the truth being that each person has an ordained role to play in the world.[4]

Moira, then, is a cosmic order that rules human affairs as well as natural events. Limit, restraint, and balance fit into this order harmoniously; excess breaks the order and is bad. *Themis* is the force that holds things in order in heaven; on earth, the force is *dikē*. Neither of the two is usually personified, though each can appear in myth as a bloodless goddess lacking all personality. Together they correspond roughly to the Egyptian *ma'at*. If one loses sight of one's proper place on earth, one will violate *dikē*, and one will be destroyed as impersonally and as certainly as a barn that happens to be in the way of a whirlwind. Nemesis, the goddess of the sacred grove (*nemos*), attacks and punishes those who violate *dikē*. The fear engendered by nemesis is so great that her personification is more convincing than that of *dikē*, but nemesis is not so much malicious as she is the abstraction of the force that inevitably punishes trespasses of proper limit.

3. As is customary, I shall speak of Homer as one person, although it is doubtful that the *Iliad* and the *Odyssey* are the work of one person.

4. F. M. Cornford, *From Religion to Philosophy* (New York, 1957), p. 21.

Hecate, engraved gem, Rome. Hecate, goddess of night and underworld, was the dark side of the goddess Artemis, and the special patroness of dark magic. Her three faces symbolize her power over underworld, land, and air, as do the three prongs of the Devil's trident.

But if transgressions of *dikē* are to be punished by nemesis, who is responsible for the transgression? Is a person as lacking in responsibility as the barn that gets in the way of the whirlwind? In Homer, particularly in the *Iliad*, that seems almost to be the case. Men trespass proper order when they are blind to the proper course of conduct. This blindness is called *atē*, *atē* being personified as the eldest daughter of Zeus. Zeus, it is implied, sends *atē* to men and then punishes them when she causes them to err. In the *Iliad*, Agamemnon argues that Zeus, *moira*, and the Erinyes all caused him to deprive Achilles of his spoil. Human responsibility is stronger in the *Odyssey*, where the gods generally inspire good thoughts rather than evil, the evil thoughts even being in one passage attributed to an evil demon whom the gods, taking on a positive moral role, combat (*Od.* 5.396–399).

But the ambivalence of the gods persists in later writings. Aeschylus speaks of the *prōtarchos Atē* in the *Agamemnon*, a blindness sent by the gods, a blindness which, when it strikes, drives one to inevitable ruin (*Ag.* 1192). In plays of both Aeschylus and Sophocles the inscrutable will of the gods can ruin an entire family even unto the last generation. Aeschylus argues that fate is the equivalent of the will of Zeus, and that Zeus is responsible for all that happens everywhere. In *The Persians* (*Pers.* 93) he says that no mortal can escape the insidious guile of the God. In *The Libation Bearers*, Aeschylus' point of view is even clearer. Orestes is driven to revenge by the Erinyes of his father, but when later he does succeed in avenging his father on Aegisthus and Clytemnestra, the same spirits pursue him on behalf of his mother. To his pleas that this torment is unjust the Eumenides reply that if he is released the house of justice will fall. The gods compel us to a necessary action and then of necessity punish us. Aeschylus, like the writer of the Book of Job, here presents without mitigation the stark awesomeness of the God. Orestes has, after all, no legitimate complaint, for to his mother's earlier pleas for mercy he had replied only that Fate required her death.

Certain vices, such as eris (strife), phobos (fear), and kydoimos (uproar) are personified in Homer, but their appearance in embodied form seems merely a poetic device. The responsibility of men continues to grow in early Greek literature and theology, but not necessarily as opposed to that of the gods. When a human being commits an evil deed, both he and the gods are responsible for it. In the *Oedipus* of Sophocles, Apollo causes Oedipus and Jocasta to do evil, yet this fact in no way mitigates their own guilt (*Oed.* 1329–1333). The problem of

theodicy seems very much present, but at the back of the mind: it is by no means clear how the universe is constructed in such a way that both men and gods do evil as well as good.

Of what does their evil consist? In one sense, Homer answers the question only tautologically: it consists in violating the honor (*timē*) of a god. In the *Iliad*, Zeus punishes men who forswear, not because forswearing is morally wrong, but because it violates his *timē* as Zeus Horkios, lord of oaths. Oeneus sacrifices hecatombs to the gods, in error forgetting Artemis; but unintentional though his error was, Artemis must avenge her slighted *timē* by sending a wild boar to ravage the land. Odysseus is obliged to blind the Cyclops in order to rescue himself and his men from a horrible death, but Poseidon's *timē* is injured by the attack upon his servant, and he sends a storm to wreck Odysseus' ships. It is dangerous to offend the gods, that is clear, but it is not at all clear why one thing and not another should offend them. In the *Euthyphro*, Socrates says that the gods appear to disagree among themselves about what they will for mankind.

Side by side in Homer with this conception of evil is the idea that evil is a matter of social custom. In the *Iliad* especially, the positive terms *agathos* and *aretē* and the negative term *kakos* correspond almost exclusively to the virtues and vices of a noble warrior class: competent generalship, for example, is *agathos*, cowardice in battle *kakos*. In the *Odyssey*, in Hesiod, and in the later classical writers, a gradual transformation occurs. As society becomes more settled, virtues and vices, rather than remaining peculiar to a class, become generalized: there are now general human standards for what is good and what is evil. As they become generalized, these standards begin to apply to the gods as well, for if standards are universal, the gods are felt to be responsible for upholding them. This is the beginning of a moral good and evil and of a general conception of justice.

The move in the direction of morality and justice was not the only movement of thought in the early classical period. The idea of pollution, which played little part in Homer or Hesiod, grows very important in the work of Aeschylus (*The Seven*

Against Thebes) and Sophocles (*Oedipus at Colonnus*). In *The Seven*, for example, the pollution of Oedipus brings about the fall of the City of Thebes. The origin of the idea of pollution is hard to trace, but in the classical dramatists *miasma* (pollution, as opposed to *katharia*, purity) could be contracted by a number of acts ranging from the morally evil to the morally neutral, such as homicide, inhospitality, repugnant disease, childbirth, physical contact with corpses, and bad dreams. If not dispelled, *miasma* could destroy a person as surely as could nemesis. The remedy for *miasma* was neither placation of the angry gods nor moral reform, but ritual lustrations, often with pigs' blood or with sea water, salt being a traditional repellant of evil in the ancient world.[5]

Toward the end of the classical period, the difficulties posed by Greek theodicy become evident in the work of Euripides, where man struggles in the grip of an irrational universe in which the gods represent no order at all. The gods make no distinction between good and evil men, treating all alike (*Herakles* 655–672). When Hecuba appeals to law and to justice her plea fails, and the *Hecuba* ends with the stark statement that "Fate spares no one" (*Hec.* 1295). For Euripides, goodness is a human virtue, not a divine one, and it consists of living a decent life in a world filled with depravity. But if goodness is a human virtue, so is evil a human vice. No evil spirit in Euripides urges men on to their ruin; the evil of men and women is their own, and Helen, mightily though she tries to shift her guilt onto the gods in *The Trojan Women*, does not free herself from responsibility for enticing men to warfare and slaughter. This somberly naturalistic view of the world also appears in Thucydides, who wrote as the glory of Athens was coming to an inglorious end. The cynical debates of the Athenians with their victims the Melians and the Mytilenians, who call in vain upon justice, reflect the dour thoughts of a historian who knows that there is no proper order in the world. Order is ever disrupted by the viciousness of mankind, a viciousness generally manifested in

5. For a discussion of the origins of pollution in Greece, see A. W. H. Adkins, *Merit and Responsibility* (Oxford, 1960), p. 92.

hubris, the arrogant pride that inevitably leads to downfall. Though the Athenians successfully intimidate or destroy their victims, their success leads them only to further transgressions against proper limits until at last they are crippled by their foolhardy effort to conquer distant Sicily. Later generations know, as Thucydides suspected, that the ultimate end of the Athenian bid for empire would be the enslavement of Athens by Sparta. All classical Greek thought from Homer to Euripides and Thucydides echoes the ancient theme, attributed to Apollo and inscribed at his oracle in Delphi: "nothing in excess." But there is no Spirit of Excess; such a personification would itself be an excess, a movement away from balance and monism in the direction of dualism, a struggle, rather than a harmony, among the divine powers.

Yet such dualism and such a struggle become a commonplace among the successors of Plato and are already prefigured in the mythological structure of the poet Hesiod, whose work may be as old as that of Homer. For the pain and destruction in the world, Hesiod offers a number of mythological explanations—explanations embroidered poetically but reflecting a serious element of Greek thought that continues in the work of playwrights and philosophers. One such story, that of Deucalion and the flood, has many similarities to the flood stories of the Ancient Near East. Zeus visits the king of Arcadia, who unfortunately feels some doubt that his visitor is really who he says he is. In order to test his guest's omniscience, the king serves him a dish in which the entrails of a baby are mixed with other meat. Zeus, tasting the food, immediately knows what has been done and in punishment sends a flood that sweeps over the earth, leaving only Deucalion alive to begin anew the race of men. In another story, evil is the result of natural degeneration, almost entropy, built into the universe by the God, who first created a golden race, then a silver, then a bronze, then an age of heroes, and finally the last age, the current age in which we live, an age of baseness and decay. There is a similarity to the five ages of men in the Book of Daniel. Another story is that of Pandora, a minor goddess who has been imprisoned in the underworld. Released onto the earth, she brings with her a jar (*pithos*), pulls out the bung, and lets a horde of evils escape to infest the world.

The story of Pandora is part of a larger story of warfare among the gods, a motif also found in Indian, Hittite, and Iranian myth. The Greek version is told in many forms by the poets and philosophers and is seldom consistent even within the works of any one author. In its broad outlines, it is usually related as follows: In the beginning Chaos produced Ouranos, the sky, a male, and the sky's mother, sister, and wife, Gaia, the earth. For eons earth and sky lie in close sexual embrace (as they did in Egypt), so close that the children borne by the earth are trapped by their father's body and lie compressed in the hills and valleys of the earth.[6] Urged by her desperate children, Gaia resolves to free them. She fashions a sickle and gives it to her son Kronos, who castrates his father, thereby ending the sexual embrace of earth and sky and permitting their separation. This separation is the true end of chaos and the beginning of the world.[7] Some drops of blood from the mutilated Ouranos fall upon the prostrate earth, and from these drops are born the twelve Titans and Titanesses, the brothers and sisters of Kronos. This group of deities become the discredited elder gods of Greece, like the asuras in India and the devas in Iran. Kronos embraces the goddess Rhea, who bears him a series of children. But where Ouranos kept his children imprisoned, Kronos or Chronos, devouring time, eats his. Rhea at last devises a stratagem to save Zeus, her youngest and favorite child, and gives the hungry father a rock to swallow in place of his

6. The imprisonment of the children of Ouranos in the valleys at the beginning of time can be compared with the imprisonment of the Jewish Watcher angels in the valleys of the earth as punishment for their sin with the daughters of men as well as with the fate of the Titans after their defeat by Zeus.

7. Kronos was in his origin different from Chronos, "Time," but the two are confounded in Greek thought, so that it is legitimate to take Kronos/Chronos as a personification of time, who both creates and castrates, builds and destroys. Kronos/Chronos is sometimes called the youngest, and sometimes the eldest, son of Ouranos and Gaia, just as Zeus later is sometimes the eldest and sometimes the youngest son of Kronos.

son. Zeus then emerges from hiding and slays his father. Zeus
and his siblings then do battle with the brothers and sisters of
Kronos, the Titans, at last defeating them and chaining them
beneath the earth in Tartarus. Zeus and his cohorts emerge as
the Olympian gods most worthy of veneration by mankind,
and the Titans, usually identified with the giants, become the
sinister Old Ones inimical to the gods. Chained in the underworld, and increasingly identified as evil, the Titans begin
to acquire chthonic characteristics. Allied with them is another
monster, Typhon, whom Gaia bore to avenge herself on Zeus
after his defeat of her elder children. Typhon lives under the
earth and causes fiery eruptions; from the hips downwards his
body is formed of two serpents, and masses of serpents issue
from his shoulders, as with some of the evil asuras in India. He
marries Echidna, a hideous giant woman, and together they
produce Cerberus, Hydra, Chimera, Sphinx, the Nemean
Lion, and other monsters. Typhon also pits himself against
Zeus in a never-ending wrestling match.

But though the Titans are wholeheartedly inimical to the
ouranic gods, their attitude toward humanity is not altogether
malicious. Insofar as the heavenly gods may be unfriendly toward men, men and Titans can make common cause. And so
they do. Aeschylus recounts the story in *Prometheus Bound.*
After Zeus has defeated the Titans, he decides also to destroy
mankind and begin anew with better materials (cf. the story of
Deucalion). But Prometheus, the son of the Titan Iapetos, foils
him by giving man the gift of fire, itself ambivalent. Prometheus thus is first the benefactor of mankind in saving it
from destruction by Zeus; second the cause of evil by bringing
it the weapon of fire, the enmity of the gods, and toil; next the
enemy of the new gods; and finally the avenger of the old gods.
The subsequent terrible punishment meted out to him again
raised the question of theodicy in the mind of Aeschylus.
Chained to the rock, the eagle plucking at his liver, Prometheus, like so many of the race he came to help, curses Zeus as
a tyrant. Aeschylus invites us to sympathize with Prometheus
and even to identify ourselves with him: do the gods not treat

us unfairly too? The story of Prometheus was important in forming the image of the Devil in the heroic mold as he appears in Milton.[8]

The dualism implied by the struggle among the gods was explicit in what is called the Orphic tradition. Unresolved questions remain as to whether Orphism ever existed as any kind of organized religion, what the exact relationship was between Orphism and the cult of Dionysos, or to what extent dualism was autochthonous and to what extent imported from Iran. Indisputably, dualist ideas and practices began to appear in Greece as early as the sixth century B.C., and the tradition of dualism is commonly known as Orphism. The central myth of Orphism may have been the myth of Dionysos and the Titans.[9] In the beginning of the world was Phanes, the androgyne who brings all things to light. First Phanes bears Ouranos, who sires Kronos, the father of Zeus. After Zeus defeats the Titans, he swallows Phanes, thus taking into himself the original principle, becoming a creator god, and producing all things anew, including the Titans. Meanwhile Zeus fathers a son, Dionysos. Hating Zeus, and envious of the happiness of the infant Dionysos, the Titans approach the child, distract his attention with a mirror, and seize him. They tear him apart and devour him. But Athene rescues the boy's heart and brings it to Zeus, who consumes it. Zeus now has intercourse with Semele, who gives birth anew to Dionysos. Pleased with the resurrection of his son, Zeus proceeds to punish his murderers by blasting them to ashes with thunderbolts. From the ashes of the Titans arises the race of mankind.

The myth is wholly dualist. Mankind has a dual nature, spiritual and material. The material part of our nature derives from the Titans, the spiritual part from the Dionysos whom they devoured. The teachings of Pythagoras and the Pythagoreans

---

8. Hesiod also makes Prometheus the proximate cause of the loosing of the evils from Pandora's jar, for he says that Zeus sends Pandora to the earth to punish men for having acquired the gift of fire.

9. The full story is not reported until the time of Clement of Alexandria (b. 150 A.D.).

Dionysos, Tanagra, Boeotia, early fourth century B.C. The androgynous nature of the young god Dionysos appears clearly in this terra cotta protome. He holds in his hand the primeval egg from which the world hatched. Courtesy Trustees of the British Museum.

were highly influential in one development of the dualist tradition. For the Pythagoreans, soul is immortal, flesh mortal. The soul is trapped in the body like a prisoner (*sōma sēma*); our task on earth is to escape our bodily prison by means of ritual purifi-

eation. But the dualism found in these doctrines is different
from that of Iran. Iranian dualism posited a conflict between
two spiritual powers, one of light and one of darkness. Orphic
dualism posited a conflict between the divine soul and the evil,
Titanic body that imprisoned it. In Orphism the dualism of
matter and spirit, body and soul, is first clearly enunciated: its
influence upon Christian, Gnostic, and medieval thought was
enormous, and it is one of the most important elements in the
history of the Devil. To the extent that Dionysos was good and
the Titans evil, which is assumed, to that extent is the soul
good and the body evil. This interpretation grew steadily
throughout the Hellenistic period, when, influenced by Iranian
dualism, matter and the body were assigned to the realm of the
evil spirit, and soul to that of the good spirit. At that point the
two dualisms, Orphic and Iranian, were united, and the idea
that the body and the flesh are the work of cosmic evil became
implanted in Jewish and Christian minds. The majority opinion
in both Judaism and Christianity has always rejected this idea
in its explicit form, but from Gnosticism onwards it has been
the most persistent source of heresy.

The doctrine that the body was the prison of the soul caused
the Orphics to believe in metempsychosis, the transmigration
of souls. One can escape the flesh only through a series of incar-
nations during which one carefully practices ritual purity. The
process of reincarnation ceases when perfect purity is achieved
and is delayed by any relapse into carnality. The Orphics abstained from meat both because it is carnal and because an
animal might be a reincarnation of a human being. Under the
influence of Pythagoras, they also abstained from beans, which
they regarded as seed par excellence and therefore the root of
the flesh.

The ritual purity of Orphism was also associated with the
cult of Dionysos, which was very different indeed. Festivals of
Dionysos took place at night, symbol of darkness and the for-
bidden. They were often held in a cave or grotto, locales connected with moisture, fertility, and the chthonic powers. The
worshipers were primarily women, the Maenads or Bacchantes,

Maenad, Coptic ivory of the sixth century preserved on the ambo of Henry II, Aachen. The frenzied worship of Dionysos was a model for the later witches' orgies in honor of Satan. Courtesy Schwann Pädagogischer Verlag, Dusseldorf.

who were led by a male priest. The procession bore torches, a phallic image, and figs and other sexually symbolic fruits, and led a dark goat or statue of a goat. The goat, symbol of fertility, represented Dionysos, who was sometimes called "he of the black goat" and portrayed as shaggy and horned. The rite was characterized by wine-drinking, ecstatic dancing, feasting, and the tearing apart of animals. Literature sometimes rendered the last as human sacrifice, and it is possible, though not established, that the stories echoed real practice. As time went on, the rites became more orgiastic, and they may eventually have been characterized by sexual license.

How could Orphic purity and Dionysiac frenzy exist together? This question has been raised repeatedly by historians, in regard not only to the Orphics, but to the Gnostics, Catharists, witches, Frankists, and many other groups.[10] There are a number of answers. First, Orphic purity was ritual rather than moral. Second, the coexistence of ascetic restraint and frenzied worship is common in the history of religions and, psychologically, is a predictable manifestation of the shadow. Third, frenzied ecstasy is frequently an accepted way of bringing the spirit "out of" the body. Fourth, and most important, it is a manifestation of the coincidence of opposites, of the ambivalence that underlies all human thought, particularly thought about the gods. For Dionysos, like the other gods, is ambivalent. The son of Zeus and symbol of spirit against the body, he is also a horned fertility god. The benefactor, *Euergetes*, he is also *Anthroporraistes*, "crusher of men," and *Omēstēs*, "eater of raw flesh," and he rides in a black ship. Most of all he is *Lusios* or *Luaios*, the great looser or freer, who releases from all restraints and inhibitions. In the Hellenistic period he became the perfect androgyne, as the great head in the British Museum shows him. Orgy may be perceived as an urge to integration through commingling of the sexes. On

10. For example, Hans Jonas, *The Gnostic Religion* (Boston, 1958), pp. 270–274; Gerschom Scholem, *The Messianic Idea in Judaism* (New York, 1971), pp. 78–141; Jeffrey B. Russell, *Witchcraft in the Middle Ages* (Ithaca, N.Y., 1972), pp. 123–132.

the one hand the opposition of spirit and body eventually made the Devil "the lord of this world"; on the other hand the Dionysiac orgy became the model for the orgy imputed to Gnostics, Catharists, and witches.

In common with other peoples, the Greeks possessed a number of minor spirits of a malicious nature, and, as with most other peoples, none of these approached anything like the stature of a principle of evil. In dealing with the Greek spirits we encounter an unusual difficulty. Our word "demon," which is sometimes synonymous with "Devil" and always carries at least some negative connotations, is derived from the Greek *daimōn*, which did not necessarily mean an evil being. In the *Iliad*, *daimōn* is frequently used as an equivalent of *theos*. In the *Odyssey*, the term has more frequent negative than positive connotations but is still ambiguous, as is the post-Homeric equivalent *daimonion*. After Homer, a *daimōn* was generally held to be a spiritual being inferior to a god. The term's shift in connotation from neutral or at least ambiguous to evil was still incomplete at the time of Socrates, whose guiding spirit was a "demon," but it was consummated by Plato's pupil Xenocrates, who divided the good gods from the bad demons and shifted all the evil or destructive qualities of the gods onto the demons.[11] The Stoics and Plutarch followed Xenocrates, Plutarch going so far as to argue that if literature described Apollo destroying a city, it must have been a demon taking the shape of Apollo. By the late Hellenistic period the term *daimonion* had acquired an almost universally bad connotation.

Greek spirits, some of which were called "demons" and others not, might be good or evil or ambivalent; they might be spirits of nature or spirits of the dead. The Keres, for example, were ghosts who could be benign but who were more likely to cause nightmares, blindness, or madness. The Keres had gnashing fangs and blue-black, horrible faces; they drank the

11. Simone Pètrement, *Le Dualisme chez Platon, les gnostiques, et les manichéens* (Paris, 1947), p. 16.

blood of the dying.[12] Heroes were originally spirits of the dead whose activities could be baneful. Some other spirits were almost always harmful. Lamias roamed the world seeking the death of children and sexual intercourse with sleeping men, much like the Hebrew Lilith.[13] Harpies, the "snatchers," were winged women who swept the world like the storm wind and were originally wind demons. The Gorgons were demons of the underworld or of the deep sea; there were originally three of them, Medusa being the most horrible with her savage tusks and her hair of snakes. The Sirens were sea monsters related to the Gorgons and Harpies. The Hydra was a huge serpent with five to a hundred heads, and Cerberus, the dog that guarded the entrance to Hades, had anywhere from three to fifty mouths, depending on the account. The Minotaur, son of Pasiphae and the bull, was the ancient horned monster of Minoan Crete. At least in classical times most people had ceased to take these creatures very seriously. The Erinyes, the raging spirits that avenged the dead, inspired more alarm, as did the avenging ghost, the Alastor, to which they were often assimilated.[14]

Hades was considered more real as a place than as a god. Originally the underworld abode where the dead went as pale shadows to pine but not to suffer, it gradually became transformed into a pit of torment for the damned. Already in the *Odyssey*, Tityrus, Tantalus, and Sisyphus underwent torment there for their faults, and from the fate of these mortals it was assumed that all might suffer in the afterlife for their sins. The god Hades judged the dead, and the Erinyes or other terrible

12. Hermann Fränkel, *Early Greek Poetry and Philosophy* (New York, 1973), p. 111.

13. An etiological myth makes the original Lamia a queen of Libya who was loved by Zeus. Hera in jealousy slew Lamia's children, and in revenge Lamia roams the world seducing men and killing infants. W. H. Roscher, *Lexikon der griechischen und römischen Mythologie* (Leipzig, 1894–97), vol. II (2), 1818–1821.

14. The Alastor both tempts us to sin and then punishes us: Clytemnestra argues that the Alastor of Atreus caused her to kill Agamemnon: Aeschylus, *Agamemnon*, 1497–1508.

spirits punished the souls who were damned, tormenting them with fire. The underground Hades was identified with Tartarus, the terrible land surrounded by Pyrophlegethon, river of fire. The ambivalence of many of these concepts was not so much a question of good and evil as a matter of function: spirits both tempted mortals to sin and then punished them for sinning, a double role later assigned to the Christian Devil.

Greek religion, legend, and mythology thus produced a number of concepts and symbols that were influential in shaping the concept of the Devil, but nowhere any being who approximated the personification of the principle of evil. This was not because the Greeks were uniquely free from evil thoughts, but rather because the refinements of theodicy in Greece passed out of the hands of the mythologists and into those of the philosophers. It was the Greeks who first asked in a rational and systematic way the question *Pothen to kakon*: Whence does evil come? For some philosophers, evil was merely a human concept born of lack of understanding of the divine nature and the divine plan. To the God, said Herakleitos, "all things are beautiful, good, and right; men, on the other hand, deem some things right and others wrong."[15] Monism is of course even clearer in the Eleatic philosophers: for Parmenides all, including that which we call evil, is in reality an undifferentiated aspect of the One. For these philosophers, and for many who followed them, including Socrates, the Stoics and Cynics, and even the Sophists, evil therefore lay in human error, in flaws of character. Socrates found its origin in a lack of *epistēmē*, the practical knowledge of how to seek virtue and shun vice; the Cynics considered it to stem from the error of seeking happiness in worldly wealth and fame; the Sophists located it in weakness. For all of them it entailed a human lack of balance, a going beyond the proper limit. On the other hand, Pythagoras and Orphism implied a cosmic flaw: lack of limit, disorder, unformed matter, these were all visible in the universe at large as well as in the minds of men, in the macrocosm as well as in the

15. Philip Wheelwright, *Heraclitus* (Princeton, 1959), p. 90.

microcosm. And so two ideas were gradually formulated, both of which departed from monism. One was dualism, the idea that there are two warring forces in the universe. The other belief was that although there was only one divine power, it was not responsible for the creation of all things and did not command and order all things. Where monism insisted upon the totality of the God's power and dismissed evil as a formulation of a human mind too limited to grasp the nature of the God, these ideas insisted upon the goodness of the God by limiting his powers. It was Plato who wrestled with these ideas most persistently, if not always most consistently, and it was he who, with his great impact upon Christian thought, was most influential in the development of the concept of the Devil.

Plato began with Socrates' notion that evil arose from the individual's lack of knowledge of how to be good, a knowledge that he considered just as practical as that of a carpenter or a shoemaker who understands, well or ill, how to build shelves or make shoes. But Plato was not satisfied. What was the nature of the good that we are supposed to know in this practical manner? Protagoras the Sophist argued that good had no nature, and that good and evil were merely conventional and relative terms; Thrasymachus went further and argued for power or for expediency as the only possible measures of good and evil. Against such views Plato always labored, though the fruits of his labor never satisfied him and late in his life, in the *Philebus*, he seemed to withdraw from absolutes and to resign himself to the idea that the world was a *meixis*, a mixture.

Plato and those who followed him wavered between various degrees of dualism and monism. Platonists tend to be monist in their belief that all that is is a product of, or emanation from, one principle. But their monism is limited by the positing of a refractory element in the cosmos that is either (1) the lowest emanation of the one principle or (2) an element entirely independent of the one. This lowest, or independent, element is usually identified as matter. Plato's dualism also combines his Orphic distrust of matter with the notion (possibly derived indirectly from Iran) of the two opposite spirits. Plato opposes the ideal or spiritual world to the material world, arguing that the ideal world is more real than the material world and that, in consequence, it is also better. The occidental tradition has subsequently almost always followed the notion that being is better than nonbeing.

In such a world what are the sources of evil? Plato offers a number of answers. One is that evil has no real being at all. Rather, it consists of lack of perfection, or privation. The world of ideas is perfect, wholly real, and good. But the phenomenal world cannot adequately reflect the world of ideas, and to the degree that it falls short it is less real, less good, and, consequently, more evil. A withered cow that can give no milk is an evil, but the evil lies not in the being of the cow but in its *lack* of vitality and health. It is the nonbeing, rather than the being, in the cow that is at fault. Ontologically, evil does not exist, since it is only a lack or a defect. This idea, adopted wholeheartedly by Augustine and Aquinas, deeply affected Christian philosophy and theology. And in those contexts it has always posed problems. It made possible the confusion of ontological evil with moral evil. More, it led to the argument that, as evil had no being, it had no principle. From this position, later philosophers went on to argue either that the Devil did not exist or that the Devil did exist but was not truly the principle of evil: rather, he was a powerful angel whose evil lay not in his angelic being but rather in his lack of perfection, a lack magnified precisely by his great power. The root of these future problems lay in Plato's system. But neither Plato nor the Christian philosophers who followed him ever argued that the ontological nonbeing of evil meant that there was no moral evil in the world. Plato was well aware of wars, murders, exploitation, and lies. The evil of a lie was taken not to be in the ontological reality of the words themselves but rather in the *lack of truth* inherent in the words. Moral evil exists, but it exists as a lack of good, rather as the holes in a Swiss cheese exist, but exist only as a lack of cheese. Plato did not argue that the ontological nonbeing of evil removed moral evil from the world but rather that it removed the responsibility for evil from the creator.

There is no agreement on the meaning of Plato's theology, which was in itself very inconsistent and also suffered for centuries from having Christian ideas read back into it. Whether Plato argues for the existence of an ultimate God is not clear. If there is a God, it is remote and hidden. The creator, or demiurge, is a being inferior to the God. Though the creator is a spiritual being, it is not a figure of worship but an abstract principle. It is responsible for the existence of a material world that is imperfect and contaminated by evil—an idea that the Gnostics used in order to label the creator itself evil. Plato himself wished to preserve the essential goodness of the creator. But how is it that the creator made an imperfect world, a world in which evil exists, even if only as a lack of perfection? The answer is that the creator is not the cause of all motion in the universe. The creator is responsible for cosmos, that which is ordered and proper. But chaos exists as disorder and random, erratic motion. Chaos may have existed before cosmos, or they may be coeval: it is irrelevant which. The point is that the creator has never been able to bring the chaotic into order. This random irrationality in the universe is what we call evil. It exists, but it was not created, and the creator is not responsible for it. The refractory part of nature is sometimes identified with necessity. Sometimes, under Orphic influence, it is identified with matter. For Plato, matter was clearly not in any sense an emanation from the creator. It followed that either matter did not exist at all and was consigned to ontological nonexistence (*mē on*), or else it existed and was evil. It might be that unformed, limitless, chaotic part of being that resists ordering by soul. The creator found it necessary to create a world which made use of matter, but matter always proved refractory to his purposes. Bone, for example, had to be made hard in order to support the body, but the hardness of bone rendered it brittle and liable to break. Or, finally, evil may lie not in matter itself, but rather in the mixture of matter and spirit. Soul plunged into matter and entrapped there cannot cope, loses its *epistēmē*, and becomes corrupt. This is true ethical dualism. "For the good we must assume no other cause than God, but the cause of evil we must look for in other things and not in God" (*Republic*, 379c). Defects in our moral actions are the result of a defective bodily constitution, or of a bad environment, or of our free will, or of all three.

None of the above explanations involves a principle of evil that is easily personified or held morally responsible. In Book Ten of *The Laws* something more is suggested. Plato had long argued that nothing corporeal is the cause of its own motion. The ultimate cause of motion is soul. An animal moves because its soul moves it; a pencil moves because a body has moved it, that body being moved by soul. In an intricately constructed machine, thousands of parts may move thousands of other parts, but motion is ultimately imparted to that machine by soul. Matter is not the cause of its own motion and therefore cannot be the ultimate cause of evil. Evil must lie in soul. One of two alternatives follows. Either there is an erratic, imperfect, evil element in the creator, or there is a spirit other than the creator who brings disorder and evil into the world. Philosophers have long discussed this passage of *The Laws*, and it is not at all clear that Plato meant to posit either of these alternatives. He did not dwell upon them, and the existence of an evil world-soul was for him, if not for his followers, no more than a passing thought.

Amid the numerous inconsistencies of Plato, a gradual development of his thought from the psychological in the direction of the cosmic can be discerned. For Socrates, evil was a failing in practical knowledge of how to do good. Plato at first emphasized the goodness of reason and knowledge against the disrupting force of emotions. From this he passed to perceiving a dichotomy and opposition between the spirit, the seat of reason, and the body, the seat of emotions. And from there he came to conceive soul and body as manifestations of metaphysical principles of spirit and matter, goodness being ascribed to spirit and evil to matter. Plato's incoherent dualism was rendered more coherent, more metaphysical, and more religious in the thought of his followers. The development of the concept of the Devil owes much, if not directly to Plato, to the permutations of his thought in the work of the Platonists. The thought of Aristotle, which did not admit a principle of evil, demonstrates that there were important currents in Greek thought that ran against the Platonic grain.[16]

Greek culture was radically transformed in the Hellenistic period, during which Hellenic influence spread eastward as far as Egypt, Iran, and India, and westward to Italy. Historians have generally dated the period from 331 B.C., when Alexander the Great defeated Darius III at Gaugamela and established his empire over Persia, to the victory of Octavian over Antony at Actium in 31 B.C. This latter date, however, is wholly artificial, for the characteristics of the Hellenistic period persisted through the time of the Roman Empire, when, in Juvenal's metaphor, the waters of Syrian Orontes mingled freely with those of the Tiber. The sometimes radical and frightening shifts in practices and assumptions occasioned by this unprecedented mingling of cultures brought a sense of insecurity to religion and philosophy. The distinctions between the two became blurred: the philosophical schools became more transcendent, even mystical, while efforts to rationalize religion led to the creation of theology and allegory.

In religion, the old forms, if not the substance, persisted. Public worship of the old pantheon continued, and Vergil, writing at the time of Augustus, imitated the religion, as well as

16. I do not treat the work of Aristotle here for two reasons. First, the influence of Aristotle upon subsequent thought before his revival in the twelfth century was minimal in comparison with that of Plato. Second, Aristotle for the most part turned back from Plato's dualism in the direction of monism. All motion comes from the First Cause and is directed toward the Final Cause. Good and evil are not separate forms. There is nothing that is good in itself or evil in itself; good and evil can be applied to every category of nature. Evil is merely a failure in beings to be perfectly directed toward the Final Cause; this failure may be a material imperfection or a moral one. If it is a moral one it results from a departure from the golden mean either toward excess or toward insufficiency. Courage, for example, is the mean between the two evils of cowardice and rashness. There was nothing in the thought of Aristotle to encourage the concept of a principle of evil, or its personification. Unformed matter as such, *hylē*, may hinder progress toward the ultimate goal, but it cannot be considered a principle of evil.

the verse, of the Homeric epic. In the *Aeneid*, Venus tells
Aeneas not to blame Helen, Achilles, or any other human
being for the fall of Troy. It was the gods who destroyed the
city, and Aeneas sees them squatting on the toppling towers of
Ilium (2. 604–623). On the other hand, Vergil's descent into
hell is different from that of Odysseus: Book Six of the *Aeneid*
holds individuals responsible for their sins and confines them in
the underworld for punishment. On the whole, despair of justice in this world became the hallmark of Roman thought: Tac-
itus longed for a restoration of the good old days or for the pristine customs of the barbarians; Horace lamented that each
generation was more vicious than the last, and Juvenal dis-
agreed only by saying that there was no way for the sins of future generations to be worse. Beset by insecurity and depressed
by apparent decline, religion turned away from the public cults
of the polis to an emphasis upon individual salvation and upon
dualism. This world was rotten: very well, it was not the real
world.

> Sit, Jessica: look, how the floor of heaven
> Is thick inlaid with patines of bright gold:
> There is not the smallest orb that thou behold'st
> But in his motion like an angel sings
> Still quiring to the young-eyed cherubins;
> Such harmony is in immortal souls;
> But, whilst this muddy vesture of decay
> Doth grossly close it in, we cannot hear it.[17]

The real world was to be found elsewhere, through metaphysical speculation, contemplation, ritual purification, or ecstatic
rites.

The outstanding feature of Hellenistic religion was its syn-
cretism, the search for a unified religion through combination
in cult and myth of the gods of the Greeks with those of the
cultures with which they came into contact. Thus Zeus and
Jupiter and Re and Ohrmazd became one, and thus the religions of the East penetrated the West. Among the most influ-

17. *Merchant of Venice*, V.i.

Pan and nymphs, Pompeii, first century B.C. or A.D. Horned and playing his pipes, his right leg stained from grapes, Pan is here less animal-like than in his usual representations. Nonetheless a goat stands before him. Courtesy Alfonso de Franciscis, Naples.

ential eastern cults in Hellenistic Greece and Rome was that of Isis and Serapis (the name given Osiris at Rome), a cult characterized by the practice of asceticism and ritual purity. The cults of Anatolian Cybele and of the Magna Mater of Phrygia were both characterized by ecstatic dancing and orgies aimed at loosing all restraints and inhibitions so that the deity might enter more easily. The Roman version of Dionysiac worship, the Bacchanalia, became especially notorious for its license and was outlawed by the Senate in 186 B.C. The worshipers, at first only women, then both men and women, met at night and celebrated with torchlight rites that included orgiastic drinking and, at least according to the probably exaggerated account of Livy, sex. The Bacchanalia, or rather the version of it described by Livy, became an important part of the literary tradition of the orgy and a commonplace in accounts of medieval heresy and witchcraft.

The most widespread cult in the Roman Empire, other than Christianity, was Mithraism, a religion combining the doctrines of the Iranian Magi with those of the fertility cults. According to the central myth of Mithraism, the principle of the world is Aiōn, everlasting time (cf. Zurvan). Aiōn engenders heaven, the male principle, whose name is Ohrmazd or Jupiter; earth, the female principle, whose name is Spenta Armaiti or Juno, and the spirit of the underworld, Ahriman, who was equated with Pluto or Hades. The identification of Pluto-Hades with Ahriman reinforced the connection of the evil principle with the underworld and so contributed to the image of the Devil. Ahriman, envious of the glory of the heavenly king, Ohrmazd/Jupiter, attempts to storm heaven. Ohrmazd defeats him and casts him and his demons down into the underworld. Some of them escape, however, and wander through the world seeking the ruin and destruction of mankind. Meanwhile Mithras, god of the sun and of light, is born by the power of Ohrmazd/Jupiter from a rock. At the same time Ohrmazd also produces the primeval bull. By order of Ohrmazd, Mithras slays the bull, thereby creating the material world, for from the bull's dead body spring the fruits of the earth. Ohrmazd ap-

Head of Mithras, Romano-British, probably second century A.D. The soldier's god of light, Mithras typifies what the men of the West demanded of their gods in the dualistic milieu of the Hellenistic and Roman worlds. Courtesy the Museum of London.

points Mithras as leader of the heavenly powers and of mankind in their struggle against the shadow that is Ahriman. Through long ages they struggle, but Ahriman's power gradually increases and the human race comes more and more under his domination, until he becomes lord of this world. But just before the end of the world, a great bull will reappear, the reincarnation of the primeval beast, and Mithras will descend to do final battle with Ahriman and his forces. The dead will rise from their graves, and Mithras will judge them, separating the good from the evil. Ohrmazd will send down an annihilating fire upon the wicked, and upon Ahriman and his demons. An endless reign of happiness and goodness will ensue. The resemblance to Christian eschatology is striking, as is the similarity between Ahriman and the Judeo-Christian Satan. Mithraism and Christianity appeared at about the same time, and one may postulate a mutual influence of their ideas one upon the other, at least at a popular level. Their similarity mainly arises from their common dualist background in Orphic and Iranian thought.

The cult of Mithras also presents elements assimilated into the later concept of the heretic and the witch, although, unlike those of most of the fertility cults, the worshipers were exclusively male. The Mithraists met secretly in the dark, using torches, often in caves or crypts—when the cult became widespread and wealthy these became the vast Mithraeums—and there partook of liturgical meals. The central rite was the taurobolium, in which the postulant crouched under a platform on which a bull was sacrificed in imitation of Mithras' slaying of the primeval bull. The blood of the bull, running down upon the neophyte, initiated him into the sect. Darkness, torches, underground meetings, animal sacrifices, and ritual banquets also marked the rites of the more mystical and religiously inclined among the Neopythagoreans at Rome and elsewhere. The underground darkness and torchlight, apart from their theatrical effects, expressed creative power, the cave signifying fertility and the darkness and torches death and resurrection. Neither among the Mithraists nor among the Pythagoreans, however, was ecstatic dancing or orgiastic sex part of the ritual. Yet it is not difficult to understand why such activities should have been ascribed to the cultists by their adversaries, and with these embellishments the Hellenistic mystery cult became the

Mithras slaying the bull, Roman relief, second century A.D. Mithraism was a Roman religion drawing upon Mazdaist and Hellenistic mythologies. Here Mithras slays the sacred bull, releasing its life force for the service of mankind; in Mazdaism, however, the killing of the bull had been one of the first and most grievous sins of man. Courtesy Musée du Louvre.

type for the heretical meetings and witches' sabbats of the Middle Ages and the artificially revived witch cults of the present.

Quite different was another influence upon the iconography of the Devil, Charun, the Etruscan god of death. Although theirs was not a Hellenistic culture, the Etruscans, before and after their conquest by the Romans, influenced Roman religion significantly. Charun derives his name from the Greek Charon, the boatman of the dead, but the Etruscan god far exceeded in horror the grizzled ferryman of Greek myth. In most societies

Charun, fresco of the fourth century B.C. Charun, the Etruscan personification of death, is shown with the saturnine face, hooked nose, goatee, and wings that passed into the iconography of the Christian Devil. Courtesy Scala, New York.

death is considered an evil, often the greatest of natural evils. Seldom, however, has the spirit of death been taken as the apotheosis of evil itself; and in the Middle Ages, for example, death and the Devil were seldom identified either theologically or iconographically. Nor is there any reason to assume that Charun was to the Etruscans the personification of the principle of evil. Yet he compellingly personified at least one evil, death, and the attributes assigned to him, passing from Etruscan into Roman art and legend, had their ultimate influence upon the Christian iconography of the Devil. Charun has a huge, hooked nose, similar to a bird's beak; he has a shaggy beard and hair, with long, pointed, bestial ears, grinding teeth and grimacing lips; his color is often dark blue. (It is possible that the hairy shape was derived from the Greek satyrs or Pan). Sometimes he is shown with wings or with serpents growing from his body. All these characteristics are found in medieval and modern figures of the Devil. Some of his other attributes had little or no influence. Charun commonly carried a huge mallet with which he struck the head of a person about to die. This implement is more to be identified with the scythe put into the hand of Death by Christian iconographers than with any attribute of the Devil, although Charun's mallet is sometimes replaced by a hook, which could have influenced the Devil's trident, pitchfork, or kreuel.

Hellenistic philosophy and theology influenced the direction of the concept of the Devil at least as much as Hellenistic cult and mythology. Theology, the deliberate effort to explain and elucidate religious principles through the use of reason, first became widespread in the Hellenistic period, a natural response to the need to find rational bases for the syntheses of the cults. If Zeus was Ohrmazd, in what way was he Ohrmazd, or what principle or principles did both represent? If a sacred scripture was the revealed word of the God, how to interpret that word? What did the God mean to say? Religion's need for rational underpinnings was eagerly met by philosophies whose own direction was decidedly religious.

Many of the early Hellenistic philosophies did not posit basic principles of good or evil. For Epicurus (b. 341 B.C.), the universe was a chance concurrence of atoms, and good and evil were wholly relative human constructs. Wrongdoing was concern for the things of this world, which were meaningless: right thought was avoidance of pain by avoidance of caring. For the Skeptics, founded by Pyrrhon and Carneades (213–129 B.C.), all knowledge was impossible, including that of good and evil.

The Stoics, whose founder was Zeno of Citium (336–254), and whose influence upon Christian moral thought was immense, also avoided a dichotomy between good and evil, their teachings being rooted in the ancient tradition of monism. One Power emanates the material world, and the world in time will return to the One Power. Right thought lies in detachment from material things. Human beings possess free will, but freedom consists in following the will of the One. Mortal failing comes from turning the will away from the design of the One, a resistance that is futile, because we are obliged to fulfill our role in any event and by opposing that role we assure ourselves only of inevitable unhappiness. Avoid excess; freely and happily fill your allotted place in the cosmos: these Stoic doctrines are in line with Greek moral thought as far back as Homer. The man who through hubris batters himself against the appointed order of things is doomed to inevitable ruin. The later Stoics addressed themselves specifically to the question of evil. Epictetus (50–138 A.D.) argued that good and evil did not lie in things of themselves, but only in human use of them for good or evil ends. Marcus Aurelius, emperor from 161 to 180, agreed. There is nothing evil according to nature, he said; evil arises from human choice based upon ignorance that thwarts the intention of the God.

Epicureans, Skeptics, and Stoics alike therefore rejected the idea of cosmic good and evil in favor of strictly human responsibilities, explaining evil either as illusory, a mere human construct, or the futile endeavor to thwart the will of the One. Such lofty philosophical sentiments could not wholly satisfy a world in which disorder and destructiveness beyond the control of the individual seemed to be pressing in from all sides. There

Head of Charun, Tarentum, fourth century B.C. Courtesy Alinari Baglioni, Florence.

must, it was felt, be some cosmic explanation of evil, and some way to escape it, either in this world or another. Such cosmic explanations tended to be rooted in the dualism of the Orphic tradition that stretched from Pythagoras to Plato.

The Neopythagoreans of the second and third centuries A.D.

argued that the One, the Monad, was wholly good. By a process of emanation, the Monad produced the Dyad, the phenomenal world, which is evil. The Monad is simple spirit, the Dyad a multiplicity whose individuation derives from matter. The individual soul is confounded and tempted to wrong choice by its association with matter; our duty, therefore, is to attempt to press beyond matter to the Monad, whose being, one, simple, true, and good, lies behind the miserable multiplicity of this world. The Neopythagoreans never dealt with the ultimate difficulty in their theodicy: why the good Monad should ever have emanated the evil Dyad.

The followers of Plato developed a more explicit dualism, Eudoxos of Cnidia (fourth century B.C.) explicitly trying to reconcile the doctrines of Plato with those of Mazdaism. Xenocrates (fl. 339–314), like the Neopythagoreans later, posited a conflict between Monad and Dyad. Monad was the male principle, the prime god, rational intelligence; Dyad was the female principle, irrationality and evil. This dualism was reflected in opposition on a lower level between the Olympians, who were produced by the Monad, and the Titans, children of the female principle. On yet a lower level, good and evil demons carried on the conflict.

Early Platonism was predominantly dualist, and the Middle Platonism of the first two centuries A.D. moved to an even more explicit dualism based on the opposition of two eternal principles, spirit and matter. The God is spirit and attempts to form matter into a rational cosmos. Refractory matter renders the God's efforts only partially successful. Evil is attributed to the resistance of matter to the divine will. Plutarch (45–125 A.D.) argued that "it is impossible that a single being, good or bad, should be the cause of all that exists, since God cannot be the author of evil . . . we must admit two contrary principles." [18] According to Plutarch, matter cannot be the cause of itself; hence it was produced by a spirit. There are therefore two con-

18. William C. Greene, *Moira* (Cambridge, Mass., 1944), pp. 309–310. Similar to Plutarch's position were those of Maximus of Tyre (fl. 180 A.D.) and Celsus (fl. 179 A.D.).

trary and eternally opposed spirits, the good God and the evil spirit, the latter being responsible for the creation of matter, which resists the will of God. Here the Mazdaist belief in the two warring spirits is neatly combined with the Orphic-Platonic doctrine that matter is the enemy of spirit, the result being a cosmic war between a good spirit that generates soul, including the human soul, and an evil spirit, which generates matter. The existence of evil in the world arises first from the creation of matter and second from the action of the human free will in choosing the pleasures of the material world over that of spirit. Plutarch offers yet another explanation of evil, but this only halfheartedly. The God, he says, produces the gods, who are wholly divine; below the gods are the demons, who are both mortal and divine; below the demons are men, who are wholly mortal. The demons are morally ambiguous (they occupy the place of the angels in the Christian conception of the great chain of being), but their existence serves to relieve the gods, and a fortiori, the God, from direct responsibility for evil. Plutarch never posited the demons as a principle of evil, however, or made them an aspect of the malignant spirit that created evil.

Neoplatonism, founded by Plotinus (205–270), turned from the dualism of Middle Platonism toward an inconsistent monism perhaps closer to the thought of Plato himself. A similarity exists between the system of Plotinus and that of contemporary Gnostics, and there was probably some interchange of ideas between them, but their differences are fundamental: the Gnostics were dualists, while the basic assumption of the Neoplatonists was monist.

For Plotinus, the principle of the universe was the One. The One is perfect, and it comprises all that is. Yet we perceive a multiplicity in the universe. How is this? The One, desiring a universe full of forms, emanates from its own substance *nous*, mind, the world of platonic ideas. Here in *nous* exists a plenitude of all the possible forms of the universe, all completely incorporeal. This was the first emanation of the One, and it was good, both because the One willed it, and because it completed the world of forms. In no sense was this first emanation evil. But here already a difficulty inheres, for of necessity *nous* is less perfect than the One that emanates it. In a second emanation, *nous* produces *psyche*, the world-soul, which is *nous* thinking itself (a doctrine similar to the Christian idea that the *logos*, the Word of God, is the Father thinking himself). This emanation also is willed by the One and is wholly good. But now a third emanation occurs, for *psyche* produces the physical universe in which sense objects exist as a combination of ideas or forms with prime matter. Again, this emanation is willed by the One. Indeed, like all the emanations, it is not only willed by the One but is truly emanated from the One, begotten not made, and of one substance with the One. There is no trace in Plotinus of the Christian doctrine of the creation of the physical universe from nothing or the idea that matter is a principle independent of and separate from the God. Matter is an emanation of the God, and therefore it is good.

But here Plotinus finds himself in a contradiction that he was never able to resolve, for matter is also totally evil. The One is infinitely perfect and good. Emanations from the One share proportionately less of the good. This is the doctrine of privation hinted at by Plato and Aristotle. The last and least emanation is matter, which is farthest from and least like the One. As the One is most perfect and most good, matter, its opposite, is wholly devoid of goodness. Sense objects resemble the higher world insofar as they possess forms, but the unformed, prime matter upon which their forms are impressed is the opposite of the One. Matter is total deficiency, total privation, total non-being, and hence total lack of good. There is a word for total lack of good: evil. And Plotinus goes further. Not only is matter evil because it is totally devoid of good, but it acts positively for evil in that it impedes perfect good, resists the design of the One, and tempts the individual soul to error.

Thus Plotinus' view of matter is like one of those optical illusions that shifts its shape as you look at it. On the one hand Plotinus is a monist, insisting that even the lowest emanation of the One, no matter how deprived of being, still retained the smallest element of being and of goodness. On the other hand he is a dualist, perceiving in matter something completely evil and therefore independent of, and opposed to, the One.

A human being is, like everything else, an emanation of *psyche*, the world-soul. But there are two elements in a human being, the individual soul, which is spirit and relatively close to the world-soul, and the body, which is matter, remote from the world-soul, and evil. The body acts as a drag upon the soul, weighing it down and holding it back from its search for union with the spiritual realm. Two chief sources of evil thus exist in the world. One is matter itself, whose evil lies in its total privation of good. The other is the wrong choice of the human soul, tempted and corrupted by its union with the body. The former bears responsibility for natural evils such as earthquakes and disease, the latter for moral evils such as war, murder, and adultery. To an individual moral evil, say the murder of a child, Plotinus responds that you have done the deed because the passions proceeding from your material body have blinded you to your proper purpose in life, which is the pursuit through contemplation of the higher world that has emanated your soul.

Plotinus' ideas had an immense effect upon later thought. The implications of a great chain of being already existed in Plato. They became explicit in Plotinus, and from him they passed on to Augustine, Aquinas, and all Western thought, showing up finally in temporalized form in the Darwinian scheme of evolution.[19] And in the great chain as described by Plotinus lurks a contradiction that the Christians who followed him never resolved.

The contradiction arises from a confusion of the ontological with the moral scale of values. To begin with, the One is all perfect. Each emanation is less perfect than the one preceding it. Imperfection is introduced at the point that the One emanates the world-mind. But Plotinus balks at the implications of this and prefers to assume in some vague way that world-mind

19. The classical work is Arthur O. Lovejoy, *The Great Chain of Being* (Cambridge, Mass., 1936). See also J. Den Boeft, *Calcidius on Demons* (Leiden, 1977).

and world-soul reflect the perfections of the One. True privation, then, is introduced only at the last emanation, which
produces matter. Plotinus first speaks of evil in connection with
matter. But this first inconsistency is followed by a more important one.

A spectrum, or a scale, or a chain, exists, with the One at
one end and unformed matter at the other. The world of sense,
the universe as we perceive it, fits into that scale, and individual
beings in the universe fit into the scale at different points. But
Plotinus designed the scale in two ways. The first is ontological, in which the One is most real, and matter is least real. The
scale looks something like this:

> *The One* = Being = Infinite Being = Perfection
> *Nous*
> *Psyche*
> *The Material Universe*
>   Humans
>   Animals
>   Plants
>   Inanimate Objects
> *Unformed Matter* = Nonbeing = Infinite Privation

The higher a being is on the scale, the more it partakes of
spirit, and the closer to the One and hence to perfection it is.
The lower a being is on the scale, the more it is deprived of
spirit, the more it is material, and the closer to nonbeing it is.
Beings higher on the scale are more real; those lower on the
scale less so. Matter, at the bottom, is so nonreal that it becomes nonbeing and totters on the edge of complete nothingness. In the ontological scale it is difficult to speak of a principle
of evil. Evil is privation, lack of good, and it "exists" only in the
sense of excluding true existence, just as holes in the Swiss
cheese are lack of cheese and exist only by virtue of excluding
cheese. The top of the scale is infinite reality. Each succeeding
step down is less reality, until the bottom, which is no reality at
all. The scale proceeds downward from an infinite score at the
top to a score of zero at the bottom.

But there is a second way of constructing the scale, calibrating it not by ontology but by moral value:

The One = Perfection = Infinite Good
Nous
Psyche
The Material Universe
    Humans
    Animals
    Plants
    Inanimate Objects
  Unformed Matter = Total Imperfection = Infinite Evil

Here the value assigned to the top of the scale is infinite good. Each descending step is less good, hence more evil, until the bottom of the scale possesses no good at all and is totally evil. The score of the top of this scale is still a positive infinity, but each step down adds a negative ($-x$, $-x - 1$, $-x - 2$, $-x - 3$, and so on). In other words, where the ontological scale is positive, descending from infinity to zero, the value scale is negative, subtracting from good at each step, until the greatest possible negative is reached. In this scale it is possible to conceive of a principle of evil, that principle being the negative of unformed matter.

The two scales, though similar, are distinct, but Plotinus and those who followed him mislaid the distinction. For them:

      The One = Being = Perfection = Good
      Unformed Matter = Nonbeing = Evil

Yet another confusion is inherent, and though it did not afflict Plotinus himself, it plagued his successors. It arises when individual morality is incorporated into the value scale and, by attraction, into the ontological scale. This incorporation results in absurdity. On the ontological scale, a horse is less real than a man, because it partakes more of matter and less of spirit. We then (by elision with the value scale) say that a man is better than a horse. But what of a man who robs and tortures other people? Is he better than a strong and faithful horse? Or is he more evil, and consequently less real? Or, dealing with men themselves: according to the ontological scale, the most intelligent person, partaking more of spirit than his fellows, is the best person. (In some academic circles this is believed today.) But we know that an intelligent man can be cruel, avaricious, and deceitful, while another person, much his inferior in intelligence, can be generous, kind, and loving.

These confusions have blurred the development of the concept of the Devil. On the one hand, evil does not exist, and thus there can be no principle of evil. Some theologians argue that evil, being nonexistent, does not constitute a real problem, and, because evil is not real, the Devil cannot exist. This is the consequence of Plotinus' ontological monism. But if the value scale is used, then the opposite of absolute good is indeed absolute evil. A principle of evil does exist, and such a principle can be personified by the Devil. In a system such as that of Plotinus, the status of the principle of evil is unclear. On the one hand it is the lowest order of being or lacks being altogether. Ontologically it scarcely exists. But when the moral element is introduced, it is possible to conceive of a being of high ontological status making a choice for evil. This idea, though an implicit possibility in Plotinus, was never an explicit option for him, but it eventually became part of Christian tradition.

The religious spirit of Hellenistic philosophy and the philosophical spirit of Hellenistic religion offered Judaism a theological approach quite different from the mythological spirit dominating the Apocryphal and Apocalyptic works. Of this approach Philo of Alexandria (c. 20 B.C.–40 A.D.) was the most important exponent. Philo made two assumptions: that Scripture was true, and that reason led to truth and to the Lord. It thus became necessary to apply reason to Scripture. This had three results. First, Philo created the first coherent theological system in Judaism. Second, he introduced into the interpretation of Scripture an allegorical method that influenced later Jewish and Christian thought. Finally, Philo drew heavily upon the Greek philosophers, especially Plato, and succeeded in synthesizing Greek and Jewish thought in a manner later imitated by the Christian Apologist Fathers.

For Philo, the God is Yahweh, the Lord, and the God is good. In the mind of the Lord exists the *logos*, the Word, the domain of ideas, what the Platonists called *nous*. Prime matter coexists eternally with the God. By itself it is wholly void and without form. In the act of creation, the God imposes forms upon matter. Matter is recalcitrant, and to the extent that it resists the work of the God, it may be considered evil. The sins of mankind result from the corruption and contamination of the soul by matter, but also from free will, because each of us is free to resist the demands of matter upon us. Philo's assumption that the material world is the source of evil was combined by later writers with the Apocalyptic belief in the domination of the material world by evil spirits to produce the concept that Satan was the lord of this world. For Philo, however, this world, being the work and the will of the Lord, is intrinsically good, being evil only insofar as the material principle resists the Lord's will. Philo asserted the existence of demons but did not make of them the principle of evil. He followed the Septuagint's assumption of an order of spirits between the God and mankind, and its distinction between good spirits sent from the Lord (*angeloi*) and evil spirits (*daimones* or *daimonia*). Philo resisted the temptation to identify the pagan gods with the evil spirits. A Jew or Christian could take one of three main positions in regard to the pagan gods. First, he could deny their existence. In a world where the ubiquity and multiplicity of spirits was assumed, this was not often done. Second, he could identify them, as Philo did, with the angels. Finally, as most Christian writers did, he could identify them as demons, evil spirits, some of whose attributes could then be transferred to the Devil. That process will be described later.

These mythological and theological efforts to explain the mystery of evil all contributed to the concept of the Devil. The ordinary Greek or Roman might find in them some comfort, but the fundamental question, *Pothen ton kakon*, Whence does evil come?, had not been answered. On a tombstone a Greek father wrote: *Dōdeketē ton paida patēr apethēke Philippos enthade tēn pollēn elpida Nikotelēn:* "Here Philip buried his son of twelve years, his Nikoteles, his great hope." To the burial of this father's hope, or of ours, no theodicy has ever spoken convincingly.

In what ways did the Greek and Hellenistic experience advance the development of the tradition of the concept of the Devil? The Greeks for the first time conducted a rational investigation of the universe, producing philosophy and, by application of philosophy to the gods, theology. The problem of theodicy accordingly became for the first time explicit rather than enshrouded in mythology. Through philosophical and literary reflection, the Greeks obtained a generalized and moralized view of good and evil. There were general standards of behavior to which both men and gods, and beyond them, even the God itself, were supposed to conform. If the God disapproved anything, it was not by whim, but because the thing was intrinsically evil. If there was a principle of universal good, there might be a principle of universal evil. The principle of evil could then become not merely something opposed to the gods but something morally evil, and the Devil could be defined as the principle of *moral* evil. A rational and universal law governed the cosmos, and moral evil consisted of failure to conform to this law. Moral evil was typically viewed as an excess, a transgression of proper limits, a refusal willingly to comply with the cosmic plan. Its most typical expression was hubris, arrogance. Men were capable of moral evil, and so were the gods. What of the God himself?

There were strong currents of monism in Greek and Hellenistic thought. When considered rationally, monism offers a limited number of responses to the question raised by theodicy, and all these explanations were at one time or another presented in Greek thought. The first is a straightforward acceptance of a morally ambivalent God who can do both good and evil. The philosophers, with their desire to equate the God with goodness, did not seize this nettle, but it was implicit in Greek mythology. The gods are manifestations of the God, and, taken as a whole or as individuals, the gods are both good and evil, both beneficent and malevolent. The second monist theodicy argues that the God either does not exist or is morally neutral, in which event evil is merely a relative or human construct; Epicurus and the Skeptics expressed this point of view. The third position is that evil is necessary in the plan of the world, that is in an unavoidable by-product of a creation for the most part good. A usual corollary of this explanation is that evil is itself nonexistent, that it consists only of privation, of lack of perfection. The fourth is that the power of the God is limited: he wishes to create a good, orderly cosmos, but he is prevented by the existence of something refractory, such as matter. This particular theodicy is really not monist, for it leads naturally to the search for the principle limiting the action of the God. As soon as you introduce such a principle—whether an evil spirit or matter—as coeternal and coexistent with the God, you move away from monism in the direction of dualism.

Tetradrachm of Demetrios, Hellenistic coin, second century B.C. Horns here appear on the head of a Hellenistic ruler as a sign of his divinity. The twofold association of horns, divine and bestial, combined in the iconography of the Devil, connecting him with divine awesomeness on the one hand and fertility worship on the other. Courtesy Propyläen Verlag, Berlin.

In fact, though monism always remained dominant, Greek thought contained a strong element of dualism as far back as Pythagoras. Influencing Plato and the later philosophical schools, Greek dualism was of enormous importance in the formation of the late Jewish and Christian conceptions of the Devil. The Greeks combined the two kinds of dualism into one, ascribing matter to the work of a malevolent spirit. Matter in general and the body in particular are the work of an evil being, the individual's duty being to free himself from corrupt matter and to unite himself to that ethereal realm visible on earth only as the patines of bright gold shining through the pierced vault of dark heaven. This double or compound dualism, which had already appeared in Apocalyptic Judaism and would be pronounced in Gnosticism and Christianity, enabled the full development of the concept of a spiritual principle of evil, easily personified as the Devil under one of his numerous names. The idea of the Devil as lord of this world may also have received support from the eschatology of Mithraism, where Ahriman's power over the world increases until at last the Lord Mithras returns to revive the world, judge the living and the dead, and bring down the fire of Jupiter to destroy Ahriman and his evil cohorts.

The concept of the Devil was also aided by the development of the concept of evil demons. Again, this was a movement of Greek thought in the direction of dualism. At first demons are, like the original gods, morally ambivalent. Then two groups of demons are distinguished, one good and the other evil. Finally, a shift in vocabulary occurs. In the Septuagint, the good spirits are called angels and the evil spirits demons. Plutarch also opposes the demons to the gods. Both identify the demons as wholly evil spiritual beings. These are now easily amalgamated with the Devil, either lending their traits to him, or being spirits subordinate to him, just as the Watcher angels in the Apocalyptic literature became subject to Satan or Mastema.

The demons, then, were in part personifications of the evil attributes previously associated with the gods. They also acquired some of the characteristics previously ascribed to monsters, characteristics that passed on in iconography and legend to the Devil himself. Thus pictures of medieval demons show traces of the leg wings of Hermes Psychopompos; the serpents associated with the Gorgons, Typhon, and Hydra; the goatlike or donkeylike features associated with Dionysos, Pan, the sa-

Pan and Olympus, Pompeii, first century A.D. Pan teaches the young god Olympus to play the syrinx. Courtesy Mansell Collection, London.

tyrs, and Charun; and the beaked nose, grimacing lips, and dark blue hue of Charun, as well as the weapon he carried.

Also influential were Hades the god and Hades the place of punishment. The underworld, originally a shadowy place in which the pale ghosts of the dead flitted in a dull half-life, later combined Hades and Tartarus and became a fiery pit for the punishment of sinners. The god Hades, at first a shadowy spirit of the underworld, became judge of the dead and commander of a force of spirits whose job was to torment the damned. This concept, allied with the late Jewish concept of Gehenna, lay at the basis of the Christian hell over which the Devil presided on his throne (though in Christianity Christ, not the Devil, judges the dead).

The underworld's association with fertility as well as with death, and the conjoining of the two in myth and in cult tied the Devil to sexuality as well. Rites associated with Dionysos, the Magna Mater, Cybele, Mithras, Isis, and Pythagoreanism contained elements that were later to become standard in the practices, real or alleged, of heretics and witches. As has been noted, the orgy itself was not present in the cults of Isis, Mithras, or Pythagoras. Orgy naturally occurred (or at least was inferred) in cults whose membership was mixed, or, as with the Bacchantes, largely female.[20] But in Greece the female principle was never identified with the principle of evil, in spite of temptations from philosophy (the Dyad) and from religion (Hecate, the Erinyes, and the Lamias). The Lamias easily merged with the Semitic Lilith to create the image of the lewd and murderous female spirit who ventures out at night seducing men and killing infants, an image that the Middle Ages gradually shifted from the supernatural to the natural realm, fixing it finally upon the witch. Here as elsewhere, the assumption may have been that women were naturally inferior to men and therefore could not be elevated to the status of principle of evil. It is instructive that in the classical world high, intellectual

20. See Mark W. Wyndham, "The Concept of the Gnostic Heretic in Patristic Literature" (Dissertation, University of California, Riverside, June 1975), ch. three.

magic was ascribed primarily to men, while low, practical magic was considered the province of women.[21]

Mythologically and philosophically, powerful currents in Greek thought advanced the movement from religious monism to dualism. These currents were to some extent anticipated, and to some extent followed, in the thought of the Hebrews.

21. Wyndham, ch. two.

5 Hebrew Personifications of Evi

Woe unto them that desire the Day of Yahweh! What do you
look for from the Day of Yahweh? It will be darkness and not
light.

—Amos 5:18

"I create the light; I create the darkness": so boasts the God
Yahweh (Isaiah 45:7). In pre-exilic Hebrew religion Yahweh
made all that was in heaven and earth, both of good and of evil.
The Devil did not exist. The Hebrew concept of the Devil developed gradually, arising from certain tensions within the concept of Yahweh. Since Judaism and Christianity are live options for many of us, it is more difficult here than elsewhere to
avoid a confusion between the metaphysical and the historical.
What I intend is a discussion of the historical development of
the concept rather than a metaphysical statement. One implica-
tion for theology should be made explicit, however, for its opposite has been frequently and vigorously stated. The fact that
the Devil is not fully developed in the Old Testament is not a
ground for rejecting his existence in modern Jewish and Christian theology. That would be the genetic fallacy: the notion
that the truth of a word—or a concept—is to be found in its
earliest form. Rather, historical truth is development through
time. Another difficulty arises in discussing the concept in Hebrew religion. I have defined the Devil as the personfification of
evil in any culture. But the word "Devil" derives through Latin
from the Greek *diabolos*, which is a rendition of the Hebrew
satan. Conceptually, the Hebrew Satan is one manifestation of
the Devil, not the Devil *par essence*.

This chapter is concerned with the development of the concept of the Devil in Hebrew religion from the Old Testament through Apocalyptic and Qumran literature. The Old Testament was compiled over a long period from about 900 B.C. to about 100 B.C. Most of its books were written down in their present form during and after the period of the Babylonian Captivity (586–538) and show traces of Canaanite, Babylonian, Iranian, and Hellenistic influence. Neither the dates nor the sources of most Old Testament books are firmly established.[1]

The Apocrypha are scriptures excluded from the Hebrew canon of the Old Testament. Debates as to which of the many alleged holy books extant were truly inspired arose as early as the fourth century B.C., and the final form of the Hebrew canon was not established until the first century A.D. In the meantime, the scriptures were translated into Greek about 250 B.C. This work, the Septuagint, was expanded over the centuries to contain a number of books that were ultimately rejected from the Hebrew canon. These books, many of which reflect the misery of the Jews under Syrian and Roman oppression, were written from about 200 B.C. to about 150 A.D., and though they were excluded from the canon, they had great influence.

The suffering of the Jewish people in this period also produced a variety of literature generally described as Apocalyptic. These writings, a few of which were deemed canonical, consisted largely of visions in which the end of this world was

---

1. Scholars have long agreed, for example, that the Hexateuch is based on four major (as well as some minor) sources: the Yahwist (c. 900 B.C.), the Elohist (c. 800), the Deuteronomic (c. 680), and the Priestly (450–400), but assignation of materials to these sources is tentative. See the review of Frank Moore Cross's *Canaanite Myth* by Cyrus Gordon in the *American Historical Review*, 79 (1974), 1149. "Apocrypha" derives from the Greek *apokryptein*, "to hide"; "Apocalypse" derives from *apokalyptein*, "to reveal." These writings are also called the Pseudepigrapha because their authors ascribed them to the ancient patriarchs and prophets. Sometimes they are also called "apocrypha," but none of them ever found their way into a canon. The Qumran literature can properly be considered in the same context as the Apocalyptic: see Harold H. Rowley, *The Growth of the Old Testament*, 3d ed. (London, 1967), and David S. Russell, *The Method and Message of Jewish Apocalyptic* (Philadelphia, 1964).

prominent. Some of these works expressed the view that the oppression of the Jews indicated that the world was now in the power of the Devil. In the old days, patriarchs and kings had ruled, but in the latter days the Devil had established his rule over the earth. Soon, however, the kingdom of the Devil (the "old eon") would perish before the time of the Messiah, who would bring a "new eon," a reign of justice and light. Into the mouths of ancient patriarchs or prophets the Apocalyptic authors placed their own prophecies of the ruin and regeneration to come. As these prophecies were based upon events that had already occurred in the time of the real authors, they had of course already partly come true and so gained further validation in the minds of those who heard them. In opposition to Apocalyptic literature, that of the rabbis was little concerned with demonology, which accounts for the fact that the Devil has been much less important in modern Jewish thought than in Christian.

At least four interpretations of the origins of the Hebrew Devil have been influential in modern times. The first is that Satan was a demon among demons who rose to the position of their chief. This interpretation fails in many respects. There is no evidence of any kind that there ever was a petty demon named Satan, and although there are many manifestations of evil among Hebrew demons, no demon (with the one exception of Azazel) ever approaches the lofty position of apotheosis of evil. The second is that Satan is a personification of the evil impulse within man. In this argument, he is an earlier, parallel, and more personal expression of the Rabbinic *yetser ha-ra*, "evil inclination." It is true that all cosmic conceptions may ultimately be psychological projections, but at least some of the Old Testament authors themselves considered Satan an objective reality, and this argument fails. The common assumption that Satan was one of the God's functionaries whose morals and motivations continually declined is less an explanation than a description that fails to say why this process should have occurred. The fourth explanation best grasps the historical metabolism of the concept: Satan is the personification of the dark

Moses presenting the law to the Jews, manuscript illumination, France, fourteenth century. The horns of Moses were originally horns of power; later Christian tradition made them the symbol of the supposed alliance between the Jews and the horned Satan. Courtesy Bavarian State Library, Munich.

side of the God, that element within Yahweh which obstructs the good.

Whatever the origins of Hebrew monotheism, the Old Testament writers had come to identify Yahweh, the god of Israel, with the one God of the cosmos. Since Yahweh was the one God, he had to be, like the God of monism, an "antinomy of inner opposites."[2] He was both light and darkness, both good

2. Carl G. Jung, *Answer to Job* (London, 1954), p. 369. This has been recognized by a number of writers over the past century, beginning with Gustav Roskoff, *Geschichte des Teufels*, 2 vols. (Leipzig, 1869); Paul Volz, *Das Dämonische in Jahwe* (Tubingen, 1924); Gustav Mensching, "Teufel: Religionsgeschichtlich," *Religion in Geschichte und Gegenwart*, 3d ed. (Tubingen, 1957), VI, 704–705. It was Jung who put the point most clearly, and his work was followed by one of his pupils in the best explanation of the origin of Satan: Rivkah Schärf Kluger, *Satan in the Old Testament* (Evanston, Ill., 1967), first published under the author's maiden and European name: Rosa R. Schärf, *Die Gestalt des Satans im Alten Testament* (Glarus, 1948), and then under the name of Rivkah Schärf, "Die Gestalt des Satans im Alten Testament," pt. 3 of C. G. Jung, *Symbolik des Geistes* (Zurich, 1953). Her book is admirable, but it has two limitations: on occasion, it takes the Jungian interpretation farther than the evidence warrants; and it does not deal adequately with the personification of evil by the Hebrews in the Apocryphal and Apocalyptic

and evil. We are accustomed to thinking of Yahweh in his creative aspects, but let us now consider his shadow.

In the early Old Testament traditions, the morality of the Hebrews was linked to transgressions of tabu more than to violations of social justice. The Old Testament condemns transgressions against Yahweh, such as idolatry, blasphemy, profanation of the Sabbath, and oath-breaking. The books of Leviticus and Deuteronomy testify to the importance of ritual and tabu. Insofar as the Israelites were enjoined to justice, it was primarily in regard to their dealings with other Israelites. Toward the Gentiles their behavior was as fearsome as that of Ashurnasirpal to his victims.

When the Israelites invaded Canaan, Joshua "captured the city [of Hazor] and put its king to death with the sword. [The Israelites] killed every living thing in it, and wiped them all out; they spared nothing that drew breath, and Hazor itself they destroyed by fire. . . . The Israelites plundered all these cities and kept for themselves the cattle and any other spoil they took; but they put every living soul to the sword until they had destroyed every one; they did not leave alive any one that drew breath." The Israelites attributed this policy to the will of Yahweh. If the Canaanites, perhaps forgivably, attempted to block the conquest of their homeland by the savage Israelites, it was

---

works. I am deeply indebted in the present chapter to Kluger's work, which is an example of the utility of Jungian thought in illuminating the history of concepts. Robert Gordis, in his *Book of God and Man* (Chicago, 1965), pp. 69–71, argues that the separation of the Lord and Satan occurred under Mazdaist influence. There is danger of simplification in equating Yahweh with the God. One of the earliest scriptural traditions is that of the Yahwist, who refers to the one God as Yahweh; but the Elohist uses the term Elohim. The latter is usually translated "Lord." Our term "God" of course has Germanic rather than Hebrew linguistic origins. The two terms Yahweh and Elohim were assimilated by the compilers of the Pentateuch as references to one being; but the fact remains that two different terms were used, and it is not self-evident that the Yahwist and the Elohist had the same concept in mind when they wrote. The word "Elohim" has the curious quality of being plural in number, as if the Elohist considered the one God to be somehow also plural. For simplicity, I shall always refer to the God of Israel as Yahweh, rather than Elohim.

Yahweh who had hardened their hearts: "It was the Lord's purpose that they should offer an obstinate resistance to the Israelites in battle, and that thus they should be annihilated without mercy and utterly destroyed." Yahweh ordered the conquest of Canaan, he then caused the Canaanites to resist, and he finally ordained their utter ruin at the hand of his chosen people. Few gods of Egypt, Babylonia, or Canaan itself were so ruthless.

And to the Israelites themselves Yahweh was scarcely more kind. When one among them had kept some of the spoil from a captured city for himself rather than giving it to Yahweh (in care of his priests), Yahweh punished the children of Israel, causing them to be defeated at the hands of the Canaanites. Joshua asked Yahweh what was to be done, and the God replied that Joshua was to discover the culprit. Lots were cast, by which the God's mind could be made manifest. The lot fell upon Achan. Achan confessed, and the Israelites took him up to the Vale of Achor, where they stoned him to death. And "the Lord's anger was abated." In reward, Yahweh delivered the city of Ai to the Israelites, and the Israelites "cut down to the last man all the citizens of Ai who were in the open country or in the wilderness to which they had pursued them," and then returned "to Ai and put it to the sword. The number who were killed that day, men and women, was twelve thousand, the whole population of Ai."[3] The logic was pitiless: the God had chosen Israel as his people, any Gentile who stood in Israel's path was to be mercilessly destroyed, and any Israelite who disobeyed Yahweh's command was likewise to be put to death.

Since the God of Israel was the only God, the supreme power in the cosmos, the orderer of all things, no deed could be done unless he willed it. Consequently, when anyone transgressed morality, it had to be Yahweh himself who caused the transgression. And so in Genesis 12:17, the God causes Abraham to pretend that Sarah is his sister rather than his wife

---

3. Josh. 7–8; 11:10–15; 11:20. The prosecution of the Holy War in Joshua follows from an idealized theological postulate owing much to the utopian thinking of the Deuteronomist. Cf. the Qumran War Scroll (1 QM).

while he is in the land of Egypt, and when Pharaoh falls in love with Sarah and wishes to marry her, innocently believing her to be Abraham's sister, the God punishes Pharaoh, striking him "and his household with grave diseases." In Exodus, Yahweh repeatedly hardens the heart of Pharaoh, causing him to deny the Hebrews' request to leave Egypt. Yahweh visits the unfortunate Egyptians with plague after plague. Each time, when Pharaoh begins to yield, Yahweh hardens his heart to resist further and to bring further disasters down upon himself and his people. At last the God punishes him by slaying all the firstborn of Egypt, passing over the children of Israel and sparing them alone.[4]

If ever the Hebrews showed mercy to their enemies, the God upbraided them for neglecting his will (Judges 2:1–2). Nor was it only Gentiles against whom the God raised his hand. When Achitophel sought to persuade Absalom to reconcile himself with David his father, Yahweh led the young man astray, for it was his "purpose to frustrate Achitophel's good advice and so bring disaster upon Absalom (2 Samuel 17:14)." Yahweh could even treat all Israel as he did the Egyptians. He said to the prophet Isaiah, "Go, and tell this people, hear ye indeed, but understand not; and see ye indeed but perceive not. Make the heart of this people fat, and make their ears heavy, and shut their eyes; lest they see with their eyes, and hear with their ears, and understand with their hearts, and convert, and be healed. Then said I, Lord, how long? And he answered, until the cities be wasted without inhabitant, and the houses without man, and the land shall be utterly desolate" (Isaiah 6:9–11). At this stage of Hebrew religion there is no significant distinction between the ambivalence of the God Yahweh and the ambivalence of the God of monism.

The figure with whom Jacob struggled at the ford of Jabbok may be the evil aspect of Yahweh (Genesis 32:22–32). The shadow of the God appears even more clearly in Exodus 4:24–26, where the God seeks to murder Moses on his journey

4. Exod. 3:19; 7:13–22; 9:12, 35; 10:1, 20, 27; 11:10; 13:15.

back to Egypt from Midian: "During the journey, while they were encamped for the night, the Lord met Moses, meaning to kill him, but Zipporah picked up a sharp flint, cut off her son's foreskin, and touched him with it, saying, 'You are my blood-bridegroom.' So the Lord let Moses alone." In Deuteronomy 32: 41–42, Yahweh sounds much like destroying Sekhmet or Anath:

> When I have whetted my flashing sword,
> when I have set my hand to judgement,
> then I will punish my adversaries
> and take vengeance on my enemies.
> I will make my arrows drunk with blood,
> my soul shall devour flesh,
> blood of slain and captives,
> the heads of the enemy princes.

The savage nature of Yahweh in preprophetic Hebrew religion reflects the savage mores of the wandering, conquering Israelites. As the Hebrews became more settled, they moderated their morality. The ethical teaching of the prophets emphasized mercy and care for the poor, widowed, and homeless, and it insisted upon the responsibility of the individual for avoiding promiscuity, drunkenness, bribery, and lying. The Hebrew sense of good and evil shifted from its previous emphasis upon ritual tabu in the direction of a practical and humane ethic of mutual human responsibility. As this occurred, Yahweh's characteristics changed.[5]

No longer easy in their minds about ascribing rapine and destruction to the will of their God, the Hebrews sought new theodicies. One was that evil was the result of the sin of hu-

5. It is more difficult to use figurative language when speaking of Yahweh than when speaking of Marduk, Horus, or Ahura Mazda, because of the old assumption of Western civilization that the God of the Bible, and only the God of the Bible, is the idea of the God as he exists objectively. Atheists as well as believers have made this assumption. I do not make it here. When I say "Yahweh did," I mean the phrase exactly as if I were saying "Marduk did." In other words, I use "Yahweh did" as an abbreviation of, for example, "the writer of Joshua believed or said that Yahweh did."

manity. Yahweh made the human race happy in the Garden of Eden, but the first couple disobeyed him and in consequence were expelled from Paradise. The Old Testament did not make of this story the basis for a doctrine of original sin, as later the Rabbinic, and even more, the Christian writers would, but it did follow the theme of human perversity and sin through Cain, Sodom and Gomorrah, the faithlessness bringing punishing flood at the time of Noah, and the repeated inconstancy of the Israelites during the settling of Canaan and in the period of the kingdoms.[6] The idea that humanity had alienated itself from the God was already firm in Genesis 6:5–6: "When the Lord saw that man had done much evil on earth and that his thoughts and inclinations were always evil, he was sorry that he had made man on earth." The constant backsliding of the Hebrew kings and people from the Covenant caused the Lord further regrets and inclined him to chastise his people repeatedly. Yet both sins and punishments were so frequent and so great that they seemed disproportionate to the powers of puny man

6. The interpretation of the story of the expulsion of Adam and Eve in Gen. 3 continues to be the subject of lively debate. Modern scholars reject the notion that the writer of Gen. 3 intended to equate the serpent with the Devil. Only in Apocalyptic and later literature does the serpent become the tool of Satan or Satan himself. Of recent interpretations of the sin of Adam and Eve some of the most useful are in Martin Buber, *Good and Evil* (New York, 1953); George Wesley Buchanan, "The Old Testament Meaning of the Knowledge of Good and Evil," *Journal of Biblical Literature*, 75 (1956), 114–120; W. Malcolm Clark, "A Legal Background to the Yahwist's Use of 'Good and Evil' in Genesis 2–3," *Journal of Biblical Literature*, 88 (1969), 266–278; Joseph Coppens, *La Connaissance du bien et du mal et le péché du paradis* (Louvain, 1948); A. M. Dubarle, *The Biblical Doctrine of Original Sin* (New York, 1964); J. M. Evans, *Paradise Lost and the Genesis Tradition* (Oxford, 1968); Robert Gordis, "The Knowledge of Good and Evil in the Old Testament and the Qumran Scrolls," *Journal of Biblical Literature*, 76 (1957), 123–138; Cyrus Gordon, *The Ancient Near East*, 3d ed. (New York, 1965), pp. 36–37; Julius Gross, *Entstehungsgeschichte der Erbsündendogmas; von der Bibel bis Augustinus* (Munich, 1960); Herbert Haag, *Is Original Sin in Scripture?* (New York, 1969); F. R. Tennant, *Sources of the Doctrines of the Fall and Original Sin* (Cambridge, 1903); Norman P. Williams, *The Ideas of the Fall and of Original Sin* (London, 1927). The doctrines of the fall and of original sin have been less consistent than flexible in the hands of mythographers and theologians. See Evans, p. 10.

to displease the deity. And always at the back of their minds the Hebrews wondered how it was that the God, all powerful and all knowing as he was, would permit humanity to sin. The corrupt will of human beings seemed insufficient to explain the vast and terrifying quantity of evil in the world.

For an answer, the Hebrews turned to another explanation: the instigator of evil was a malignant spirit whose power to offend was far greater than that of mere mortals. The malignant, destructive aspect of Yahweh was subtracted from him and ascribed to a different spiritual power, the Devil. In effect, a twinning occurred in the divine nature, similar to the twinning in the God of Egypt or of Canaan. The one God split into two parts. One, the good aspect of the God, became "the Lord." The other, the evil aspect, became "the Devil." At the same time that the Hebrews continued to insist upon monotheism as the essential element of their religion, they moved unconsciously toward dualism. Explicitly they were monotheists: there was only one God, and his name was Yahweh. The God was omnipotent. But now the God was wholly good; evil was alien to his nature. Yet evil still existed. To explain the existence of evil, the Hebrews had to move in the direction of dualism. They were never fully aware of what they had introduced into a religion in which any retreat from monotheism was the greatest blasphemy. Even the Apocalyptic literature stops short of explicitly asserting that the Devil is totally evil in origin and essence. This tension between explicit monotheism and implicit dualism became characteristic of Hebrew and Christian religion.

This theodicy was hindered—or helped—by an important blurring of distinctions. Before, Yahweh had been the God, the antinomy of inner opposites. Now, Yahweh became the Lord, the good aspect of the God. The name Yahweh, and the loyalty of the Hebrews to Yahweh, was applied strictly to the good twin. What of the evil twin? In a strict monotheist religion he could not be a god. What was he then? The answer proved difficult for both Jewish and Christian theologians. Historically, the answer is best provided by examining the way in which the twinning of the divine nature took place.

The God divided, to change the metaphor, along two geological fault lines. The first fault line is that provided by the *bene ha-elohim*; the second that represented by the *mal'ak Yahweh*.

There seems to be evidence of the survival of some elements of Hebrew polytheism in the Hexateuch, where the Elohist source consistently uses the plural *Elohim*, "Lords," to refer to God.[7] In Genesis 3:5 the serpent tells Eve that she and Adam will become as *gods* if they eat the fruit of the tree. The God sometimes uses a pronoun "we" that is more than a mere royal convention. He appears both in the Pentateuch and in later writings as the God of Hosts surrounded by a heavenly council, a *sod*.[8] This heavenly court is often called the *bene ha-elohim*, "sons of the Lord," comparable to the "sons of the God" in Canaanite religion. In Canaan these "sons" are gods, manifestations of the divine principle.[9] Clearly the original idea in Hebrew religion was that Yahweh was surrounded by a pantheon comparable to that of Zeus or Wotan. The idea of a pantheon was displeasing to a strict monotheism, and the *banim* (*bene ha'elohim*) became shadowy figures. Yet they retained an important function in separating the evil aspect of the divine nature from the good.

The Book of Genesis relates that early in the history of the human race, the *bene ha-elohim* looked upon the daughters of men and found them beautiful. They had intercourse with these women and by them begot a race of giants called *nephilim*.[10] These offspring of the *banim* and women were "the

7. The Elohist source is usually dated about 800 B.C. See Aubrey Johnson, *The One and the Many in the Israelite Conception of God*, 2d ed. (Cardiff, 1961).

8. Kluger, *Satan*, p. 101, n. 54, shows that scholars do not agree as to the correct interpretation of the term *Yahweh Seba'ot*. The *sod* is clearly implied in 1 Kings 22:19–22 and Isa. 6.

9. Theodore M. Gaster discusses the Canaanite parallel to the *banim* in his *Myth, Legend, and Custom in the Old Testament* (New York, 1969), p. 79.

10. Gen. 6:1–4. The passage appears in the course of a discussion of the life of Noah, but it is not clear that the author intended to say that the event took place in Noah's time. *Nephilim* may derive from the Hebrew *nerfal*, to fall.

heroes of old, men of renown." Following these events, the Lord sent the deluge upon the earth, but this punishment was ascribed not to the sins of the *banim* but to those of men, who "had done much evil on earth" (Genesis 6:5). The Book of Psalms says that "God takes his stand in the court of heaven to deliver judgment among the gods themselves" and concludes "Gods you may be, sons you all of the Most High, yet you shall die as men die; princes fall, every one of them, and so shall you."[11] Here the Lord judges the members of his heavenly court and causes them to fall for their sin. The fall may consist of the passage from immortality to mortality, or a fall from power, or both. It does not appear to imply a fall from heaven. There is no indication what the sin of the gods was. The passage of Psalms is at least five hundred years removed from that of Genesis and written in a very different intellectual context. Yet each passage indicates the existence of the heavenly court and the sin of at least some of its members. It was left to the writers of the Apocalyptic period to develop these ideas.

The Jews of the Apocalyptic period did not understand why Yahweh had abandoned Israel. If he had, they mused, then there could be no more hope for Israel as a nation among nations. Evil ruled the world in their time; the Messiah, they thought, must soon come; and in the meanwhile each individual must do his own duty to the Lord. In those dark days individual morality was increasingly conceived as a matter of avoiding sin rather than of practicing virtue, and this brooding presence of sin and evil lingered in Rabbinic and Christian thought. The

11. Ps. 82:1–7. This psalm dates from the third or second century B.C. In the midst of this passage are a few verses that textual criticism has shown are independent and inserted by the final editor of Psalms from a different context. These intercalated verses refer to human princes rather than to the *banim*. See Bernard Bamberger, *Fallen Angels* (Philadelphia, 1952), pp. 10–11. These verses had great influence upon both Latin and Greek Christianity. In the Vulgate, the key phrases are "Deus stetit in synagoga deorum. . . . Ego dixi; dii estis, et filii Excelsi omnes." In the Septuagint, they are: "Ho theos estē en synagōgē theōn. . . . Egō eipa, theoi este, kai hyioi hypsistou pantes." "God" is a translation of the Hebrew *El*, and "gods" of the Hebrew *elohim*. The "Most High" is *Elyon* and may be translated "a high god."

evil of the world could no longer be attributed to Yahweh, who now said: "Call heaven and earth to witness; call them to witness, for I have left out evil and created good, because I live, says the Lord." [12]

One of the earliest and most influential Apocalyptic accounts of the ruin of the *bene ha-elohim* is the First Book of Enoch. [13] In this book, Enoch is taken on a journey of inspection around the earth and to Sheol. [14] During the journey he sees the sons of God in their ruined state and learns their story. Enoch's account is in the nature of a gloss upon the original passage in Genesis. According to Enoch, "the angels, the children of the heaven, saw and lusted after" the daughters of men. The Apocalyptic writer here has taken a long step in the development of the Devil. He reaffirms the original closeness of the *bene ha-elohim* with the Lord—they are children of heaven—but by demoting them to the status of angels, Enoch has safely removed them beyond the limits of the divine nature itself, and this in turn allows him and his fellow Apocalyptic writers a free

12. 4 Ezra 2:14.

13. This is the book known as 1 Enoch or Ethiopic Enoch because it is fully extant only in an Ethiopian version. It is composed of a number of elements dating from about 200 B.C. to about 60 B.C. The relevant chapters are 6–36. For this and other references to the Apocalyptic literature, see R. H. Charles, *The Apocrypha and Pseudepigrapha of the Old Testament*, 2 vols. (Oxford, 1913), II: *Pseudepigrapha*.

14. Sheol appears first in Num. 16:30 and then in Job 30:23. It is beneath the earth and is "the land of destruction, forgetfulness, and silence" (Charles, p. 230). The spirit of the dead individual exists there disembodied in a joyless, lonely, shadowy state. Both the good and the evil go there at death. From the second century B.C., during the Apocalyptic period, the original concept was changed by the idea of the last judgment and retribution. Since the Apocalyptic writers came to limit resurrection from the dead to the righteous and to leave the unrighteous below, Sheol began to be thought of as a place of punishment. At that time it was assimilated to the idea of Gehenna. Gehenna (Ben-hinnom) is a valley near Jerusalem originally associated with the worship of Moloch. Jeremiah curses it (7:31–32; 19:2, 6; 32:35), and Isaiah (66:24) says that rebellious and apostate Jews suffer punishment there by fire. In Ethiopic Enoch it remains a place of punishment for apostate Jews. For the Rabbis it was a place of eternal damnation for the Gentiles and of temporal punishment for rebellious Jews. Once the ideas of Sheol and Gehenna fused, the composite was adopted as the Christian idea of hell.

William Blake, "Satan before the Throne of God," 1820. God is surrounded by the court of heaven, the *bene ha-elohim*, as Satan appears before
him to ask permission to tempt Job. Courtesy Dr. J. Street, Fitzwilliam College,
Cambridge.

hand in bringing out their evil nature. And it now becomes clear, as it was not in Genesis or Psalms, that these fallen beings are evil indeed.[15]

The Watcher angels—as they are now called—have a leader, whose name is Semyaza.[16] The names of the Devil vary, particularly in the Apocalyptic period: he is Belial, Mastema, Azazel, Satanail, Sammael, Semyaza, or Satan.[17] These names have different origins, and the beings they denote differ in their origins and functions one from another. But gradually they coalesce. The Devil becomes a spiritual being personifying the ori-

15. The late Jewish inclination to take the Genesis passage as referring to "angels" is reflected in the Septuagint, where the original translation of the *bene ha-elohim* of Genesis was *angeloi*—thus it appears in Philo—and was changed later to the more correct reading *hyioi*.

16. Semyaza is first called their leader in En. 6:3; the term "Watchers" is first used in 10:7 and is the most common term employed by the Apocalyptic writers. It appears in the Old Testament only in the Book of Daniel, which is itself an Apocalyptic book written 166–164 B.C.

17. Belial (Gk: Beliar) may derive from *beli*, "without," and *ya'al*, "profit," and so mean "worthless." See Theodore H. Gaster, "Belial," *Encyclopedia Judaica* (New York, 1970), 4, 427–428; Hans W. Hupperbauer, "Belial in den Qumrantexten," *Theologische Zeitschrift*, 15 (1959), 89. In the Qumran texts, the term is used in a number of ways, sometimes merely as an adjective connoting evil, other times as a name of the personification of evil. In the Old Testament, Belial appears in Deut. 13:13; Judg. 19:22; 20:13; and 1 Sam. 1:16; 2:12; 10:27; 25:17, but he has little or no personality. The term *belial* is often simply a common noun signifying people who act reprehensibly, as in Deut. 13:14; Prov. 19:29; Nah. 1:11. Belial appears in the Apocalyptic and Qumran literature as the prince of evil. He is completely absent in Rabbinical literature. See J. Michl, "Katalog der Engelnamen," *Reallexikon für Antike und Christentum*, V (1962), 209. Mastema may derive from the Hebrew *mastemah*, "enmity," or the Aramaic *mastima*, "accuser," and so is related to Satan. Mastema does not appear in the Old Testament but is a prince of evil in the Apocryphal period: Michl, p. 221. Azazel or Asasel appears in Lev. 16:8 and 10:26, where his personality is ill defined; there he seems to be the principle of impurity. Later he becomes a prince of evil. His name may derive from *'azaz* and *'el* and mean the "strong one of the God." He was originally a god of the desert and may derive from the Canaanite god 'Asiz, who caused the sun to burn strongly. There is a possible influence of the Egyptian Seth on Azazel. See Kluger, p. 41; Roskoff, I, p. 183; Michl, pp. 206–207. Satanael or Satanail is derived from Satan; he does not appear in the Old Testament but is a prince of evil in the Apocalyptic period: Michl, pp. 232–233. Sammael, whose name derives from *sami* ("blind"), first appears in the Amoraic period. See Michl, p. 231, and Gershom Scholem, "Sammael," *Encyclopedia Judaica*,

gin and essence of evil: there can be only one Devil. Previous studies that have concentrated exclusively upon the name of Satan have obscured this fact. As the Devil has many names in different religions, so he has many names within the Judeo-Christian tradition itself.

Of all these names, that of Satan became the greatest. "High on a Throne of Royal State, which far / outshone the wealth of Ormus and of Ind . . . Satan exalted sat." The reasons for this pre-eminence are: (1) the word *satan* appears more frequently and more prominently than the names of the others, and (2) it appears at a number of crucial points. The victory of "Satan" over "Azazel" or "Belial" is less the victory of one kind of *being* over another than the victory of one *name* over the others. Satan, Azazel, Belial, and Mastema were none of them in their origins a principle of evil, but in the Apocalyptic literature they converge in that direction. What is important is the development of the *concept* of the principle of evil, with which the name of Satan was linked more closely than any other.

The Hebrew word *satan* derives from a root meaning "oppose," "obstruct," or "accuse." It was translated by the Greek *diabolos*, "adversary," whence it passed into Latin *diabolus*, German *Teufel*, and English *devil*. The basic denotation of the term, then, is "opponent." In this simple sense the word *satan* appears as a common noun several times in the Old Testament in reference to a human opponent, as when David says to the sons of Zeruiah, "What right have you . . . to oppose me today?" or "What right do you have to play the opponent against me?" [18]

14, 719–722. Semyaza, whose name may mean "rebel" or "watcher," appears briefly as leader of the evil angels in the Apocalyptic literature: Michl, p. 234. Beelzebub or Beelzeboul appears in the Old Testament as a god of Ekron in 2 Kings 1:2–6; 16. The Septuagint and New Testament translated the Hebrew as Beelzeboul, which was adapted by the Vulgate as *Beelzebub*. The origin of the name is uncertain. See Edward Langton, *Essentials of Demonology* (London, 1949), pp. 166–167. Beelzebub appears frequently in the New Testament as a name of the Devil, but not as yet in the Old Testament or Apocalyptic literature.

18. 2 Sam. 19:22. Here the Vulgate translates: "Cur efficimini mihi hodie in satan?" Other appearances of *satan* as a common noun in the Old Testament: 1 Sam. 29:24; 1 Kings 5:4; 11:14–25; Ps. 109:6 (LXX: *diabolos*; Vulg:

But also in an early passage, an angel of the Lord blocks the road on which Balaam seeks to travel riding an ass. Since the angel obstructs the road, he is referred to as a *satan*. Here for the first time a supernatural being is called a *satan*, but again the sense is clearly that of a common noun. The angel is not a *being* called a *"satan"*; he merely acts in this particular instance as an obstructor of the road (Numbers 22:22–35). A third dimension of the word *satan* appears in Zechariah 3:1–2: "Then he showed me Joshua the high priest standing before the angel of the Lord, with the Adversary standing at his right hand to accuse him. The Lord said to the Adversary, 'The Lord rebuke you, Satan, the Lord rebuke you who are venting your spite on Jerusalem.' " [19] This passage is a striking development. Although the presence of the Hebrew article indicates a common rather than a proper noun ("the satan"), the idea of personality is still conveyed. Here is a supernatural being who not only acts as obstructor but whose nature and name are those of an obstructor. Next, this being shows himself in overt hostile opposition to at least one man, for the adversary stands before the God to accuse Joshua. Satan appears here in the specific sense of an *accuser*, a sense broadly accepted in Apocalyptic Judaism and Christianity owing to the connotations of the Greek *diabolos*. There is a hint of Satan's opposition to Yahweh as well as to

---

diabolus). The psalm was composed in the third or second century B.C; the earlier passages have pre-exilic origins and were compiled in the post-exilic period. Kluger, pp. 34–35, sees even in these passages a hint of the personality of Satan in that all these adversaries are opposed to right and proper order. There is a possible connection between the name of Satan and the verb *sut*, "to roam," which would emphasize the role of Satan as a spy. Harry Torczyner, following Adolphe Lods in *Mélanges syriens*, suggests that "the figure and role of the Satan derives from the Persian secret service. . . . We now understand that there are in God's service, as in that of any earthly king, secret roving officials, who go and come and report to him on the doings of his subjects" (Torczyner, *The Book of Job* [Jerusalem, 1957], pp. 38–45). Lods argues that Satan, viewed this way, is an obstructor only of unlawful deeds. But this still leaves unanswered the question why the God declares certain deeds unlawful rather than others. The Devil still appears as the agent of God's destruction.

19. Here "Satan" is translated by *diabolos* in the Septuagint and *Satan* in the Vulgate. The passage is early post-exilic, dating from about 520–518 B.C.

human beings, for the God reproaches him for his activities. Yet Satan appears merely to be punishing Joshua for his sins; rather than having any malicious intent, he may simply have failed to understand that Yahweh intended to be merciful. Yahweh permits Satan to stand before him and speak to him in the heavenly court: the Satan is one of the *bene ha-elohim* and thus in some indirect way a manifestation of the God himself.[20]

Before examining further the development of the character of Satan in the context of the Book of Job, I return to the Watcher angels and their leader. Semyaza encourages the Watchers to make a formal, mutual agreement that none will falter in his desire to slake his lust for the daughters of men. The Watchers descend (they do not fall) from heaven of their own free will, alighting upon Mount Hermon, and take human wives to whom they teach the arts of magic and agriculture. Another Watcher, Azazel, variously Semyaza's lieutenant, equal, or superior, also teaches men to manufacture weapons tempting them to violence and ornaments tempting them to vanity.[21] The Watchers here play a role very similar to that of the Titans in Greek myth: they increase the knowledge of mankind, but they do so against the will of the God, who regards their instruction as sinful. In the Hebrew story, the lust of the Watchers is additional proof of their vice, as is the nature of their offspring. The children of women and Watchers are giants who turn upon mankind, destroying possessions and devouring human flesh. Humanity now complains to the Lord, saying, "Thou seest what Azazel hath done, who hath taught all unrighteousness on earth. . . . And the whole earth has been corrupted through the works that were taught by Azazel: to him ascribe all sin."[22] The Lord answers the prayers of mankind and sends down the four archangels, Uriel, Raphael, Gabriel, and Michael (aspects of the protective side of the divine nature)

20. If the second part of the passage is translated to mean that Satan is "venting his spite" on the holy city of Jerusalem, the hint of opposition to Yahweh is stronger. But the original meaning of the passage is very unclear.

21. The name Azazel derives from the scapegoat story of Numbers, but the Azazel of Ethiopic Enoch is now a definite personality.

22. Ethiopic En. 9:6; 10:8.

to rescue them. The archangels slay the giants, whose ghosts remain to "afflict, oppress, destroy, attack, do battle, and work destruction on the earth."[23] The avenging angels attack the Watchers themselves: Raphael binds Azazel and casts him through an opening in the desert into the darkness; other Watchers are cast into the deep valleys of the earth; and their punishment will endure until the day of judgment.[24]

The myth of the Watchers as told in Enoch thus squarely attributes sin to the angels and describes their punishment. Though they descend from heaven voluntarily, their latter end is a true "fall": they are cast down into pits of darkness by the avenging angels of the Lord. Are the Watchers then the ultimate cause of sin on earth? Enoch is not at all certain. In the first place, their descent occurs long after the expulsion of Adam and Eve from Eden and the sin of Cain against Abel, and Enoch declares that "sin has not been sent upon the earth, but man himself has created it."[25] And if the Watchers sin, the heart of their sin may be in subjecting themselves to Azazel or Semyaza, who is the origin of all evil.[26] The ambivalence of the Book of Enoch, written over a period of a century and a half by a number of authors, indicates that in the Apocalyptic period the concept of the origin of evil was very much in flux.

A number of other accounts of the Watchers appeared in the Apocalyptic period. The Book of Jubilees says that in the days of Jared, the Watcher angels descended to the earth.[27] They did not come to earth for the purpose of sinning but rather "that they should instruct the children of men, and that they should do judgment and uprightness on the earth."[28] Only after they

---

23. Ethiopic En. 15:11.

24. Note that the author of Ethiopic Enoch does not use the flood as the means of punishment, another indication that the Genesis story does not intend the deluge as a punishment for the *banim*.

25. Ethiopic En. 98:4.

26. Ethiopic En. 54:6, a later addition, names Satan both as their leader and as their punisher.

27. Jubilees was written between 135 and 105 B.C. by a Pharisee who expected the immediate arrival of the Messianic kingdom.

28. Bk. Jub. 4:15.

arrive on earth do they lust after the daughters of men and defile themselves. The ambivalence of these angels is clear: their original intent is good, but they yield to sin. Once they have sinned, their works are evil. Their leaders are Belial and Mastema; their children are giants who wreak destruction and entice people to sin. The Lord punishes the Watcher angels by binding them in the depths of the earth, and he causes their children the giants to do battle with one another to their mutual destruction.[29] The spirits of the slain giants remain upon earth, doing evil and tempting mankind to sin. Noah therefore prays to Yahweh for help, and Yahweh replies by ordering the spirits to be bound in the darkness. But then Mastema arises and goes before Yahweh and says, "Lord, Creator, let some of them remain before me, and let them hearken to my voice, and do all that I shall say unto them; for if some of them are not left to me, I shall not be able to execute the power of my will upon the sons of men." And Yahweh replies: "Let the tenth part of them remain before him, and let nine parts descend into the place of condemnation." And so the angels of the Lord bind nine of ten of the evil spirits in the darkness but the tenth part of the angels are spared so that "they might be subject before Satan on the earth."[30] The function of these beings, sometimes equated with demons, is to tempt humanity to abandon the ways of the Lord for sin: later, Isaac will be able to promise Jacob that for the sake of the Covenant "the spirits of Mastema shall not rule over thee or over thy seed to turn thee from the Lord."[31]

In Jubilees, then, the Watchers do not introduce sin, for they come in the days of Jared, five hundred years after the creation. Yet they and their progeny exacerbate the sins of the world. Their leader Mastema or Satan, as prince of the fallen angels and leader of the tempters of mankind, has now acquired a pronounced diabolical cast. Yet Yahweh himself has not only permitted the sin of the Watchers and the temptation of men, he

29. Bk. Jub. 5:6–11.
30. Bk. Jub. 10:1–12. Mastema and Satan are to be considered identical.
31. Bk. Jub. 19:28.

has explicitly granted Mastema the right to keep one of ten demons in order to continue to exert his will over man. Mastema is the leader of the fallen Watchers, but he appears also to be the lieutenant of Yahweh. The author of Jubilees cannot forget that Yahweh himself must be the ultimate author of the ills of the world.

Two other Apocalyptic works add significantly to the myth.[32] The Testament of Reuben contains some details that eventually become important in witch lore.[33] As Eve tempted Adam, Reuben says, so did women allure the Watchers by using seductive makeup and hair styles: the burden of sin is placed upon man, or rather upon woman. The Watchers, being spiritual creatures, cannot themselves beget children, so they appear to women while the women are having intercourse with their husbands. Lusting after the Watchers, the women conceive alien forms from the seed of men. A variant of this incubus myth appears frequently in the history of medieval witchcraft: the witch conducts her revels while appearing to be safely in bed with her husband.

The Book of the Secrets of Enoch adds to the myth the significant new element that the angels rebelled on account of pride.[34] The key passage is: "And one from out the order of

32. In addition, the Testament of Dan (109–106 B.C.) reports that Satan is the leader of the Watchers (5:5–6); the Damascus Rule (Qumran), ch. 2, says that the Watchers fell "because they walked in the stubbornness of their heart": Geza Vermes, *The Dead Sea Scrolls in English*, 2d ed. (Harmondsworth, 1970), p. 99. Later both Josephus and Philo refer to the Watchers and the giants, but without developing the myth. The Testaments were written in Hebrew probably about 109–106 B.C.; the texts contain some Christian additions.

33. T. Reub. (109–106 B.C.), 5:6–7.

34. The Book of the Secrets of Enoch is also called Slavonic Enoch or 2 Enoch. Its only complete extant version is in Slavonic. There are two elements in Slavonic Enoch. The first is a short core, originally in Greek (the text now lost) and possibly as early as the first century A.D. The second is a long elucidation that may date as late as the fifteenth century and betrays Christian influence or even origins. See A. Vaillant, *Le Livre des secrets d'Hénoch* (Paris, 1952). Vaillant argues that the longer element, which contains most of the interesting material relating to Satan, must postdate the Apocalyptic period. Many modern scholars do not accept the argument of Vaillant

angels, having turned away with the order that was under him, conceived of an impossible thought, to place his throne higher than the clouds above the earth, that he might become equal in rank to any power. And I threw him out from the height with his angels, and he was flying in the air continuously above the bottomless."

The combination of the motifs of rebellion and lust melded two originally discrete sins, and two originally different motives for sin, on the part of the angels.

In yet another way the idea of a prideful fall was added to the concept of the Devil. In the Book of Isaiah it is written:

> How you have fallen from heaven, bright morning star,
> felled to the earth, sprawling helpless across the nations!
> You thought in your own mind,
> I will scale the heavens;
> I will set my throne high above the stars of God,
> I will sit on the mountain where the gods meet
> in the far recesses of the north.
> I will rise high above the cloud-banks
> and make myself like the Most High.
> Yet you shall be brought down to Sheol,
> to the depths of the abyss.[35]

This "bright morning star," or perhaps more literally translated from the Hebrew *Helel ben-shahar*, "bright son of the morning,"

---

and continue to date the content, though not the present form, of Slavonic Enoch to the Apocalyptic period. See Albert Marie Denis, *Introduction aux pseudépigraphes grecs de l'Ancien Testament* (Leiden, 1970), pp. 28–29. The key passage is 29:4–5. If the story in Slavonic Enoch of the pristine revolt of Satan through pride is later than the Apocalyptic period, this would help explain the lack of clarity and agreement on the subject in the New Testament and the Fathers, most of whom followed the story of the lust of the angels rather than their pride. It is possible that not until Origen in the third century was there a clear account of what has come to be Christian tradition: that Satan's sin was pride, that he fell before the creation of Adam, and that he was the tempting serpent in the garden. See Otto Eissfeldt, *The Old Testament: An Introduction* (New York, 1965), pp. 622–623. Eissfeldt says that the book in its present form is Christian but "appears to rest upon an older Jewish original . . . before A.D. 70" (p. 623).

35. Isa. 14:12–15.

has often been considered a reference to a king of Babylon or Assyria, metaphorically likened to the morning star whose brightness is erased by the rising of the sun. It now appears that the roots of the passage are in Canaanite legend and literature. The Ugaritic poem of Shachar and Shalim tells of two divine children, Shachar, dawn, and Shalim, dusk, who were born as a result of the intercourse of the god El with mortal women. The original story of Shachar is thus related to that of the Watchers: both involve a hierogamy in which a divine being descends to a mortal woman.[36]

Whatever the intention of Isaiah, the Apocalyptic writers took the passage as a reference to the fall of one of the heavenly host. In the Book of Enoch, the falling angels are likened to stars falling from heaven. The identification of angels with stars is not uncommon in the Old Testament, but the imagery of Enoch indicates that a certain overlap between the Watchers myth and the passage in Isaiah may already have begun.[37]

36. G. R. Driver, *Canaanite Myths and Legends* (Edinburgh, 1956), pp. 22–23. The preferred transliteration of the Hebrew is *Helel ben Shachar*.

37. A fundamental inconsistency of these myths is the chronology of the fall. The Watcher angels fell *after* Adam and Eve had already left Eden and produced many generations of children, the sin of the Watchers being placed in the time of Noah. The Watchers seduce the daughters of men, and they also teach mankind useful knowledge. But mankind's acquisition of this knowledge is displeasing to the Lord. The myths of the fall of Adam and Eve and that of mankind at the time of the Watchers can from the structural point of view be considered the same myth with the meaning that humanity acquired knowledge that the Lord wished to hide from them. The myth is typologically similar to that of the Titans in Greece. For Adam and Eve were tempted by an evil angel, Satan. And if logic and chronology were followed, this temptation would be impossible, since the angels had not yet fallen. The efforts of modern scholars to build in a consistency by speaking of a distinction between the Watchers and Satan has led to an artificial separation of the two: Satan or the *satans* and the other evil angels are essentially the same. The Christians would resolve the ambivalence by gradually forgetting the story of the Watchers altogether and emphasizing the fall of Satan through his envy of the Lord *before* the creation of Adam. Such refinements are not necessary to understand the myth, which, like most myths, should not be expected to be logically or serially consistent. Another apparent inconsistency is that evil spirits are sometimes perceived as the ruined angels themselves, sometimes as the giants whom their intercourse with the daughters of men produced, and sometimes as the ghosts of the giants after they were slain by the avenging

Four ideas, hitherto separate, are now united: (1) the sin of the Devil as pride; (2) the ruin of the Watchers through lust; (3) the fall of the *Helel ben-shahar* from heaven; (4) the descent of the Watchers for the purposes of sin. The falling or fading star, equated now with Satan, gives a new name, Lucifer, to the Devil, and substantially enriches the myth. In the New Testament (Luke 10:18), Satan falls from heaven like lightning. Luke seems to have united the idea of the fallen angels with Lucifer and so identified Satan, chief of the ruined angels, with the fallen one cast down from heaven.[38]

To sum up: the *bene ha-elohim* are the heavenly court, the pantheon of the Lord. But some of them sin, through lust or pride. If through pride, they are cast down from heaven; if through lust, they descend voluntarily but are then cast down into the pit as punishment for their sins. They are imprisoned in the darkness, either in the earth (in its valleys or beneath its surface) or in the air. They not only sin themselves but also tempt humanity to sin. Their chief is the chief of tempters. Sometimes all sin is attributed to him, yet Yahweh explicitly grants him the right to continue to do mischief. As far remote from the divine nature as Azazel or Mastema might appear to be, they still have the function of servants, arms, tools of the God. They still represent an aspect of the God's personality. The *bene ha-elohim* are progressively differentiated from the good side of the God and so progressively become more evil. But their original relationship to the God can still be perceived.

The second great fault line upon which the nature of the God divided was that of the *mal'ak Yahweh*. The *mal'ak Yahweh* is the emissary or messenger of the God. Like the *bene ha-elohim*, the *mal'ak* is an aspect of the divine nature. But he differs from the *banim* in one important respect: they remain in heaven with the God, but the *mal'ak* roams the world in his ser-

---

angels. Again, if understood as myth, the story is comprehensible without being consistent.

38. See Karl Schmidt, "Lucifer als gefallene Engelmacht," *Theologische Zeitschrift*, 7 (1951), 161–179.

39. See Kluger, pp. 55–76.

vice.[39] The *mal'ak* is the voice of the God, the spirit of the God, the God himself. That the *mal'ak* is identical with the God is seen in Exodus, where Moses is addressed from the thornbush in Exodus 3:2 by the *mal'ak* and in Exodus 3:4 by Yahweh himself. The concept of the *mal'ak* was meant to represent the side of Yahweh turned toward men, or the aspect of Yahweh that men perceive, or the manifestation of Yahweh in his relationship with human beings. The term *mal'ak* is invariably translated in the Septuagint as *angelos:* "messenger." It is usually singular, though occasionally the plural *mal'akim* appears. It is possible that the *mal'ak* tended to become plural by attraction of the concept of the *bene ha-elohim*. In the Apocalyptic period, the idea that there were a number of angels was fully established. In the Old Testament the *mal'ak* was clearly an aspect of the God himself.

The God was ambivalent, and so was the *mal'ak*, who could be either good or evil. In Exodus 12:23, when Yahweh is slaughtering the firstborn of Egypt, it is also the *mal'ak*, "the destroyer," who does the job. Yahweh in his relationship to mankind can be terrifyingly cruel.

The elision of the concept of the *mal'ak* with that of the *bene ha-elohim* and the tendency of both to become identified with evil are most clearly illustrated in the Book of Job.[40] The more the *banim* and the *mal'ak* were seen as distinct from the God,

40. It is insufficient to dismiss the framing story of Job—Job 1–2 and 42:7–17—as a mere folktale artificially joined to the poem. The probable order of composition is (1) the tale, about 550 B.C.; (2) the poem, about 450 B.C.; (3) the combination of the two in the present form of Job, about 450–350 B.C. But even if the tale is substantially older than the poem, the poet used it, and it cannot be dismissed as foreign to his thought any more than one can dismiss the stories that Shakespeare consistently utilized in his plays as foreign to the playwright. Clearly the writer of Job found the idea of the heavenly court germane to his purpose. At least a minor part of that purpose was to suggest an alternate theodicy, which he found in the concept of a heavenly court of which at least one member might act as an adversary to man. To be sure, the author rejects that theodicy as ultimately insufficient: the responsibility of Yahweh remains, and it is absolutely and forever unfathomable by human reason. The Book of Job at any rate is markedly later than the passage of Zechariah. The Septuagint translates "Satan" by *diabolos*, and the Vulgate by *Satan*.

the more it was possible to thrust upon them the evil elements in the divine character that Yahweh had discarded. In Job, that process is manifestly incomplete; Yahweh and Satan are still working closely together:

The day came when the members of the court of heaven took their places in the presence of the Lord, and Satan was there among them. The Lord asked him where he had been. "Ranging over the earth," he said, "from end to end." Then the Lord asked Satan, "Have you considered my servant Job? You will find no one like him on earth, a man of blameless and upright life, who fears God and sets his face against wrongdoing." Satan answered the Lord, "Has not Job good reason to be God-fearing? Have you not hedged him round on every side with your protection, him and his family and all his possessions? Whatever he does you have blessed, and his herds have increased beyond measure. But stretch out your hand and touch all that he has, and then he will curse you to your face." Then the Lord said to Satan, "So be it. All that he has is in your hands; only Job himself you must not touch." And Satan left the Lord's presence.

Job's family and possessions are destroyed, and

Once again the day came when the members of the court of heaven took their places in the presence of the Lord, and Satan was there among them. The Lord asked him where he had been. "Ranging over the earth," he said, "from end to end." Then the Lord asked Satan, "Have you considered my servant Job? You will find no one like him on earth, a man of blameless and upright life, who fears God and sets his face against wrongdoing. You excited me to ruin him without a cause, but his integrity is still unshaken." Satan answered the Lord, "Skin for skin! There is nothing the man will grudge to save himself. But stretch out your hand and touch his bone and his flesh, and see if he will not curse you to your face."

Then the Lord said to Satan, "So be it. He is in your hands; but spare his life." And Satan left the Lord's presence, and he smote Job with running sores from head to foot, so that he took a piece of a broken pot to scratch himself as he sat among the ashes.

As in Zechariah, Satan is now a personality with the function of accusing, opposing, and harming human beings. He is not yet the principle of evil, which remains with the God. He is still one of the heavenly court and does nothing without the God's consent and will. Yet, also as in Zechariah, there are hints here of an opposition between Satan and the Lord. Rather than simply acting as an instrument of the Lord's will, Satan must persuade the God to work evil upon his faithful servant Job. The God agrees only reluctantly and with reservations, later reproaching Satan for having tempted him. Satan is the shadow, the dark side of the God, the destructive power wielded by the God only with reluctance. Further, it is Satan himself who goes down to smite Job. Satan "ranges the earth," and when the God makes the decision to put Job to the test, he says to Satan, "All that he has is in your hands." Later Satan leaves the God's presence and smites Job "with running sores from head to foot." Satan now is the personification of the destructive power of the God.[41]

Later, in the Hellenistic Book of the Wisdom of Solomon, Satan has even more evidently become the opponent, not only of man, but of the Lord: "God created man for immortality, and made him the image of his own eternal self; it was the devil's spite that brought death into the world, and the experience of it is reserved for those who take his side."[42] This is another dimension of the development of the word *satan*: Satan as the opponent of the Lord as well as of humanity. The Wisdom passage contains another important element: death, that natural phenomenon most feared by the Hebrews, is now linked with Satan and attributed to him. It is not the Lord who willed death for mankind, nor is it the folly of people that has brought it upon them, but rather the wicked will of the Devil. The destructive power once wielded by the God now belongs

41. But the poet of Job is not satisfied with shifting the burden of destruction to Satan, for he knows that the God still bears the responsibility for it: "Wherefore do the wicked live and why are they raised up and comforted with riches?" he asks (21:7). And, "Behold the Lord is on high in his power and none is like unto him in his acts. Who shall ponder his ways, or who can say to him: Hast thou done iniquity?" (36: 22–23). The poet recognizes that ultimately his theodicy must be a mystery.

42. Wis. 2:24; LXX: *diabolos*; Vulg.: *diabolus*.

Eugène Delacroix, "Jacob Wrestling with the Angel," 1856. The *mal'ak Yahweh* is a spirit sent out from the God, or the manifestation of the God in his dealings with men. In his origins, Satan, like the angel wrestling here with Jacob, was a *mal'ak*. Courtesy Bureau des Monuments, Paris.

in the hands of the Devil, while the God's good aspect has become the Lord.

In Job, Satan is clearly one of the *bene ha-elohim*, for he was there in the court of heaven in the presence of the God. Yet Satan does one thing in Job that the *banim* do not ordinarily do: he leaves the presence of the God and roams the world as the

God's messenger or angel. In this action Satan is much more
the *mal'ak Yahweh* than one of the *bene ha-elohim*. It is in the development of the *mal'ak* that the decisive movement occurs in
the development of the Devil of the Israelites.

A spirit behaving like the *mal'ak* appears in Judges 9:22–23:
"After Abimelech had been prince over Israel for three years,
God sent an evil spirit to make a breach between Abimelech
and the citizens of Shechem." In 1 Samuel, an evil spirit from
the Lord vexes Saul, causes him to prophesy against his will,
and incites him to hurl a javelin at David.[43] The equivalence of
Yahweh and his murderous *mal'ak* is even more clear in 2 Samuel 24:13–16: "Is it to be three years of famine in your land,"
Yahweh asks David through the mouth of the prophet, "or
three months of flight with the enemy at your heels, or three
days of pestilence in your land?" David in desperation chooses
pestilence as the least evil, "so the Lord sent a pestilence
throughout Israel . . . [and] 70,000 of the people died. Then
the angel stretched out his arm towards Jerusalem to destroy it,
but the Lord repented of the evil and said to the angel who was
destroying the people, 'Enough, stay your hand.' "[44] Here the
destroying *mal'ak* almost gets out of control, and the Lord re-
strains him at the last moment. Another way of saying the same
thing would be that the Lord repented. But the imputation of
evil to the *mal'ak* rather than to Yahweh himself enabled the
Hebrews to shirk the problem of theodicy. On one level, they
knew that the *mal'ak* was Yahweh, but on another they could
begin to imagine the *mal'ak* as a separate entity. The separation
of *mal'ak* from Godhead is clearer in the dialogue of 1 Kings
19–22. Michaiah says, "I saw the Lord seated on his throne,
with all the host of heaven in attendance on his right and on his
left. The Lord said, 'Who will entice Ahab to attack and fall on
Ramothgilead?' One said one thing and one said another; then a
spirit came forward and stood before the Lord and said, 'I will
entice him.' 'How?' said the Lord. 'I will go out,' he said, 'and

43. 1 Sam. 16:14–16; 18:10–11; 19:9–10.
44. This passage is repeated almost verbatim in the later 1 Chron.
21:11–15.

be a lying spirit in the mouth of all his prophets.' 'You shall entice him,' said the Lord, 'and you shall succeed; go and do
it.' "[45] The similarity of this passage to the prologue of Job is
striking.[46] The evil spirit appears in the company of the *bene ha-
elohim* but then goes out over the earth as a *mal'ak.* Here the
mal'ak does not have to persuade Yahweh to destroy Ahab, for
that is already the God's intent. But if in this way he is less independent than the Satan of Job, in another way his independence of Yahweh is even more distinct: "I will go out," he said,
"and be a lying spirit in the mouth of all his prophets." The evil
mal'ak is not only an opponent of the human race, but he is a
lying opponent, the prince of lies and the lord of deceit.

The Hebrews were at least on one level aware of the gradual
distinction that was being made between Yahweh and his
mal'ak. In 2 Samuel there is an account of David's sin in taking
a census of the Israelites: "Once again the Israelites felt the
Lord's anger, when he incited David against them and gave him
orders that Israel and Judah should be counted." Yahweh had
declared such a census a sin, but now he commands David to
take one in order that he might have reason to punish the people of Israel. This text is wholly understandable in terms of the
original ambivalence of the God. But the redactor of the Books
of Chronicles, which derived from Samuel and Kings and were
compiled in the fourth century B.C., could no longer understand this ambiguity. The Lord, he reasoned, could not have
willed his people to sin, so he revised the passage to read:
"Now Satan, setting himself against Israel, incited David to
count the people."[47]

Gradually the *mal'ak* obtained its independence from Yahweh; gradually its destructive aspect was emphasized; finally it
became the personification of the shadow of the Lord, of the
dark side of the divine nature. The *mal'ak* was now the evil
angel, Satan, the obstructor, the liar, the destroying spirit.

45. The passage is repeated almost identically in the later 2 Chron.
18:18–22.
46. They may be almost contemporaneous.
47. 2 Sam. 24:1; 1 Chron. 21:1.

This crucial development in the history of the Devil was to be further advanced in the Apocalyptic period.

In the Book of Jubilees the evil *mal'ak* is wholly independent of the Lord. The prince of the evil spirits, Mastema, and his followers tempt, accuse, destroy, and punish mankind, taking onto themselves all the evil characteristics once attributed to Yahweh. They lead astray "the children of the sons of Noah . . . to make them err and destroy them." Where the *mal'ak Yahweh* or Yahweh himself had in the Old Testament slain the firstborn of Egypt, that carnage is now Mastema's work.[48] And where Yahweh's power had mysteriously worked against his own followers, that power is now ascribed to Mastema. In Jubilees, Mastema, rather than Yahweh, meets Moses in the desert purposing to kill him.[49] Mastema puts Abraham to the test, rather than Yahweh's doing it himself: "And the prince Mastema came and said before God, 'Behold, Abraham loves Isaac his son, and he delights in him above all things else; bid him offer him as a burnt offering on the altar, and Thou wilt see if he will do this command.' "[50] Kierkegaard perceived that the original tale of Mount Moriah (Genesis 22:1–19) was one of the most powerful in the Old Testament in revealing the inscrutability of the divine nature. As in the Book of Job, a just man is put sorely to the test and proves faithful. The author of Genesis 22 did not hesitate to ascribe this variety of temptation to the God himself, but Jubilees has both cut it away from Yahweh and given it to the evil *mal'ak*.

Yahweh does not himself do evil; evil is done by the *mal'ak*. Yet Yahweh has created him and even specifically grants him the power to tempt and to destroy. Why? The Apocalyptic literature moves in the direction of a new answer: that the Lord permits evil only for a while. As in Iran, where after eons of struggle Ohrmazd finally destroys Ahriman, so after eons of struggle the Lord will destroy the evil angels. At the end of the

48. Bk. Jub. 48:9–15; 49:2.
49. Bk. Jub. 48:1–3; cf. Exod. 4:24.
50. Bk. Jub. 17:15–18:12. The prince Mastema has an interesting afterlife in the Midrashim. See Shalom Spiegel, *The Last Trial* (New York, 1967).

world the Messiah will come and judge Mastema. The power of the evil angels will be destroyed, and they will be bound and imprisoned forever so that they may no longer accuse the children of Israel.[51]

The chief problem with this Apocalyptic theodicy is the question with which Friday puzzled Robinson Crusoe: if the Lord has the power to destroy the Devil and wishes him destroyed, why does he wait till the end of the world? This is a version of the question that has always tormented theologians: why does the God permit so much evil? For if the God permits, even authorizes, another spirit to destroy in his service, is not the God responsible for the destruction? Does he not ultimately will it himself? The efforts of the Hebrews and the Apocalyptic Jews to remove the responsibility from the God only blur the question. What Mastema does, that also Yahweh does.

The solution proposed by Apocalyptic and Christian literature is dualist. At the end of the world, evil will be negated. Now, since no part of the divine can be negated, it follows that evil is not part of the divine nature. And as the divine nature is ultimately that which is, evil has no real being of its own. Drawing upon converging arguments in Greek philosophy, the Christian theologians would argue that evil is nonbeing, literally nothing, no thing, a mere lack of goodness. Evil exists in the cosmos like holes in a Swiss cheese: the holes are there, but they are there only as noncheese and have no existence apart from the cheese. As one cannot eat a cheese and discard the holes into a box, one cannot remove good and put evil into another category. Evil is merely the absence of good. These later theological assumptions are not explicit in the Apocalyptic literature, but they are implicitly present. They thus pose a paradox: evil is done by the *mal'ak* who is a subject (if not a part) of Yahweh; evil must therefore be willed, if only indirectly, by Yahweh; and yet evil is eradicated by Yahweh at the end of the world and has no eternal being. Evil is part of Yahweh and yet not part of him.

51. Bk. Jub. 10:8; 23:29; 48:15–16.

Ethiopic Enoch refers to "*satans*" in the plural as well as to a singular Satan,[52] and some critics have argued that the *satans* are a class of angels one of whose functions was to tempt the Watcher angels and to cause them to fall.[53] In fact there is no convincing evidence that Enoch thought of the *satans* as a class apart from the Watchers, or that the sin of the Watchers was the result of their temptation by *satans* or by Satan. The only indication to this effect is in 54:6, which speaks of the Watchers' "unrighteousness in becoming subject to Satan and leading astray those on the earth." But here subjection to Satan seems to mean subjection to the power of evil. The functions of the *satans* and of the Watchers blur, and in effect *satans* and Watchers are mingled as one group of fallen angels. Thus Satan and Azazel are to be taken as two names for the same prince of evil: both are the Devil.[54]

The evil angels function both as the tempters of men (65:6; 69:6) and as their accusers (40:7) and punishers (53:3). They are opponents of humanity, but as in Jubilees, their opposition to the God is more ambiguous. As accusers and punishers, they are the tools of the Lord, but as tempters they stand against him. Azazel is set in marked opposition to the deity, for he has "taught all unrighteousness on earth and revealed the eternal

52. See W. O. E. Oesterley's Introduction to Charles's translation of The Book of Enoch (London, 1917), p. xiv. Ethiopic Enoch was in its original form composed by a number of writers over a period from about 200 to about 60 B.C.

53. Ethiopic En. 40:7; 65:6. Reference is made particularly to 69:4 in which it is written that "Jeqon" is the "inciter who led astray all the sons of God, brought them down to earth, and led them astray through the daughters of men." But the context makes it clear that Jeqon is a leader of the Watchers and one of the Watchers himself, not a member of a different class of angels.

54. Semyaza appears as the prince of the Watchers in Ethiopic Enoch 6:3, but otherwise plays a subsidiary role. By assuming that Satan and Azazel are both one Devil we can resolve the discrepancies in Enoch, where sometimes Azazel and sometimes Satan is named as the prince of evil. The Azazel passages appear throughout Ethiopic En., but the Satan passages occur only in chapters 37 to 71, the section probably written last. Apparently the later writer preferred the name of Satan, which was gaining in popularity in the first century B.C., to that of Azazel, used a century earlier in the Book of Noah section of Ethiopic En.

secrets," and "the whole earth has been corrupted through the works that were taught by Azazel: to him ascribe all sin."[55] To Azazel—not to Yahweh, nor yet to mankind—ascribe all sin. Here is the strongest expression of dualism found in Hebrew religion to that time.

As in Jubilees, the wicked angels suffer punishment. They are tormented with fire in the valleys of the earth, and at the end of the world when the Messiah comes they will be cast down under the earth to be bound in darkness for eternity.[56]

In the Books of Adam and Eve, Satan, or the Devil, successfully tempts Adam and Eve to fall, appearing to Eve in the shape of a beautiful angel.[57] When Satan has successfully tempted her, Eve cries out and says, "Woe unto thee, thou devil. Why dost thou attack us for no cause? . . . Why dost thou harry us, thou enemy [and persecute] us to the death in wickedness and envy?"[58] The displacement of evil from Yahweh to the Devil is clear. No longer does Abraham or Job seek to understand the inscrutable will of the God; now it is the Devil whom one must ask why there is evil in the world.

55. Ethiopic En. 9:6; 10:8.

56. Ethiopic En. 10:4; 12; 21; 55:3–56:8; 64:1–2; 67:4–7; 88.

57. The Books of Adam and Eve, conjoined with the Apocalypse of Moses, exist in a Latin and in a Slavonic version. They were written before 70 A.D. by a Jewish author, though there are some later Christian interpolations. The Devil's ability to take the form of a beautiful angel was explained by later theologians in terms of his angelic nature. Angels have no bodies, or spiritual bodies merely, so that in order to communicate with human beings they assume a form of their choice. They are able to change their apparent forms, and Satan and the evil angels use this ability in order to deceive, taking a handsome form, or a humble one, or whatever they please. Historically speaking, the Devil's assumption of the shining form is probably in part due to the assimilation of the figures of Lucifer and Satan that was already under way. The Devil's ability to change forms later reinforced the idea, derived from folklore, that witches could shift their shapes. In another passage (Apoc. Moses 15–23) it is the serpent who tempts Eve, but the serpent is merely the tool of Satan, who, as a shining angel, tempts the serpent to share his envy of the happy first couple. This version introduces a hitherto unusual emphasis upon sex in the fall: the serpent "poured upon the fruit the poison of his wickedness, which is lust, the root and beginning of every sin."

58. Lat. 11.

Adam joins Eve in her complaint, and Satan obliges the first pair with an explanation.

And with a heavy sigh, the Devil spake: "O Adam! all my hostility, envy, and sorrow is for thee, since it is for thee that I have been expelled from my glory. . . . When thou wast formed, I was hurled out of the presence of God and banished from the company of the angels. When God blew into thee the breath of life and thy face and likeness was made in the image of God, Michael also brought thee and made [us] worship thee in the sight of God; and God the Lord spake: 'Here is Adam. I have made thee [Adam] in our image and likeness.' . . . I will not worship an inferior and younger being [than I]. I am his senior in the Creation; before he was made was I already made. It is his duty to worship me."[59]

As in the story of the Watchers, the Devil's fall occurs after the creation of human beings. Now, however, it is not the beauty of the daughters of men that tempts the angels. It is not a matter of lust but one of pride. The Devil, being an angel, stands above Adam in the order of nature and was created before him. Adam is made in the image and likeness of the Lord in a way that the angels are not, and so the angels must worship him. In his pride the Devil refuses. The Devil falls in pride and envy, but envy of man, not of God.[60]

Michael rejects the Devil's arguments, warning him that unless he joins the other angels in worshiping Adam, the Lord will be angry. And Satan said, "If he be [wroth] with me, I will set my seat above the stars of heaven and will be like the Highest." Satan has now translated his envy and hatred of man into envy and hatred of the Lord.[61] The Lord, filled with wrath,

59. In what way Adam might be more similar to the Lord than are the angels continued to bother theologians for centuries. See Charles Trinkaus, *In Our Image and Likeness* (Chicago, 1970).

60. There is more than a hint in this of the common conflict in myth between the elder and the younger brother, where the elder, who works long and hard to please his father, is hurt and outraged by the father's preference for the younger son. Note that the Qur'an follows this version of the myth, saying that Iblis fell because of his envy of Adam.

61. Lat. 15:3. Again there is evidence of the intrusion of the Lucifer myth in the reference to the stars of heaven.

banishes Satan and his angels, hurling them to the earth.[62] Cast down from heaven, the Devil envies the joy of Adam and Eve in the Garden, "And with guile I cheated thy wife and caused thee to be expelled through her [doing] from thy joy and luxury, as I have been driven out of my glory." Adam, appalled at the power of his great enemy, prays to the Lord to banish "this Adversary far from me, who seeketh to destroy my soul."[63]

This version of the myth presents Satan as one of the greatest and earliest creations of the God, a creature who falls through envy and pride from his high estate, a creature whose love of the God is turned to hatred by the God's preference for his younger offspring. The Devil appears less as an *Urprinzip* of evil than as a being hurt by and alienated from his parent. Once having rebelled, however, he is thrust by the sheer weight of his power further into enmity against the Lord. The division between the two steadily widens. The Devil threatens to raise up his throne against the God, and he attempts to divide the universe with him, informing Adam that "Mine are the things of earth, the things of heaven are God's"; when the God in anger casts him and his followers down to earth he continues to work his wiles against man and against him in whose likeness man was created.

The Testaments of the Twelve Patriarchs name Belial or Satan as chief of the evil angels. These are but two names for one concept, a concept to which no better name can be assigned than that of "the Devil."[64] The Lord is closely associated with ethical good, and the Devil with ethical evil. The Devil is the personification of sin, and he commands at his right and left hands the spirits of wrath, hatred, and lying.[65] He is lord also of fornication, war, bloodshed, exile, death, panic, and destruction.[66] He tempts humankind to error, and "if fornication over-

---

62. Note that the fallen angels are hurled *onto* the earth, and not under it. This is usual in the Apocalyptic literature: the fallen angels are punished in *this* world; only at the end of time are they bound under the earth.

63. Lat. 12–17.

64. For Belial as evil see Test. Jud. 25:3; Test. Iss. 7:7.

65. Test. Sim. 5:3; Test. Gad. 4:7; 5:1–2; Test. Dan. 3:6; 5:1.

66. Test. Ben. 7:2.

Gustave Doré, "Satan Enthroned in Hell," 1866. Having fallen into the pit
with the other evil angels, Satan encourages them to further resistance.

comes not your mind, neither can Beliar overcome you."[67] He rules the souls of the wicked, who "cleave unto Beliar," but at the end of the world the Messiah will free mankind from captivity to the Devil.[68]

The ethical conflict between the Lord and the Devil brings the two into a cosmic opposition that is almost completely dualist. As in the strongly dualist Qumran documents, the works and will of the Lord are contrasted with those of Belial. Each has his own kingdom; that of the Lord is light while that of Belial is darkness.[69] Those who attend Belial cut themselves off from the Lord, and it is the Devil's plan to lure Israel away from Yahweh to serve Belial; but at the end of the world Israel will repent, and the Messiah will bring the kingdom of the Devil to an end.[70] Satan now rules a wretched world nearing its doom, but that evil kingdom will itself come to an end when the Messiah saves Israel by establishing in its place the kingdom of the Lord upon the earth.[71] The end of the individual, like the end of the world, is the occasion of a mighty struggle between the angel of the Lord and the "angel of Satan," a struggle that becomes a theme of medieval art and homiletic.[72] The use of the term "angel of Satan" indicates how far the Apocalyptic literature had moved from the concept of Satan as the *mal'ak Yahweh*, for the Devil is now so independent of his father that he has his own *mal'ak* or angel. The Lord and the Devil stand each at the head of a heavenly host girded for the final conflict at the end of the world.

The other Apocalyptic works add little to the concept: the forces of evil, led by Belial, Sammael, Satan, Mastema, or Azazel, prevail for a little while but at the end of the world will be shattered by the Messiah, "and then Satan shall be no

---

67. Test. Reub. 4:11; Test. Jos. 7:4; Test. Ash. 1:8; 3:2.
68. Test. Iss. 6:1; Test. Zeb. 9:8. This motif became very important in Christian theology.
69. Test. Lev. 19:1; Test. Naph. 2:6; 3:1; Test. Jos. 20:2; Test. Dan. 6:2–4.
70. Test. Dan. 6:1–7.   71. Test. Lev. 18:12.   72. Test. Ash. 6:4.

more."[73] Only the Greek Apocalypse of Baruch introduces a new element, which did not have lasting influence: the tree that led Adam and Eve astray, says this peculiar work, was the vine, for "from the drinking of wine come all evils."[74] Of all the sins of the flesh, only drunkenness and lust have been associated with the fall of man, and only the latter becomes a part of the tradition.

The Qumran literature, which is a part, though a distinct one, of the Apocalyptic tradition, helped to move the concept of the Devil in the direction of dualism. The dualism of the Qumran documents is not merely a psychological conflict within the individual between the good inclination and the evil inclination. It is a dualism in which good and evil people are led by good and evil spirits of cosmic dimensions.[75] "From the God of knowledge comes all that is and shall be. . . . He has created man to govern the world and has appointed for him two spirits in which to walk until the time of his visitation: the spirits of truth and falsehood. Those born of truth spring from a fountain of light, but those born of falsehood spring from a source of darkness. All the children of righteousness are ruled by the Prince of Light and walk in the ways of light; but all the children of falsehood are ruled by the Angel of Darkness and walk in the ways of darkness."[76] This passage from the Common Rule expresses the fundamental anthropology of Qumran. Two opposing spirits, one goodness and light, the other evil and darkness, are warring for the world and for the individual soul. Nor are the spirits abstractions, but individual entities of terrible power: the Prince of Light, the Lord of Israel on the one hand, and on the other hand the Prince of Darkness, the Destroying Angel. Those who follow the Lord of Light are

73. Assumption of Moses 10:1. See also the Sybilline Oracles; the Martyrdom of Isaiah; the Acts of Abraham; the Hebrew Apocalypse of Baruch (2 Baruch); the Acts of Abraham; the "Zadokite Fragment."

74. The Greek Apocalypse of Baruch (3 Baruch) 4:17.

75. Herbert G. May, "Cosmological Reference in the Qumran Doctrine of the Two Spirits and in Old Testament Imagery," *Journal of Biblical Literature*, 82 (1963), 1–14.

76. The Common Rule, 3, in Vermes, *Dead Sea Scrolls*, pp. 75–76.

the children of light; those who follow the Angel of Darkness are the children of darkness. The merciless war between the two spirits and their followers is in deadly and ageless earnest. Yet, terrible though the conflict is, it is not absolute; the two principles are not wholly divorced as in Iran, and their conflict affects the will of mankind, not that of nature. For "from the God of Knowledge comes all that is and shall be" and later, "[The Lord] establishes all things by his design, and without him nothing is done."[77] The Lord of Light has created all things and directs all things, even the Prince of Darkness himself. Attenuated though it has now become, a sense of the ancient role of the Devil as the *mal'ak Yahweh* still remains.

The conflict between the two armies is eternal, but in the latter day it has become more sharp. The legions of darkness are now active as never before, and for forty years fierce battles shall rage over the earth.[78] The present age has been delivered over to the Devil: it is the age of Satan or Belial, an "age of tribulation and war during which Satan would do his utmost to lead astray the chosen of God."[79] The end of the world is shortly to come, and Satan is expending his utmost energies to destroy the universe before the inevitable triumph of the Lord of Light. These latter days are thus the worst that the world will ever know, for now Satan's power is at its height and his malice at its most cruel. "During all those years Satan shall be unleashed against Israel."[80] "As long as the dominion of Satan endures . . . the Angel of Darkness leads all the children of righteousness astray": all the sins of Israel are the result of Satan's dominion, and Satan is made manifest in the evil inclination, the *yetser ha-ra*, within men.[81]

Yet the message of Qumran is optimistic. Because this is the worst of all ages, because Satan now walks the earth in brazen triumph, the Lord will arise and smite him, and a new age will

---

77. Common Rule, 11 (Vermes, p. 93).   78. Vermes, p. 48.
79. Vermes, p. 47. For Satan as the leader of the host of darkness see the War Rule 4, 11, 13 (Vermes, pp. 128, 138, 140–141).
80. Damascus Rule, 4 (Vermes, pp. 100–101).
81. Community Rule, 1–3 (Vermes, pp. 73–76).

dawn in which pure goodness and light will reign. For the Lord
of Light has never lost control of the evil *mal'ak*. "The Angel of
Darkness leads all the children of righteousness astray," and
"all their unlawful deeds are caused by his dominion," but it is
"by his dominion *in accordance with* the mysteries of God."[82]
"[God], Thou hast created Satan, the Angel of Malevolence, for
the Pit; his [rule] is in Darkness and his purpose is to bring
about wickedness and iniquity."[83] The Lord has created Satan
and has used him as an instrument of his vengeance against sinners.[84] But the Lord, having created him, will now cast him
down, and forever "in the darkness bind him." The Messiah will
save the righteous elect, the children of light, and will lead
them into an earthly kingdom of peace, happiness, and prosper-
ity. But the others—the Gentiles and the faithless Jews—will
remain with Satan and his angels to be punished with them and
by them for ever and ever.[85] And so the old Eon, the age of
Satan, comes to an end, and the new eon dawns, the age of the
Lord. The use to which the Christians put this concept is evident. More important for present purposes, Qumran in the end
shrinks from the absolute dualism of Iran and insists that even
the Prince of Darkness is the creature of the Lord and inhabits
a universe that the Lord has made, including the principles of
light and darkness. This theodicy has the same ultimate
weakness as the previous solutions offered by the Hebrews: for
if the Lord creates darkness and allows it to rule, for whatever
length of time, he must have ultimate responsibility for it.
Satan is still the *mal'ak Yahweh*, no matter how headstrong, envious, and hostile. For the people of Qumran, however, the
weakness of their theodicy was obscured by their immediate
conviction that the Messiah would come at any moment and
that their salvation from the hands of Satan was imminent. In
such a state of mind, when the Lord was tarrying no longer,
they did not think to reproach him for the long reign of Satan

82. Community Rule, 3 (Vermes, p. 76). Italics added.
83. War Rule, 13 (Vermes, p. 141). See also War Rule, 4 (Vermes, p. 128)
and 11 (Vermes, p. 138).
84. Damascus Rule, 2; 8 (Vermes, pp. 98, 105).   85. Vermes, p. 48.

now soon to vanish into the past. The hopes of Qumran were high and its trust firm in the Lord. The historian can only reflect with sadness that its history ended not with the coming of the Messiah and the kingdom of God, but rather with the coming of the legions of the emperor Titus and the destruction of the Temple. The old eon seems, two thousand years later, still to be with us.

The minor malicious spirits that appeared from time to time in Hebrew religion resemble those of other cultures and were in large part derived from those of Canaan. Some were personifications of single evils, such as pestilence, plague, and famine. These nature-demons were partly autochthonous, partly borrowed from Canaan and Mesopotamia (the name of pestilence, Resheph, derives directly from Canaan).[86] There were the hairy and goatlike *se'irim*.[87] Lilith and her followers roamed the world seducing men and attacking children with murderous intent, and other she-demons went about at night strangling sleeping men.[88] Asmodeus appears in Tobit; his name may be derived from the Iranian Aeshma Daeva, but he does not seem to act in Aeshma Daeva's role as prince of the host of demons.[89] There are a number of presences who may have been thought of as demons in the sense of personifying certain evils or whose

86. The host of Hebrew demons owes much to Babylonian and Canaanite influence, and possibly some to Iranian. The Septuagint translates the Hebrew *shed* as *daimonion*, deliberately avoiding *daimōn*, which has some positive associations, in favor of a term that connotes the destructive. The Latin and English *demon* has retained an exclusively negative connotation. See Gaster, *Myth*, pp. 574–576; 764.

87. The *se'irim*: Lev. 16:1–23; 17:7; 2 Chron. 11:15; Isa. 13:21; 34:14. The word is derived from Heb. *sa'ir;* "hairy one" or "he-goat." See Kluger, pp. 43–44.

88. Lilith appears in Isa. 34:14. Related typologically to the Greek Lamia and Empousa, she derives directly from the Babylonian Lilitu. See Gerschom Scholem, "Lilith," *Encyclopedia Judaica*, 2, 245–249. See also Harry Torczyner, "A Hebrew Incantation against Night-Demons from Biblical Times," *Journal of Near Eastern Studies*, 6 (1947), 18–29. On the Ugaritic background of these female night-demons, see Theodore H. Gaster, "A Canaanite Magical Text," *Orientalia*, N. S., 11 (1942), 41–79.

89. Tob. 3:7–9; 6:14–19; 8:2–3. Here the demon slays the seven husbands of a Persian woman.

names may merely be the common names of natural evils.[90] Sheol is not only a dwelling-place for the dead but a voracious being with mouth gaping to devour souls, an image that later appears in Christian iconography as the hell-mouth.[91] In the Apocrypha the spirit Sammael bears a spear tipped with gall and is preceded by howling dogs as he goes about spreading death.[92] Leviathan, derived from the Canaanite Lotan and related to the Babylonian Tiamat and the Greek Hydra, was a seven-headed dragon that haunted the sea. The monster Behemoth, a spirit of the desert, is associated with Leviathan.[93] The Hebrew demons could cause illness, death, pollution, and sins both moral and ritual.[94]

Some of these beings, such as Leviathan, could represent a diffused concept of evil, but the influence of these lesser demons on the figure of the Devil was limited mainly to the transfer of some demonic attributes—the goat shape of the *se'irim*, for example. Such a transfer is the result of a vague but nonetheless real similarity between the demons and the Devil: both are perceived as supernatural forces of evil. Satan "stands

90. Cf. the *'alukah* of Prov. 30:15 and the *shedim* of Deut. 32:17 and Ps. 106:37–38.

91. Isa. 5:14.   92. Sir. 25:24; cf. also 3 Baruch 4:8; 9:7.

93. For Leviathan, see Job 3:8; Ps. 74:12–17; Isa. 27:1; 51:10; Ethiopic En. 60:7; 4 Esdras (Ezra Apocalypse) 6:49. See Gaster, *Myth*, p. 577, Kluger, pp. 43–44, and Cyrus H. Gordon, "Leviathan; Symbol of Evil," in Alexander Altmann, ed. *Biblical Motifs: Origins and Transformations* (Cambridge, Mass., 1966), pp. 1–9. For other conflicts of Yahweh with the sea, cf. Hab. 3:8; Ps. 74:13–14; 89:9–10; 93; Job 7:12; 26:12–13. For Behemoth, see Job 40:15; Ethiopic En. 60:8; 4 Esdras 6:49. The term may be derived from the Egyptian for "water buffalo." See Kluger, pp. 43–44. For another monster, Rahab, see Isa. 51:9; Job 9:13; 26:12–13; Ps. 89:10. Various interpretations of all these monsters exist in Rabbinic literature. G. R. Driver, "Mythical Monsters in the Old Testament," *Studi orientalistici in onore di Giorgio Levi della Vida* (Rome, 1956), I, 234–249, shows that both Leviathan and Behemoth are imaginary monsters corresponding to no known animal. See also A. Caquot, "Sur quelques démons de l'Ancien Testament: Reshep, Qeteb, Deber," *Semitica*, 6 (1956), 53–68.

94. The spirits of the dead were called up to predict the future. Possession was ambivalent: it might be the spirit of the Lord or an evil spirit who takes hold of a person, as when Saul was possessed during his search for David and compelled to stand and prophesy (1 Sam. 19:20–24).

in a dialectical confrontation with God. The animal attributes 'grew' on him only later."[95]

By the end of the Apocalyptic period, then, the Devil was more firmly and more permanently than ever associated with the following characteristics found in Hebrew demonology and folklore: darkness, the underworld and the air, sexual temptation and molestation, the goat, the lion, the frog or toad, and the serpent or dragon. Only one common mythological aspect of the serpent fails to adhere to the Hebrew Devil: the feminine.

The development of the idea of the Devil in Hebrew thought, particularly in the Apocalyptic period, is striking. The historiography dealing with the origins of the idea is, however, anything but united. Scholars have found traits of the Hebrew Satan or Belial in Canaan, Babylonia, Greece, and, most com-

95. Kluger, p. 51. Azazel: Lev. 16:8–26; Ethiopic En. 6:7; 8:1; 9:6. For a thorough discussion of the symbolism of good and evil in Old and New Testaments, see Otto Böcher, *Dämonenfurcht und Dämonenabwehr* (Stuttgart, 1970). Water means life but may also be associated with destruction (Leviathan; the story of Noah). Blood can confer both life and death (Lev. 3:17 and 7:26). Air can symbolize the spirit of the individual or of God (*ruach*) but it can also be a destroying whirlwind (Job 1:19). The fallen angels of Apocalyptic literature dwell in the air. Fire as well as air can be an instrument of the anger of the God (Nah. 1:2–3; Jer. 7:20). A mountain is the frequent location of theophanies, either of the Lord or of an evil deity (1 Kings 12:31; 2 Kings 21:3). The desert is usually a place of fear, but it can also be a place where the Lord manifests himself as when he led the people through Sinai to the promised land. Night is often a time of demonic visitation (Job 4:13–15), and in the Apocalyptic and Qumran literature darkness becomes the chief symbol of evil (Ethiopic En. 108:11–12). The color black (as opposed to absence of light) is not a symbol of evil in the Old Testament or in the Apocalyptic period. Rather, the symbolism of the three basic colors of the Ancient Near East, red, black, and white, is ambiguous. Even where color symbolism is striking, as in the Book of Enoch, neither red nor black becomes symbolically fixed as evil as both would do in Christian iconography (see Ethiopic En. 85). Animals, notably the bull, the lion, the wolf, the goat, the frog, and the serpent, appear as symbols of evil (bull: Ps. 22:12; 68:30; lion: Ps. 22:14–22; Jer. 5:6; wolf, Jer. 5:6; Si. 13:21; goat: identified with *se'irim* and with the apocalyptic beast in Dan. 8; frog: Exod. 8). Though the serpent may be equated through the dragon with Leviathan, the abyss, and chaos, the evil of the serpent in the story of Eden has been exaggerated in tradition. In Apocalyptic literature, Satan uses the serpent as his tool; sometimes the serpent and the Devil are equated. None of this appears at all in the original story of Gen. 3. The

monly, Iran.[96] Of the influences that may have existed, the Iranian is usually considered most likely on two grounds. First, Ahriman and Satan show certain intrinsic similarities, and second, these similarities become striking in Hebrew thought following the exile, when Hebrew writers could easily have come into contact with Zoroastrian ideas in Babylonia. But much of the development of Mazdaist thought took place in the post-exilic period, and there may have been some influence in the other direction—of Jewish ideas upon Iran—as well. In any event, all must rest upon speculation. There is no conclusive evidence of wide external influence upon the Hebrew concept, and it is possible to explain it as a natural development within Yahwism itself.

Nonetheless a consensus exists among historians that Iranian influence can be seen in the Apocalyptic and Qumran literature if not in the Old Testament, and certain similarities are indeed remarkable.[97] In the Apocalyptic and Qumran documents on the one hand and in Zoroastrianism on the other, the Devil is the head of a host of evil spirits who, like the good spirits, are arranged in orders and ranks. Both the Hebrew and the Persian Devil are associated with the serpent. The chief functions of

---

precise meaning and function of the snake in the story are unclear, but it was probably meant to symbolize human guile and cunning. See Umberto Cassuto, *A Commentary on the Book of Genesis* (Jerusalem, 1961–1964), I, 140–142. The term *'arum*, "cunning," used of the serpent in Gen. 2–3, also means "naked."

96. For a strong argument for Greek influence on the Jews in the Hellenistic period see T. F. Glasson, *Greek Influence in Jewish Eschatology, with Special Reference to the Apocalypses and Pseudepigraphs* (London, 1961). Cyrus Gordon has argued for the influence of Canaan, and Rivkah Schärf Kluger for the derivation of the accuser concept from Babylonia, where each individual had a personal accuser god and accuser goddess. See Kluger, pp. 134–135.

97. For this argument, see Helmer Ringgren, *The Faith of Qumran: Theology of the Dead Sea Scrolls* (Philadelphia, 1963), p. 78, and David Russell, pp. 238–239. In the Old Testament, Zechariah was written immediately after the exile, and Job certainly existed then in its present form. The image of Satan here, and the role of the Satan of 2 Chronicles as opponent of God, may have been influenced by Iranian thought. A strong indication of such influence appears in the Book of Tobit, where the demon Asmodeus appears to be a form of Aeshma Deva. But even this influence has been questioned.

the Hebrew Devil, to seduce, accuse, and destroy, are also those of Ahriman. The cosmos is divided into two forces of light and darkness, which are locked in deadly combat. The children of light war against the children of darkness. Toward the end of the world, the Prince of Darkness seems for a while to increase his power, and there is a dark and miserable age, but that age is followed by the triumph of the Prince of Light and the perpetual imprisonment (if not destruction) of the Prince of Darkness. The fundamental discrepancy between the doctrine of Israel and that of Iran lies in the limited nature of Hebrew dualism. But though the Hebrews, even the Qumran sect, never completely divorced the Devil from the God, the Apocalyptic Satan or Belial often acts *as if* he were a principle of evil independent of the God. The concept of the Hebrew Devil approaches dualism, and it is fair to say that to at least some Apocalyptic minds such dualism would have seemed within the framework of tradition. On their side, Zervanism and other Zoroastrian movements edged away from the complete separation of the God from the Devil. If the mainstreams of the two religious traditions remained different, the tributaries often ran close together, and may have mingled.

Whether parallel to the movement of vectors in Iran or whether under Iranian influence, the concept of the Devil moved strikingly in Hebrew thought, particularly in that of the Apocalyptic period. This motion had already begun powerfully in the post-exilic period of the Old Testament, when the relentless courage of the Hebrews in insisting that there was no other god than Yahweh forced them to consider their theodicy very carefully. In the pre-exilic period, all things in heaven and earth had been attributed to Yahweh, including destruction and violence. Yahweh was a divine antinomy, both good and evil. During and after the exile, when the trials of the Hebrews forced them into a deeper consideration of the meaning of their religion, the God twinned and became a divine doublet consisting of a good and an evil principle. Neither in the Old Testament nor in Apocalyptic literature was that twinning complete; always some sense was retained of the underlying integrity and oneness of the God. Both attracted to and shrinking from dualism, the thought of the Israelites manifests an ambivalence that persisted into Christian thought.

The Hebrew position stands between the monism of the Hindus and the dualism of the Zoroastrians. It refuses to acquiesce in the idea that evil as well as good proceeds from the divine nature; on the contrary it shuns and fiercely rejects evil. But it also declines to adopt the severing of the two principles, equally fiercely insisting that one god and one god alone can be worshiped and that one god and one alone exists. It may be that the confusion and ambiguity of the Hebrew position, rather than being inferior to the clarity and consistency of the other two, mark it as superior, because it is founded in a creative tension. It allows us to sense the hidden harmony of the cosmos while urging us at the same time to spurn the blandishments of evil. That myth may be most true which presents reality under a number of aspects at one and the same time.

The movement of Hebrew thought was an effort to obtain a satisfying theodicy. So long as the evil principle was dependent upon the divine nature, the God was in some way responsible for wars, plagues, and tortures. And when the good Lord is confounded with the God, theodicy buckles under the strain. So long as the inherent inconsistencies were expressed mythologically and taken mythologically, the problem was not acute. With the efforts of Christian and Rabbinic theologians to elucidate it rationally, it became unmanageable.

6 The Devil in the New Testament

Yet there is One who holds all this falling in his hand, gently
and without end.

—Rilke

The ideas of the New Testament derive in part from Hellenistic thought and in part from that of contemporary Judaism,
especially the Apocalyptic and Rabbinic traditions.[1] Christianity synthesizes Greek and Jewish concepts of the Devil, and
the New Testament's diabology and demonology are essentially
those of Hellenistic Judaism. The New Testament was composed by a number of writers over a period of half a century,
and its point of view is not homogeneous. I shall point out differences between the synoptic, Pauline, and Johannine interpretations of the Devil. These variations are not great; as
always, the motion of the development is what is essential.[2]

1. It is generally recognized that the earliest Christian writings as we now
have them spring from even earlier oral, and possibly also written sources.
The books of the New Testament were written over a period from about 50
to about 100 A.D. Those of the Christian Apocrypha are of diverse origin and
chronology, some originating as early as the second century and some dating
as late as the fifth.

2. The dominant thrust of biblical criticism in the past half-century has
been to scrutinize the New Testament with the tools of historical criticism in
order to discover the historical Jesus. The success of this enterprise is open to
question, considering the vast disagreement in which the critics find themselves. It is the thrust and motion of the concept, its development, that constitutes reality for the historian, who feels puzzlement at the assumption that the
truth about Christianity is to be found only in its most primitive origins.
Rather, the truth about Christianity is the history of Christianity. And so
with the Devil. The "demythologizing" of Scriptures, which has yielded a
Jesus who did not consider himself divine, has left critics in a curious posture.

Christian theodicy posed the question of evil and of the Devil
more sharply than ever before. The figure of Satan in the New
Testament is comprehensible only when it is seen as the counterpart, or counterprinciple, of Christ. Generations of socially
oriented theologians dismissed the Devil and the demons as
superstitious relics of little importance to the Christian message. On the contrary, the New Testament writers had a sharp
sense of the immediacy of evil. The Devil is not a peripheral
concept that can easily be discarded without doing violence to
the essence of Christianity. He stands at the center of the New
Testament teaching that the Kingdom of God is at war with,
and is now at last defeating, the Kingdom of the Devil.[3] The
Devil is essential in the New Testament because he constitutes
an important alternative in Christian theodicy.

Christianity posits a God who is One, omnipotent, and
wholly good. These attributes derive in part from Hellenistic
thought, which assigned ontological and moral perfection to the
One, and denied evil ontological existence or attributed it to the
lowest level of being. They derive in part also from Judaism,
which had separated the good from the evil element in the God,
calling the good aspect the Lord and identifying it with Yahweh, and demoting the evil aspect, which it called the Devil, to
the status of an inferior being or angel. The original figure of
the God had been wrenched apart. But at the same time the essential unity and totality of his being was strictly affirmed.
How then could evil be explained?

This has always been the weakest seam in Christian theol-

If Jesus is not divine, and if we can know as little about him as the de-
mythologizers claim, their own attention to Jesus is surprising, for his thought is
then much less important or interesting than that of Paul, not to mention
Philo or Plotinus. Most recently, students of Christianity have turned back in
the direction of the study of myth, an approach that is proving much more
fruitful.

3. A forceful statement of this argument is Richard H. Hiers, "Satan,
Demons, and the Kingdom of God," *Scottish Journal of Theology*, 27 (1974),
35–47. Also see Morton Kelsey, *Encounter with God* (Minneapolis, 1972),
pp. 242–245. Kelsey notes 568 references to demons and the Devil in the
New Testament as compared, for example, to 340 to the Holy Spirit and 604
to miracles.

ogy, the spot at which generations of atheists have forcefully struck.[4] Their argument usually runs something like this: (1) If God exists, he is all good and all powerful; (2) such a God could have no morally sufficient reason to allow evil; (3) but there is evil in the world; (4) therefore God does not exist.[5]

The objections to the Christian definition of God are older even than Christianity, for philosophers had raised them against the Jewish and Hellenistic definitions. Over the centuries, Christians have evolved a number of responses. I offer some of them here with some of the basic arguments for and against them. As I indicated in Chapter 1, I do not think that the traditional separation of natural from moral evil has ultimate validity, since natural evil can be perceived as the God's choice to inflict suffering upon his creatures.

(1) The first argument is similar to that of monism: what is perceived as evil is necessary for the greater good. Beyond the apparent discords of the universe is a hidden harmony directed by Providence. Human criteria of good and evil cannot be applied to God. If one only knew enough, one would perceive that what one assumes to be evil is part of a benevolent divine scheme. Bertrand Russell once contemptuously suggested that this argument be presented to a mother whose child is dying of leukemia. But Russell's reply is not preemptive: would you prefer to tell the mother that the child's suffering is meaningless, that there will be in all eternity no reward or justice for her child, or for her, or for any human being, because the universe is gratuitously cruel? The point is that the horror of the evil of the universe is not removed, or even palliated, by the abolition of the concept of God. Camus and other sincere athe-

4. See for example Wallace I. Matson, *The Existence of God* (Ithaca, N.Y., 1965).

5. This argument works, if it works at all, against the idea of the Christian God, but not against a monist God, from whose being evil is not excluded. Some atheists address themselves, rather reluctantly, to the problem of monist theodicy, but most have paid Christianity the curious compliment of insisting upon a Christian definition of the deity. Matson, for example, dismisses unorthodox theism as a refusal to play by the rules of the game. The rules of the game, as Matson sees them, consist in defining God in such a way that Matson will be able to disprove his existence.

ists have admitted this: facing the problem of evil squarely is as difficult for the atheist as it is for the Christian.

(2) Evil is real, but it is the necessary by-product of the creation of an essentially good universe. Since the finite cannot be perfect, God is obliged in creating a finite world to render it imperfect. This is the best of all possible worlds, in the sense that it is as perfect as God can make it. (The unsophisticated objection that if God is all powerful there is nothing he cannot do is specious: God cannot do or be that which is self-contradictory; he cannot and will not break his own rules.) In this argument the cosmic harmony overwhelms the discords of evil. The corollary is that the world could be much worse than it is: it could, as one writer put it, be Lovecraftian. The question is not why is there evil, but rather, why is there good? The existence of any goodness at all implies a benevolent Providence. (3) A variant of (2) is the argument that evil has no ontological existence. Evil is nonbeing. It is mere privation, privation in the universe being necessary for the plurality of forms. The world is perfect insofar as it has being, but it is necessarily laced with pockets of nonbeing, as the Swiss cheese is laced with holes. Again, this is the best universe that God could make, for there was no way he could create a differentiated cosmos without these pockets of nonbeing. The good outweighs the evil. To both these arguments an atheist can grant the premise that some evil may be necessary but then go on to ask why there needs to be as much as there is. Suppose God could not make a cosmos without a certain amount of evil in it; still, the amount and intensity of evil seem to exceed that which can be reconciled with a perfectly good and omnipotent creator. Suppose, for example, that change, dissolution, and death are necessary. Need they entail so much pain? A possible response is that if the amount of evil of which we are capable were limited, the amount of good might be also. This response argues that goodness is greater to the degree that it rises above the evil.

(4) A recent theodicy has arisen from process theology: granted that the universe is imperfect, God is drawing it toward perfection. God could not have made a better world, for

God is himself in the process of development toward perfection. God does not want stasis, and change implies passage, transfer, and death. Whether this new theodicy will last remains to be seen; it stands so far outside the lines of tradition that it does not enter into this history of the Devil.

(5) Another recent argument, one with deep roots extending as far back as medieval nominalism and even the Greek Skeptics, argues that the question of theodicy is semantically meaningless and that it is therefore a pseudoquestion. This position, however, also excludes as meaningless any discussion of God, the Devil, or evil itself. Such flights of intellect, however exciting to philosophers, will satisfy neither the historian nor anyone who is aware of the suffering he encounters in life. This response is an evasion. (6) Equally an evasion, and a simpleminded one at that, is the old parry of Christian theologians backed into a corner: the existence of evil is a mystery, shrouded forever from human understanding. In one sense, of course, everything is a mystery, for we can know nothing with certainty. But if life is to be meaningful at all, we must investigate everything to the best of our ability to do so. The only thing that ennobled this evasion was the idea that God himself on the cross participated with us in a suffering whose ultimate meaning we do not know.

To an extent, all the preceding answers, or pseudoanswers, are evasions, because none of them faces the existential reality of a universe in which a soldier shoots the head off a baby or a little girl is disfigured for life by napalm dropped on her from an anonymous airplane. Once the suffering of that little girl is immediately felt and intellectually grasped as real, once her suffering becomes our suffering, once we really face up to the monstrousness of this world in which we exist, we are bound to dismiss these answers as intellectual games.

The answers that follow face suffering squarely. (7) Suffering is terrible, but it is necessary to test us, to instruct us, to permit us to mature. Without suffering we would be spoiled children, selfish, insensitive, and irresponsible. Through suffering, through our "fortunate fall" from grace, we acquire wisdom

and maturity. Very well, but what price wisdom and maturity?
Dostoevsky asked whether it might be better for the whole
world not to exist than for that one innocent child to suffer. Or,
again, if some evil, some suffering, is necessary, why so much?
Can there be any sufficient moral reason for the abundance of
evil, the intensity of suffering? (8) Suffering exists to punish us
for our sins. It is possible that our sins do in fact merit such
punishment, though the argument has always been difficult to
apply to infants. But in any event the inevitable question is
why God permitted sin to enter the world to begin with. (9)
Evil is the result of sin, and sin proceeds from free will. The
postulate is that God creates the world in order that a moral
goodness other than his own should exist. Two things are req-
uisite for an act of moral goodness: the existence of a real choice
between good and evil, and real freedom to choose between
them. It is true that God might have created a world in which
no person was allowed to wish to hurt another person; but in
that event we would be robots programmed to do no wrong,
our actions would have no moral value, and goodness would
not have been increased. Or God might have created a world in
which an external force always frustrated our intentions to
hurt; but in that event, no real alternative would be presented
to us. We would have no perception of the effects of an evil act
since none would ever have occurred. The point is that God
cannot create a world in which human beings are truly free to
choose evil and at the same time prevent evil from happening.
The evil that exists in the world is not God's fault but ours.
The objections to this argument are two. (a) Again, why is the
degree of suffering so great? Would it not be sufficient to God's
purpose to allow us to slap or kick one another without using
knife and napalm? (b) It leaves untouched the question of natural evil, of tornadoes, of cancer. (Natural phenomena such as
storms on Venus or rocks exfoliating in a remote mountain
valley are processes of change and dissolution that cannot be
considered in any sense evil. Natural evil is the pain inflicted
upon sentient beings by natural processes.) The traditional
argument that natural evil entered the world consequent upon

the fall of Adam and Eve enjoys some tenuous scriptural under-pinnings but carries little weight. However the story of the fall is interpreted, the notion that the activity of storms and bacteria, not to mention stellar disturbances, results from any deeds of human beings on this planet is completely at variance with current understanding of the enormous size, age, and complexity of the cosmos; it is a quaint, metaphorical relic of an anthropocentric age. In only one way does the argument still have validity: as a result of our vast numbers, our advanced technology, and our contempt for the earth, we can and do inflict great destruction upon other living things.

The last argument, in one form or another, is common in Christian tradition. Evil entered the world through freedom of the will. Evil results each time that individual human beings freely elect evil over good. It also comes about through the free will of intelligent beings other than humans; in traditional Christian terms this meant the angels. Evil is the fault partly of fallen man and partly of fallen angels. To the extent that the fallen angels, and their chief, the Devil, are responsible for evil, the Devil plays an important, but not necessarily essential, role in Christian theodicy. Man might have fallen without any help from the Devil at all.

This view ignores a central thesis of the New Testament, which is that the powers of darkness under the generalship of the Devil are at war with the power of light. In other words it ignores the dualist element in Christianity. Ever since the suppression of the Albigensians, indeed since the rejection of the Gnostics, Christians have been at pains to deny, or at least to minimize, the dualist element. There is but one God, the argument goes, and therefore but one principle. The argument fails. It fails because Christianity has the virtue of taking the problem of evil seriously. The hidden harmony theme is decidedly minor in Christian tradition. The conflict between good and evil stands at the center of New Testament Christianity. The argument also fails because traditional monotheist theodicy has proved gravely unsatisfactory: how indeed can there be one, all-powerful, perfectly good creator who allows the abundance of evil and the intensity of suffering that we perceive in the world? Finally, it fails because it leaves the conception of the God incomplete. The God has been divided in two: the good Lord and the evil Devil. If the Devil is dismissed, the deity is left unbalanced, and the concept of the good Lord loses identity through the abolition of its antithesis. *Sine diabolo nullus Dominus.*

Other Christian theodicies have existed and will exist, but no theodicy that does not take the Devil fully into consideration is likely to be persuasive. In spite of the efforts of generations of theologians to reduce or abolish the role of Satan, the concept of the Devil has persisted. Christianity is in fact a semidualist religion. On the one hand it rejects the full dualism that asserts the opposition of two eternal cosmic principles. But it has also generally rejected the monist complacency of the hidden harmony. The tension between monism and dualism has led to inconsistencies in Christian theodicy. But the tension is also creative. Creativity arises whenever meaning strains against the bounds of form, when novelty strains against the strictures of tradition. Water is drinkable only when held in a container. Precisely in its willingness to confront the problem of evil without recourse to the simpler solutions of either dualism or monism, Christianity advanced the motion of the concept of the Devil creatively.

The New Testament inherited several concepts of the Devil. The Devil is a fallen angel. The Devil is the head of a demonic host. The Devil is the principle of evil. Evil is nonbeing. These and other elements had to be absorbed, refined, and, to the extent possible, rendered consistent. "Who say you that I am?" Jesus asked his disciples. The Devil might have asked the same question. Who, according to the New Testament, is the Devil?

The names given the Devil in the New Testament reflect the double background of Hellenism and Apocalyptic Judaism. Most often he is "Satan," or "the Devil" (*diabolos* being a translation of the Hebrew *satan*); he is also "Beelzeboul," "the enemy," "Belial," "the tempter," "the accuser," "the evil one," "the ruler of this world," and "the prince of demons."[6] The Devil's connection with the demons is paralleled by his association with the fallen angels (Revelation 12:4; 12:7ff.; and Ephesians 2:1–2), which makes it clear that he is to be regarded as a spiritual being. These conceptions have their roots in both Apocalyptic and Rabbinical Judaism. Although the fallen angels are likened to fallen stars in Revelation 12:4, the name Lucifer, light-bearer, already attached to the head of the fallen angels in Apocalyptic literature, is not used in the New Testament, where the "bearer of light" is the Christ.

The function of the Devil in the New Testament is as counterprinciple to Christ. The central message of the New Testament is salvation: Christ saves us. What he saves us from is the power of the Devil. If the power of the Devil is dismissed, the Christ's saving mission becomes meaningless.[7] The Devil occupies a central position in the New Testament as the chief

6. One Greek rendition of the Hebrew *satan*, e.g., *Satanas*, appears 33 times in the New Testament, e.g., 2 Cor. 12:7 and Matt. 12:26. *Ho diabolos* also appears 33 times, cf. Matt. 4:3 and 13:39. *Ho echthros*, "the enemy," also appears; cf. Matt. 13:25, 39; Luke 10:19. All three of the above titles appear in Jewish Apocalyptic. *Beelzeboul*, which does not appear in Jewish Apocalyptic and only once (under the less correct form *Beelzeboub*) in the Old Testament (2 Kings 1), appears 6 times, e.g., Matt. 10:25, Luke 11:15. It derives from the Canaanite "Baal the prince," but its popularity in the New Testament, given the lack of contemporary Jewish references, has not been explained. *Belial*, 2 Cor. 6:15, is the Apocalyptic Belial or Beḷiar. *Ho tou kosmou archōn*, "prince of this world," or similar phrases appear especially in John: cf. John 12:31; 14:30; this term reflects the great struggle between the two kingdoms. *Ho peirazon*, "the tempter," appears in Matt. 4:3 and 1 Thess. 3:5. For *Ho katēgoros*, "the accuser," cf. Rev. 12:10. *Ho ponēros*, "the evil one," cf. Matt. 13:19; 1 John 5:18, may also be intended in the Lord's Prayer (Matt. 6:13), where the Greek can be read "Deliver us from evil," or "Deliver us from the Evil One." In the New Testament both *ho ponēros* and the neuter *to ponēron* frequently appear in cases that make the distinction impossible. *Archōn tōn daimoniōn*, "prince of the demons," cf. Matt. 9:34, and the similar phrase, *Archōn tēs exousias tou aeros* (Eph. 2:2), "prince of the power of the air," bring him into close connection with the demons. Mark and Paul incline to the use of the proper name of Satan; the other New Testament writers often prefer "the Devil" or the circumlocutions.

7. Good discussions of this point are in Bendt Noack, *Satanás und Sotería* (Copenhagen, 1948) and Trevor Ling, *The Significance of Satan* (London, 1961).

Christ exorcising a demon, Armenian, 1262. Christ's powers of exorcism were a sign of his power to replace the Kingdom of this World, which is the Kingdom of Satan, with the Kingdom of the Lord. Courtesy Trustees of the Walters Art Gallery, Baltimore, Maryland.

enemy of the Lord. For the New Testament writers, this opposition was both fierce and profound, and they never consciously perceived the underlying connection between the Lord and the Devil. For the problem of theodicy remained. If the Devil is not an absolute principle of evil—as he was not in the New Testament—then how and why does the God permit, condone, or ordain his destructive activities? To put it now, not in New Testament terms, but in the tradition of the concept:

the God has been divided into two parts, the good Lord and the evil Devil. Christ, the Son of God, is associated and identified with the good Lord. The opposition between Yahweh and Satan becomes the opposition between Christ and Satan. (But early Christian tradition frequently held to the doctrine of subordinationism, affirming that the Son was not coequal in power with the Father. A hint of this subordinationism is found in the New Testament teachings on the Devil. Then the counterpart of Christ is not Satan himself, but an inferior figure, such as Antichrist or even Judas, a servant of the Devil rather than the Devil himself.)

The essential scenario of the struggle appears something like this: The good Lord creates a good world, which is injured by the Devil and the demons, who bring disease and other ills. The world is also injured by the free choice of humanity, as represented by Adam and Eve, to do evil instead of good. The Devil may or may not have tempted Adam and Eve to their original sin; he has certainly been active in the world since. Through the activity of Satan, aided by the demons and by those human beings who fall into sin, the world has fallen under the domination of the Devil. The natural and moral evils of the world are the fault, not of the good Lord, but of these creatures. The conflict between this world, dominated by the Devil, and the Kingdom of God, now brought to earth by Christ, is an important emphasis of the New Testament.

To what extent in this scenario is the Devil the principle of evil? The origin of Satan is not discussed in the New Testament. A few texts seem to equate him with the head of the fallen angels, one of the good Lord's creatures whose sin, like that of Adam, arose from the misuse of his own free will. On the other hand, the cosmic struggle between the Kingdom of God and the Kingdom of Satan, deriving directly from Jewish Apocalyptic and indirectly from Mazdaism, makes the Devil almost a principle of cosmic evil independent of the good Lord. Almost, because Apocalyptic Judaism and Christianity both stopped short of dualism by insisting upon the oneness of God.

The position of the Devil therefore remains anomalous in the New Testament.[8]

Nowhere is its anomalous condition more clearly seen than in the doctrine of the fall of humanity. The doctrine of original sin is not found in the Old Testament, and it rarely appears in Rabbinical literature. Apocalyptic literature gives hints of it, but even in the New Testament its development is very rudimentary. Nowhere do the gospels mention original sin. Oblique references may be found in 1 Corinthians 15:20–22 and 44–50, Galatians 5:4, Ephesians 2:3, and 2 Corinthians 11. The only direct (but still very unclear) discussion of original sin is in Romans 5:12–21, where St. Paul explains that sin and death entered the world through the sin of Adam. The Devil's role is not mentioned at all. Other passages (for example, Romans 16:20) suggest that the serpent of the Genesis story was Satan, an identification that had already been made in Apocalyptic literature. The corollary that Satan tempted Adam to sin is implicit. Satan's sin would then precede Adam's. But what the New Testament meant on this point is far from certain, and the consensus of early Christian tradition was that Satan fell after Adam. In any event, neither the New Testament nor later Christian tradition held that the Devil forced Adam's will. If Adam had not been free, he would not have been able to sin. It follows that he could have sinned without the Devil's intervention. Once again, the position of the Devil as the fount and origin of evil is restricted.

But though the fall of man is peripheral in the New Testament, the war between the worlds is central, and in that context the Devil functions most clearly as principle of evil. Two Greek words have been translated as "world" in English versions of the Bible. One is *aiōn*, used most frequently by Paul; the other is *kosmos*, employed most frequently in the Johannine writings. They have similar, if not identical, meanings, for they are sometimes interchanged, and the Devil is called both lord of

---

8. The elements of cosmic dualism in the synoptic gospels are much stronger in Luke than in Mark and Matthew, and stronger in John than in any of the synoptics.

The harrowing of hell, manuscript illumination, Germany, tenth century. During the three days between Good Friday and his resurrection, Christ descended into hell and liberated the souls of the just. Here the mouth of hell gapes open at the right, while Christ spears the vanquished Devil. Courtesy the Pierpont Morgan Library.

the *aiōn*, or "eon," and lord of the *kosmos*.[9] The kingdom of the Devil, perceived as the world, is contrasted to the kingdom of the Lord, which is not of this world.[10] The meaning of the "Kingdom of God" has exercised Christian thinkers for two millennia, and no interpretation is without difficulty. The basic thrust of the idea, insofar as it relates to Satan, seems to be as follows. From the beginning the Devil has been increasing his power over this world, until now, at this latter day, his sway is almost complete. But the good Lord sends Christ to break the power of the old eon and to replace it with the new, the kingdom of God. Although the meaning of the latter is difficult to understand, what is meant by the old eon or "this world" is easier to grasp. The terms *kosmos* and *aiōn* are used in a number of different ways. *Kosmos* can mean the natural world; it can mean the world of men; and it can mean those people who are sinners and who because of their sin are cut off from the body of Christ and have become limbs of the Devil. *Aiōn* can mean the time allotted to the material world; the material world itself; or the present, sin-ridden time as opposed to the time of the God to come. The Devil is lord of the natural world in his power to cause death, disease, and natural disasters: the world has been disfigured from the outset by the action of sin. The Devil is lord of the world of men, because he roams it freely tempting those whom he pleases. And, most importantly, the Devil is lord of sinners. It is in the sense of sinful human society that the terms *kosmos* and *aiōn* are most often used, for the New Testament emphasizes the problem of moral evil more than that of natural evil. It affirms that the world was created by the good Lord for good purposes. Yet this basic teaching is obscured by what it says about the power of Satan. The good

9. 1 Cor. 1:20; 2:6–7; 3:18; Rom. 12:2; Gal. 1:4; 1 John 4:3–4; Eph. 2:2; 6:2; 2 Cor. 4:4; John 12:31; 14:30; 15:18–19; 16:11; 17:15–16. On *kosmos*, see Herman Sasse, "κόσμος," *Theologisches Wörterbuch*, 3 (1938), 867–896; on *aiōn*, see Sasse, "αἰών" *ThW* 1 (1933), 197–209. See also the translations in *Theological Dictionary of the New Testament*, ed. Gerhard Kettel and Gerhard Friedrich (Grand Rapids, Mich., 1964–1973).

10. The Greek is *basileia*, which translates directly and without difficulty into "kingdom." Cf. Mark 3:24; Matt. 12:26–28; Luke 11:20.

Lord's power over the world has waned for a while; or, to put it another way, the Lord has allowed Satan temporary power over the world. Now, "The whole world lies in the Evil One."[11] The original Greek can mean a number of things: "the whole world" may be taken as "all mankind," and "in the Evil One" may be simply "in evil." But these refinements would be lost on the Gnostics, who insisted that the material world was irredeemably evil and had been created by an evil deity.

The association of the kingdom of Satan with the material universe led, along lines suggested by Greek Orphic tradition, to a dichotomy between spirit and body. The body, like the rest of the material universe, is the good creation of a good Lord—this is made manifest in John 1. It is the dwelling place of the spirit, and it is taken on by the Lord himself in the person of Jesus. At the end of the world the body will be resurrected. All this the New Testament affirms, yet it also affirms an opposition between body and spirit. There are two Greek words that can be rendered "body": *sarx* and *sōma*. *Sōma* is a neutral word in the New Testament, in spite of its long tradition in Orphic thought as the prison of the spirit (*sōma sēma*). *Sarx* is a complicated term sometimes used to denote the material body, flesh itself, and sometimes the whole evil eon, the corrupt world. It has some positive uses—in Jesus the Word took on *sarx*—but usually it is pejorative. The flesh, *sarx*, stands in opposition to the work of the spirit. Saint Paul says that the desire of the flesh (*sarkos*) is in enmity (*echthra*) with God.[12] The "flesh" in the New Testament seems to be the equivalent of the

---

11. 1 John 5:19: *ho kosmos holos en tō ponērō keitai.*

12. Rom. 8:7. Cf. Rom. 8:5–6; John 3:6; 6:63. For the neutrality of *sōma*, see Rom. 8:10. On *sarx*, see Eduard Schwazer, "σάρξ," *ThW* 7 (1960), 98–151. The body is not pejorative in 2 Cor. 12:7 or 1 Cor. 15:39, and 1 Cor. 7:28 makes the point that the human being is composed of both *sarx* and *pneuma*. *Sarx* can mean the whole world of men (Rom. 1:3f.). But it more frequently is negative. It can mean temptation (Gal. 6:12f.); it can be equated with the Old Law (Phil. 3:3f.), and it can be associated specifically with sin: Phil. 3:3; Rom. 8:13f.; Gal. 4:23; 5:18–19. *Sarx* is opposed to the gospel, and the crucifixion of *sarx* yields life (Rom. 7:5; 8:8ff.; Gal. 5:24). In Eph. 2:2–3 the body is clearly equated with the old eon that opposes the Kingdom of God. See also John 8:15; 6:63.

yetser ha-ra, the evil inclination, of the rabbis.[13] The New Testament is ambivalent on the subject of the body, sometimes regarding it as part of the material world and a source of temptation, in opposition to the spirit and the kingdom of God. The Gnostics were to carry this teaching to extremes, and though the Christian tradition avoided the extremes, it bore within itself a distrust of the flesh evident over the years in the Church's attitudes toward the body and sex.

The struggle between the old eon and the new is also expressed in terms of darkness against light. To some extent this language is metaphorical, but it goes beyond metaphor to draw upon the ancient tradition of the war of darkness against light. The darkness of Satan is not only figurative; it is also literal.[14]

The Devil is prince of a host of evil spiritual powers, who may be viewed as fallen angels or as demons. The distinction between the two, already hazy in late Judaism, becomes even hazier in the New Testament. Only rarely are the fallen angels mentioned (for example, in Jude 6 and 2 Peter 2:4). The powers that Christianity attributed to demons were similar to those the rabbis and the Apocalyptic literature gave them. By the end of the New Testament period, Christian tradition made no distinction between fallen angels and demons. This development is in line with the Hellenistic practice of dividing the beings situated on a level between God and men into good and evil spirits, the latter being called *daimonia*. The name given to the evil spirits in the New Testament is most frequently *daimonion*, though *daimōn* appears once (Matt. 8:31), and there are also *archai*, *exousiai*, *dynameis*, *kuriotētes*, *thronoi*, *onomata*, *archontes*, *kyrioi*, *theoi*, *stoicheia*, and, of course, *angeloi*.

Demons appear most frequently in the gospels. Saint Paul seldom refers to them.[15] The usual view is that between God

13. See Hermann Strack and Paul Billerbeck, *Kommentar zum Neuen Testament aus Talmud und Midrasch* (Munich, 1922–1969), IV, 466.

14. Cf. the *locus classicus*, John 1:4–5, and also 2 Cor. 4:4 (light vs. blindness); Acts 26:18; Col. 1:13; Eph. 6:12.

15. I Cor. 10:20–21 is a reference to Deut. 32:17; I Tim. 4:1 is the only other place in the Pauline epistles where the term appears.

and man are spiritual beings who, like men, have the freedom
to do good or evil. The good spirits are the angels of the Lord;
the others are the minions of the Devil. The New Testament
for the most part assumes that these powers are hostile: "The
angelic powers are the equivalent of one aspect of the larger
symbol of Satan."[16] On the whole the New Testament moves
in the direction of consolidating the diverse demons of Near
Eastern and Jewish tradition into one host under Satan's power.
The distinction between the Devil and the demons who followed him, still clear in the New Testament usage of *diabolos*
and *daimonion*, becomes blurred in later Christian tradition
(probably owing to the identification of the Devil as one of the
fallen angels). Most English translations of the New Testament
also miss the distinction, rendering *daimonion* as "devil." In contemporary Rabbinical literature, demons are spiritual beings
who have been given permission by the Lord to tempt us or to
do us bodily harm for the punishment of our sins, and they
play much the same role in the New Testament. In the latter,
they are more clearly under the generalship of Satan, helping
him oppose the kingdom of God.[17] Again, demonology is central, not peripheral, to the teaching of the New Testament.

Possession is one of the most common means Satan uses to
obstruct the Kingdom of God. Ordinarily, the demons, Satan's
servants, do the possessing, though in the Johannine literature
Satan does it himself.[18] By exorcizing the demons, and by cur-
ing diseases sent by them, Jesus makes war upon the kingdom
of Satan and thereby makes known to the people that the new
eon is come: "If I drive out demons by the power of God, it is
because the Kingdom of God is come among you." Contemporary magicians and healers also exorcized demons, but the gospels point out that only Christ exorcizes through the power of
the Holy Spirit. The exorcism of demons is no quirk in the gospels, no strange and irrelevant accretion introduced from con-

16. Ling, p. 77.
17. Cf. Rom. 8:38; 1 Cor. 2:6; Matt. 9:34; 25:41; Rev. 12:10; 2 Pet. 2:4;
and especially Matt. 12:28.
18. John 6:70–71; 8:44; 13:2, 27; 1 John 3:12.

Exorcism, medieval Bilderbibel, Germany, fifteenth century. Christ drives out the demons who have possessed the woman: they emerge from her black and with wings that signify their power over the air. Courtesy Jan Torbecke Verlag.

temporary superstition. It is central to the war against Satan and therefore an integral part of the gospels' meaning. "In each act of exorcism Jesus saw a defeat of Satan, a presage of the final triumph that was soon to come to pass. . . . Jesus actualized Satan, just as he actualized God. Just as he treated with full earnest the coming Divine Kingdom, so he treated also the present dominion of Satan."[19]

The Devil is prince of evil humans as well. Evildoers are called followers or sons of the Devil.[20] Peter himself is called Satan when he tempts Christ to waver from his appointed path to the cross.[21] Curiously, Christ calls Peter the Devil for attempting to avert the Passion and Judas the Devil for working to bring it about. What these two apostles have in common is thrusting their own personal fears into the path of the divine plan of salvation.[22] Judas is most commonly associated with the Devil, and Luke says that Satan actually enters into him.[23] Judas is such a close counterpart of Jesus that one senses an analogy between their relationship and that of the doublets so often found in mythology. The Lord chooses Jesus and sends his spirit upon him, just as Satan chooses Judas and sends his spirit to enter him. The analogy may even be closer: in the great scheme of salvation the God knew from all time that Jesus would be the savior and Judas the betrayer; and as the betrayal of Judas was necessary for the Passion of Christ, the God might

19. Anton Fridrichsen, "The Conflict of Jesus with the Unclean Spirits," *Theology*, 22 (1931), 127. Fridrichsen also suggests, p. 128, that the word *biastai*, "The violent ones" in the difficult passage of Matthew 11:12 that says that the violent will bear away the kingdom of God, is best understood as applying, not to human, but to spiritual, powers, the *biastai* being Satan and his demons. For Christ exorcizing through the power of the Holy Spirit, see Matt. 12:28 and Luke 11:20.

20. John 8:44; Acts 13:10; 2 Thess. 2:3–9; Rev. 2:9; 3:9; 1 John 3:8; 3:12.

21. Matt. 16:23; Mark 8:33; Luke 22:31; cf. Matt. 4:10, where the same words Jesus uses to Peter are used to Satan himself.

22. Henry Ansgar Kelly, "The Devil in the Desert," *Catholic Biblical Quarterly*, 26 (1964), 218.

23. Luke 22:3; cf. John 6:70; 13:2, 27.

be said to have chosen Judas for his part in the act of salvation as well as Jesus for his.[24]

The New Testament Devil is a tempter, a liar, a murderer, the cause of death, sorcery, and idolatry; he hurts people physically, and he blocks and obstructs the teaching of the Kingdom of God wherever he can, assaulting us, possessing us spiritually, and tempting us to sin.[25] In all this he is the enemy of the Kingdom of God. He also retains some of his old characteristics as an agent of the God in the accusation and punishment of sinners.[26] In this respect, he has almost the same function as the Mosaic law, and Saint Paul applies similar terminology to the two.[27]

In later Christian tradition, dramatized by Dante and Milton, Satan came to rule hell, to punish people there, and to suffer there himself. None of these activities appear in the New Testament, where references to hell are both few and unclear. The two most common New Testament terms for hell are *hadēs* and *geenna*. In the Septuagint, *hadēs* usually translates the Hebrew Sheol, and the New Testament understanding of this place is similar to the Hebrew: it is under the earth, and it is the abode of souls temporarily separated from their bodies until the time of resurrection. *Geenna*, the location of which is not specified in

24. John 6:64. This irony never becomes explicit in Christian tradition, which rejects the notion that Judas was chosen, attributing his sin to his free will. Yet the implications are there to be drawn.

25. Tempter: 1 Thess. 3:5; Acts 5:3; 1 Cor. 7:5; Mark 4:15; 1 Tim. 5:15; 2 Tim. 2:26; 1 Pet. 5:8; tempter of Christ: Matt. 4:1–11; Mark 1:13; Luke 4:1–3; liar: John 8:44, and implied in 2 Cor. 2:11 and 2 Tim. 2:26; murderer: John 8:44 (here there is possible reference to Cain, who in later tradition became a demonic figure); as cause of death (cf. Wisdom of Solomon 2:24 and rabbinic tradition): Heb. 2:14; cause of sorcery and idolatry: Acts 13:10; implied in 1 Cor. 10:20; hurts people physically: Luke 13:11–16, 2 Cor. 12:7; blocks and obstructs: 1 Thess. 2:18.

26. Rev. 12:10; 1 Cor. 5:5; 1 Tim. 1:20.

27. See the argument of G. B. Caird, *Principalities and Powers* (Oxford, 1956), pp. 36–44. Trevor Ling (p. 41) argues that Paul's sending to Satan in 1 Cor. 5:5 may best be taken as expulson from the Christian community. If the world outside Christianity is under the power of the Devil, then removal from the Christian community places one under that power.

the New Testament, is a place of eternal fire and punishment for the wicked. These two concepts, related but originally distinct, merge quickly in post–New Testament thought. The relationship of Satan to hell is also ill defined in the New Testament. In Revelation 20:10 the Devil is cast into a lake of fire and brimstone, and in the later, Apocryphal works he appears both as a prisoner of hell and as a jailer of the damned.[28]

The question of hell is part of the whole question of eschatology: what happens at the end of the world, and when does the end of the world occur? To the extent that the world, the *kosmos* or *aiōn* of the New Testament, is identified with the Kingdom of Satan, it would appear that the end of the world and the defeat of Satan are simultaneous. But the New Testament speaks notoriously unclearly about when and how the ruin of Satan is effected.

One errs in reading back into primitive Christianity the notions of Dante or Milton centuries later. Several different interpretations of the fall of Satan and his fellow angels have at one time or another been put forward. The first set of differences has to do with the nature of the fall: it has been viewed as (1) a moral lapse; (2) a loss of dignity; (3) a literal ejection from heaven; (4) a voluntary departure from heaven. The second set of differences has to do with the geography of the fall: (1) from heaven to earth; (2) from heaven into the underworld; (3) from earth (or air) into the underworld. The third set is chronological: Satan fell (1) at the beginning of the world before the fall of Adam; (2) from envy of Adam; (3) with the Watchers about the time of Noah; (4) at the advent of Christ; (5) at the Passion

28. Montague Rhodes James, ed., *The Apocryphal New Testament* (Oxford, 1924), pp. 117–146. Note that the English word "hell" is a Germanic word relating to the underworld; Teutonic and other medieval concepts of hell should not be read back into the early Christian period. The New Testament uses *geenna* twelve times and *hadēs* ten; the name Tartarus seems to be behind the odd verb in 2 Pet. 2:4; and Matt. 25:41 speaks of the eternal fire prepared for the fallen angels. For the tradition of the descent of Christ into hell, see Josef Kroll, *Gott und Hölle* (Leipzig, 1932).

of Christ; (6) at the second coming of Christ; (7) a thousand years after the second coming.[29]

It is possible to find various accounts implicit in the New Testament. (1) At the beginning of the world there was war in heaven, and Michael cast out the Devil and his angels. They were plunged into the underworld, from which, however, they issued forth to tempt and persecute mankind. (2) The angels fell long after Adam, when they lusted after the daughters of men; they were cast down from heaven into the underworld but issued forth again for our harm. (3) The Kingdom of God arrives on earth with the advent of Christ; his casting out of the demons shows that the power of Satan is presently being crushed. A variant of this chronology is that the Passion of Christ on the cross hurled Satan down. (4) The Kingdom of Satan has been weakened but not finally toppled by the coming of Christ. Christ will come again, and at the last judgment Satan will be destroyed, or else cast forever into hell. This last chronology, found in Revelation, indicates the shifting faith of the Church after the first century, when it had become clear that Christ's first coming had not removed evil from the world. As his second coming was delayed further, another postponement of the ruin of Satan occurred, this also visible in Revelation. (5) At the second coming, Christ will bind Satan for a thousand years; at the end of a thousand years, he will issue forth to our harm one final time, and then finally will be destroyed.[30] The inconsistency of these stories is inherited from

29. Luke 10:18; Matt. 12:28; 25:41; John 12:31; 16:11; 2 Pet. 2:4; Rev. 9:1–3; 12:7–9; 20. The spirits in prison (1 Pet. 3:19) are fallen angels.

30. It is from Rev. 20 that all Christian millenarian dreams have come. Christian millenarianism reflects the change in late Jewish Messianic thought. Until about 150 B.C., the Jews believed that the Messiah would usher in a reign of eternal happiness on earth, and vestiges of that belief still existed at the time of Jesus. But during the terrible events of the period after 150 B.C., the Jews came to believe that the world was too evil for the Messiah to reign here and that it would have to be purified for a time before the kingdom was established. The length of time was specified as a thousand years for the first time in Slavonic Enoch 22–23, which dates from about 50 A.D. For the fire and brimstone of hell, see 1 Enoch; Test. Jud. 25:3; and the Sibylline Oracles, 3:73.

Apocalyptic Judaism, and it is irresoluble. The fall of the Devil
and his angels may be a fall from heaven to earth, or a fall from
heaven or earth to the underworld; the fall into the underworld
may mean the destruction of the Devil or merely his imprisonment; Christ has the power to destroy the kingdom of Satan,
the old eon, but it is unclear whether the old eon perishes with
the first coming of Christ or lingers until the second. These ambiguities allowed for the development in subsequent Christian
thought of a variety of legends and doctrines regarding the
overthrow of the Devil, all consistent with one or another
teaching of the Bible. The essential point, one on which there is
complete consistency, is that the new eon brought by Christ is
irreconcilably and eternally at war with the old eon of Satan.

Other eschatological adversaries of the Kingdom of God are
mentioned, whose origins and characters are even more unclear.
Toward the end of the world, when Christ is about to come
again, Antichrist will appear and lead the people of God astray.
Antichrist may be one person or a plural entity. He may be a
spiritual or a human adversary. The ambiguities of the New
Testament on the subject of Antichrist arise from the multiple
sources of his nature. In part, the figure is drawn from Beliar,
who in the Apocalyptic literature is the equivalent of Satan, the
spiritual general of the forces of evil. In part it also draws upon
the image of the tyrant at the end of the world in the Book of
Daniel and, more specifically, upon more recent political enemies of the Jewish people, such as Antiochus Epiphanes, Nero,
and Caligula.[31] Associated with Antichrist in Revelation are the
beasts and the dragon (Rev. 11–19), who again have mingled
and ambiguous characteristics. The dragon is to be identified as

---

31. See Josef Ernst, *Die eschatologischen Gegenspieler in den Schriften des Neuen
Testaments* (Regensburg, 1967), and Béda Rigaux, *L'Antéchrist* (Gembloux,
1932), for a critical evaluation of the proposal put forth by R. H. Charles that
Antichrist is a composite of three figures, Beliar, Nero Redivivus, and the
false prophet. The association with Caligula may be implied in 2 Thess.
2:1–4, where the Antichrist takes a place in the temple and pretends to be
God. Caligula had ordered a statue of himself erected in the Temple.
Though he was assassinated before the order was carried out, the memory of
the proposed blasphemy endured.

The De Quincey Apocalypse, "The Worship of the Beast," England, thirteenth century. Satan's last and greatest ally, the enthroned Antichrist orders the execution of the saints who will not adore the apocalyptic beast. From O. E. Saunders, *English Illumination* (1969), courtesy Hacker Art Books, New York.

the Devil himself, and the beasts as his servants. The beast from the sea is generally agreed to be the power of Rome, although it has mythological resonances going back to Leviathan and Tiamat.[32] The Antichrist and the two beasts are best understood as helpers of the Devil in his last struggle against Christ at the end of the world. Their close association with the Devil, given the ambiguity of the passages, permitted an assimilation of their characteristics into the image of the Devil himself. And this is proper. Together they are the old eon, the world, the force of evil that blocks and obstructs the Kingdom of God. The beast and the false prophet are cast into a lake of

32. Cf. John 3:8; 40–41; Ps. 74:14; 104:26; Isa. 27:1; Ethiopic En. 60:7–9.

fire (Rev. 19:19–20), and with the Devil are tormented day and night forever (Rev. 20:10).

The iconography of the beasts is of minor importance in the formation of the iconography of Satan. Both the dragon and the beast from the sea have ten horns and seven heads, attributes never assigned to the Devil in later tradition. The later Devil is hardly ever polycephalic, though he may have a face on belly or buttocks, and he never has more than two horns. Revelation (13:11) says, however, that the beast from the land has two horns and speaks like a dragon. Of all the possible pictures of the Devil—no horns, one horn, many horns—why did the two-horned image become fixed in the iconographic tradition? The answer is that the figure of the beast from the land matched other two-horned figures. The Devil was associated with horned wild animals, with Pan and the satyrs, with fertility and the crescent moon. And the *qeren*, the horns of power assigned to Moses and other numinous figures, are two. On an unconscious level, these images blended together in primitive Christianity to fix two horns upon the head of the Devil forever.

Demons in the New Testament are associated with a number of animals: locusts, scorpions, leopards, lions, and bears, for example; but the Devil himself has direct associations with only two animals, the serpent and the lion.[33] The lion never became a strong part of the iconographic tradition, because it was also connected with Christ himself and with the Evangelist Mark.[34] Saint Paul refers in passing to the serpent as Eve's tempter and, when taken with Romans 16:20, this would imply its identification with Satan. Revelation 20:2 makes a threefold identification of Devil with dragon and serpent. But Satan's connection

33. 1 Pet. 5:8; Rev. 12:9.
34. See Rev. 5:5 for the identification of the lion with Christ. The image was used with great success by C. S. Lewis in his Narnia series; that it could be so used without any ambivalence indicates that the metaphor of the Devil as roaring lion did not become dominant in Christian tradition. The Christian Apocrypha would associate the Devil with a number of animals, e.g., the wolf and the dog (see James, *Apocryphal New Testament*, pp. 35, 36, 82), probably through a blurring of the distinction between the Devil and the demons.

with the serpent is never emphasized in the New Testament. Later Christian tradition affirmed it, but, with the one exception of the primordial scene in Paradise, seldom portrayed Satan as a serpent. The forked tongue eventually assigned him may proceed as much from his role as father of lies in John 8:44 as from his association with the snake.[35]

The wings so often associated with the Devil in later tradition do not appear in the New Testament, but they are implied in his power over the air. This power derives from two sources. In Jewish Apocalyptic the fallen Watchers are cast down from heaven into the air, where they wander about doing mischief. In Pythagoreanism and Middle Platonism, an order of spirits (angels or demons) exists between God and men, their abode being in the air. The air, with its winds and storms, was always a dangerous element, as the Babylonian demon Pazuzu indicates. The Devil rules the air, and wings naturally become part of his navigational equipment.[36]

In the New Testament, as in the Old Testament, the salt water of the sea is generally considered evil. In Revelation, where the beast rises from the sea, where the serpent looses a flood against the mother of Christ, and where the Great Whore sits upon the waters, the ancient evil of the waters of chaos appears. Fresh water, on the other hand, is powerfully good. It cures bodily infirmities and through baptism cleanses the soul. In later Christian folklore, water offers protection from the Devil, who often is said to lack the power of crossing streams or bodies of water.[37]

In later Christian tradition, the color of the Devil is either red or black. Of the books of the New Testament, only Revelation renders the color red as evil; there it is the color of one of the dread horses, or of the Whore, or of the beast that the

35. Cf. 2 Cor. 11:3; Rev. 12; 13:2. The serpent motif is stronger in the Christian Apocrypha: see James, *Apocryphal New Testament*, pp. 44, 80–82.

36. Eph. 2:2: "the power of the air."

37. One of the many passages emphasizing the goodness of water: John 3:5. For water as evil, see Rev. 12:15–16; 13:1; 17:1. The Great Whore who sits upon the waters in Rev. 17:1 certainly counts the fertility goddesses of the Near East among her progenitors.

Whore rides, or of the dragon. Its connection with evil passed most easily into tradition from the red dragon of Revelation 12:3.[38] The blackness of the Devil arises naturally from his role of lord of darkness in opposition to the Kingdom of God and from his association with the underworld or pit where he is imprisoned after his fall. The conflict between the two kingdoms, between light and darkness, is so central to the New Testament that it permanently fixed the image of Satan as lord of darkness.[39] Although red is ambiguous, the New Testament never refers to darkness or blackness as a good color.[40] Yet nowhere does it describe Satan as actually black. Satan is a spirit, not a body; he has the power of changing his shape to suit his purposes, and he can even transform himself into an angel of light (2 Corinthians 11:14). Only in the later Apocryphal literature is blackness specifically assigned to the Devil.[41]

The New Testament does not move the tradition of the concept of the Devil strikingly beyond the position of late Jewish Apocalyptic; the two literatures are almost contemporary and arise from the same Hellenistic Jewish milieu. But it does fix many of the elements of Hellenistic Jewish tradition firmly in the concept. The Devil is a creature of God, the chief of the fallen angels, but he most of the time acts as if he had far greater power. He is lord of this world, chief of a vast multitude of powers spiritual and physical, angelic and human, that are arrayed against the Kingdom of God. Satan is not only the Lord's chief opponent; he has under his generalship *all* opposition to the Lord. Anyone who does not follow the Lord is under the control of Satan. In this capacity Satan appears very much the principle of evil. Christianity, like Apocalyptic Judaism, refused to embrace dualism, but Satan's power, attri-

38. Cf. Rev. 6:4; 17:3-4.   39. John 1:4-9; Acts 26:18; Rev. 22:5.
40. For red (or purple) as good, see Mark 15:17.
41. For the Apocrypha, see James, pp. 22, 55, 323, 345, 451, 468. As early as about 120 A.D. the Epistle of Barnabas designated Satan as *ho melas*, the black one, and by the time of the Apostolic History of Abdias and the Acts of Philip he is completely limned as black, winged, and reeking of smoke. See also the early Christian treatise, *The Shepherd of Hermas.*

butes, and ultimate fate are very similar to those of Ahriman in Mazdaism. As Satan is the opponent of the good Lord of Judaism, so he is the opponent of Christ, the Son of the Lord. As Christ commands the armies of light, Satan commands those of darkness. The cosmos is torn between light and darkness, good and evil, spirit and matter, soul and body, the new eon and the old, the Lord and Satan. The Lord is the creator of all things and the guarantor of their goodness, but Satan and his kingdom have corrupted this world. Christ comes to destroy this old world, this evil eon, and to establish a new one in its place. In the end, Satan and his powers will be defeated, cast down, and perhaps annihilated, and Christ's other world, the kingdom of goodness, of light, of spirit, will be forever established. The dualism of this view is mitigated in at least three important ways. The good God created the world, which, though corrupted by Satan, remains intrinsically good. Satan himself is a creature of God. The meaning of the created world is itself ambiguous: it is not clear whether the struggle between the two kingdoms is on a truly cosmic level or whether it occurs in human society alone. And at the end of time, Christ will win a final victory over Satan. The dualism of the New Testament is thus not the extreme dualism of Gnosticism. Yet it is even farther from monism. New Testament Christianity is best perceived as a semidualist religion, in which both the unity and goodness of the Lord are preserved, however precariously, while Satan is given almost as vast a scope as Ahriman.

Wide powers were assigned to Satan for two reasons. The first is simply that the traditions of Mazdaism, Orphism, Hellenistic religion and philosophy, and late Judaism were passed on to New Testament Christianity. But, second, these traditions were eagerly accepted and reinforced because they allowed a partial answer to the question of theodicy. To the corruption of the cosmos by Satan can be assigned natural ills, such as death and disease and storm, whether they are simply sent upon us as diabolical afflictions or are meant as punishment for our sins. Moral evil might exist in mankind without Satan, but he constantly abets it through temptation, and all those who sin are automatically under his power. Every day, in every place, in every life, Satan and his powers are working to block the kingdom of God. The Devil is the source of lies, of murder, of wars; he tempts us, accuses us, punishes us; he afflicts us with disease and even possesses us. The horns and darkness of the Devil, his association with the air and the underworld, his ability to change shapes, and the other iconographical features assigned him in the New Testament are all mere symbols of this immense power. The Devil of the New Testament is not a joke, he is not taken lightly, he is not merely symbolic, and he is decidedly not peripheral to the New Testament message. The saving mission of Christ can be understood only in terms of its opposition to the power of the Devil: that is the whole point of the New Testament. The world is full of terrible grief, suffering, and pain. But somewhere, beyond the power of Satan, is a greater power that gives meaning to that pain.[42]

42. I regret that an excellent article appeared too late for me to use it: Roy Yates, "Jesus and the Demonic in the Synoptic Gospels," *Irish Theological Quarterly*, 44(1977), 39–57.

7 The Face of the Devil

Woe unto them that call evil good, and good evil.
—Isaiah 5:20

When an ungodly man curses Satan, he curses his own soul.
—Sirach 21:27

The little girl cries out in the darkness: we live in a world in which evil appears to be gratuitous and unceasing. We perceive evil as greater than mere moral ignorance. We perceive it as transcending the individual and possessing unity of purpose and force. Over the centuries, the expression of these perceptions has formed a tradition that posits a principle of evil and accords it personality.

Hebrew-Christian thought developed this tradition most fully. The tradition, a complex blend of diverse mythological and philosophical elements, bears the following marks: (1) It is alive. Perceptions of evil continue to occur to individual minds. The bleeding soldier, the crippled child, the old woman in the devastated village, the murdered hostage, these are not abstractions but real people who truly suffer. Personifications of evil also persist, even in the materialistic world of today, as the revival of interest in exorcism and possession testifies. (2) Because the tradition is alive, it goes on developing through time. The movement of the concept is continually being reinforced and modified by new formulations. (3) Because the tradition has not as yet reached its focus, no final definition of the Devil is now possible. It is possible, however, to offer a definition of the Devil as conceived at the time of the New Testament.

The most important development in the tradition is the shift from monism in the direction of dualism. Monism posits one divine principle; polytheist monism teaches that the many gods are manifestations of that principle. The God is a coincidence of opposites, responsible for both good and evil. This ambivalence is manifested in two ways: (a) each individual deity may be ambivalent, as is the God himself; (b) two deities representing opposite principles, such as Horus and Seth, may be paired.

The first clear departure from monism occurred in Iran, where Zarathushtra's followers posited two principles, each independent of the other. One was the good god, the god of light; the other the evil god, the god of darkness. In Iranian dualism, both principles were spirits. Another dualism appeared in Greece, asserting an opposition between spirit and matter. These two dualisms—Iranian and Greek—united in late Jewish and Christian thought; the result was an association of the good Lord with spirit and the Devil with matter.

The third departure from monism appeared among the Hebrews. The Hebrews early insisted that Yahweh was the only manifestation of the divine principle: their god became the God. They wanted their one god to be all good as well, however, and so they implicitly and unconsciously separated the evil side of the God from the good side, calling the good side the Lord and the evil side the Devil. But as the essential principle of their religion was monotheism, however, they had to stop short of positing two separate principles. That left the evil spirit, the Devil, in an anomalous position. On the one hand he was the author of evil, and his existence relieved the Lord of direct responsibility for many of the evils of the world. On the other hand, he was not an independent principle but the creature and even the servant of the Lord. This anomaly led to an implicit tension between monism and dualism. The Devil, who was not prominent in the Old Testament, gained stature in the Apocryphal, Apocalyptic, and New Testament literatures. Far from being a mere accretion of peripheral superstitions, the Devil has his genesis in the God himself. He is a counterpart, a doublet of the good Lord. He is the shadow of God.

The shift from monism toward dualism was paralled by a shift in theodicy. In most of the ancient religions, theodicy was implicitly expressed in mythology. But Greek philosophical thought, and the Jewish and Christian writers influenced by it, sought a rational and explicit theodicy. The philosophers formulated a rational conception of moral law that was applicable to all intelligent beings. This permitted a rational and moral definition of evil. In mythology evil had been vaguely defined; philosophy now made the distinction between moral and natural evils and defined the Devil's role in both.

To what extent was the Devil responsible for the evil in the world? Egyptian thought, positing a perfect cosmos, needed no theodicy. In Mesopotamia and Canaan, and among the early Greeks and Hebrews, something was felt to be wrong with the world, and this evil was variously ascribed to evil spirits, to ill choices of human free will, or to the inscrutable will of the deity. Dualism radically changed this theodicy, freeing the God from responsibility for evil and assigning it instead to an independent and hostile spirit. Both late Hebrew and early Christian thought were caught in the tension between monism and dualism. Insisting on monotheism, they left the God with at least partial responsibility for evil; tending to dualism, they shifted much of the blame onto the Devil.

The relationship of demons to the Devil has always been somewhat blurred, and the demons of the New Testament are a composite of different elements. One element is the fallen angels. To the extent that the demons are fallen angels, their origin is in the *bene ha-elohim,* the sons of the God. In this context the demons share a common divine origin with the Devil, and there is reason to refer in one breath to "the Devil and the other demons," for the Devil is the first and greatest of the fallen angels. But the demons have roots in other ancient traditions as well. They are menacing spirits of the thunderstorm or the lonely grove, avenging ghosts of the dead, bringers of disease, and violent spirits who possess the soul.

```
principle of evil ---------------------- DEVIL ⎤
                                              ⎪
                                              ⎬ fallen angels
                     pagan deities ⎤ demons   ⎪
                     nature spirits ⎬         ⎦
                                    ⎦
```

In the living tradition, the characteristics of the personification of evil gradually accumulate. In Egypt and Mesopotamia the workings of the evil spirit are expressed diffusely. In Canaan the spirit of evil, Mot, signifies death and sterility. In Iran, Ahriman is destroyer and deceiver, the personification of lust and greed, the prince of darkness, the lord of lies, and the lie itself. It is curious that the deep ambivalence toward the female principle in these ancient religions did not produce a female personification of evil. The Egyptian Sekhmet, the Canaanite Anath, the Greek Hecate, are all ambivalent. The Iranian Jeh the whore and Druj the lie are evil, but they are subsumed under the general, and male, evil principle, Ahriman. The female Hellenistic Dyad was a bloodless abstraction. Other evil female spirits—Lilitu, Labartu, the Gorgons, Sirens, Harpies, and Lamias—were minor entities that never approached the dignity of the principle of evil.

The Christian iconography of the Devil has ancient precedents, although the links are not always clear. The Devil is red. Red was characteristic of the followers of Seth, but no connection has been demonstrated between the redness of Seth and that of the medieval Devil. A red serpent adorned the temple of Marduk, but again the connection is unclear. It is possible that the Devil's redness is derived from the redness of the underworld's destroying fire. Or, the Devil is black. Seth sometimes appeared as a black pig, and Dionysos was sometimes black, but the connection is uncertain. The Devil's blackness may derive from his association with darkness, which symbolized death, annihilation, and the terrors of the night. Lilitu, Lilith, and the Lamias are night creatures, and the world of the dead is dark from Egypt to Greece and Iran to Rome. Canaanite Mot and Greek Hades are lords of death and darkness. The most direct connection of darkness is with Mazdaism, where Ahriman is defined as the lord of the absence of light. Though the principle of darkness may be translated iconographically into a black hue, the Devil can also be pallid owing to his association with death and the sunless underworld. The cold and stinking nature of the Devil so prominent in medieval beliefs derives directly from the iconography of Ahriman.

· Theriomorphy, the manifestation of a spirit as a beast, is associated in India, Egypt, and Mesopotamia with ambivalent deities; in other cultures, an animal appearance was ascribed exclusively to spirits of evil. Animals associated with evil were the pig, scorpion, crocodile, dog, jackal, cat, rat, toad, lizard, lion, serpent, and dragon. Of these the pig, cat, toad, dog, and serpent appear most frequently in the Judeo-Christian tradition. The goat form of the Devil derives primarily from the image of Pan. From such theriomorphic ancestors the Devil inherited his claws, cloven hooves, hairiness, huge phallus, wings, horns, and tail.

Three of his characteristics have origins other than the bestial. Wings are an ancient symbol of divine power found on the shoulders of many Mesopotamian deities, and from Mesopotamia they passed over onto the shoulders of the Hebrew cherubim and seraphim. Ahura Mazda in Iran was represented borne aloft by mighty wings. Hermes, the messenger of the gods, wore wings upon his ankles or legs. Horns too are ancient symbols of power and fertility. The Devil's "pitchfork" derives in part from the ancient trident, such as that carried by Poseidon, which symbolizes threefold power over earth, air, and sea, in part from symbols of death (such as the mallet of Charun), and in part from the instruments used in hell for the torment of the damned.

The Devil, like gods and angels, is not restricted to any one form. He has the power to change his shape at will, and in order to deceive he may appear as a handsome youth, a beautiful girl, or even an angel of light.

The Devil's association with the underworld connects him to

both death and fertility. In Egypt, Mesopotamia, Canaan, and early Greece, and among the early Hebrews, the underworld was a place where the dead led a pale, shadowy existence; the torment of sinners did not figure prominently. With the advent of Iranian dualism, and with the Greek philosophers' definitions of morality, punishment became more prominent. In Iran, the dead had to pass over the Chinvat Bridge in order to attain paradise; lurking beneath were demons who caused sinners to fall from the bridge into a pit of torment. Among the Greeks, shadowy Hades gradually merged with the more sinister Tartarus, and the torments at first reserved only to a few (Prometheus in the world above, Tantalus and Ixion in the underworld) were extended to all the unjust. The Hebrew concepts of Gehenna and Sheol combined to produce an underworld place of torment, which in Apocalyptic literature became the abode of the Devil and his attendant demons. All these elements combined to create the Christian tradition of hell, which in the New Testament was as yet far from clearly articulated.

The individual eschatology of death and the underworld was associated with the eschatology of the cosmos, the end of the world. Before the advent of Iranian dualism, it was not necessary to assume an end of the world, a climax to cosmic events. But a universal warfare between a good and an evil spirit ending in the triumph of one and the destruction of the other renders some kind of climax inevitable. After ages of struggle, during which the power of the Devil has increased, the Lord descends, the final battle is joined, and the Devil is defeated, to be bound forever in the pit or forever annihilated. On that great day those who aligned themselves with the Devil, whether spiritual or mortal beings, will suffer the fate of their master.

But the idea of the fall of the Devil is ambiguously expressed in the tradition. Eschatology represents the final fall and ruin of the evil one. But Mazdaism offers two accounts of a previous fall. At the time of the initial war in heaven, when Ahriman first coveted the light of Ohrmazd, Ohrmazd cast him into the outer darkness, or, in another version, hurled him down from heaven through the earth into the primeval waters below. A similar eschatology is found in Mithraism. The Hebrews and Christians had a further reason to emphasize the double fall of Satan. Their tradition, though implicitly dualistic, explicitly insisted that Satan was not an independent principle coeval with the God of light, but rather a creature of the good Lord, and, like the rest of the Lord's creation, originally good. It was therefore necessary to assume an initial fall of Satan from grace, that fall resulting from his free decision to reject the will of the creator. This first fall was a moral one, but it was accompanied by a geographical descent from heaven, either by the free will of Satan and his followers, as with the Watcher angels, or because of their forceful ejection from heaven by the angels of the good Lord. When, as with the Watchers, the descent was voluntary, it was followed by a second, involuntary, motion, when the good angels thrust the evil ones down into the valleys and pits of the earth. In the version in which the evil angels' first fall from heaven was a forceful ejection, they were cast down into the air, or onto the earth, or else into the pits and valleys of the earth. Eventually Christianity would amalgamate these various descents into one stunning headlong plunge from heaven to hell.

The chief characteristics of the Devil at the time of the New Testament were these: (1) he was the personification of evil; (2) he did physical harm to people by attacking their bodies or possessing them; (3) he tested people, tempting them to sin in order to destroy them or recruit them in his struggle against the Lord; (4) he accused and punished sinners; (5) he was the head of a host of evil spirits, fallen angels, or demons; (6) he had assimilated most of the evil qualities of ancient destructive nature spirits or ghosts; (7) he was the ruler of this world of matter and bodies until such time as the Lord's own kingdom would come; (8) until that final time he would be in constant warfare against the good Lord; (9) he would be defeated by the good Lord at the end of the world. The concept of the Devil had been given its basic contours.

But Jewish and Christian traditions now began to part company. Judaism generally followed the Rabbinic tradition in limiting the role of the Devil strictly. Christianity—both erudite and popular—developed the concept much further. Christian tradition came to identify the Devil and the demons more completely with the fallen angels, removing the Devil farther from his divine origin and assimilating him to the demons as their prince. It clarified the nature and ranks of the good and evil angels, along with the extent of their powers over nature and over humankind, and it addressed the question whether they had bodies and, if so, of what kind. It set the time of Satan's rebellion and subsequent fall from grace at the beginning of time, rather than at the end, and it discussed the motives for his fall: lust, pride, envy of Adam, or envy of the Lord. It firmly identified the Devil both with the serpent of Genesis and with Lucifer. It asked whether the angels fell into the air or into the pit; it asked where hell was located, whether it was everlasting, and whether the demons suffer there or whether they merely torment the damned, their own punishment being delayed until later. It developed a complex theology of possession, obsession, and exorcism. It associated the Devil with the Antichrist, and, by extension, with heretics, Jews, and other "infidels," who came to form part of a "mystical body of the Devil." It discussed the extent to which the Lord gave power over humanity to the Devil in retribution for our sins and the manner in which Christ has freed us from his power. The Devil of the New Testament is but one stage of a developing concept, the entirety and overall direction of which, rather than any one stage, constitue the truth about the Devil.

I have tried to be clear that throughout this book I am speaking in historical rather than in metaphysical terms. As a historian, I have no direct access to the mind of the Lord or to that of the Devil, and I can investigate only the historical development of the concept of the Devil, not the question of his objective existence. Yet intellectual investigation of such a subject from any methodological point of view entails moral responsibility. I believe I am obliged to add my conclusions as a human being to my conclusions as a historian. More than that, as a

M. C. Escher, "The Encounter," 1944, illustrating the three stages of integration. At first, the two halves of the personality exist dimly together in the unconscious; then they separate and move in opposite directions; finally they meet and reunite on the conscious level. Courtesy Escher Foundation, Haags Gemeentemuseum, The Hague.

whole and integrated human being, I am obliged to avoid a gap between the personal and professional, the intellectual and the humane. It follows that my personal view about the Devil is an extension, not a contradiction, of my historical view.

Does the Devil really exist? This question can be considered on four levels. (1) On the first level, no certainty, no absolute knowledge, of anything at all exists. Even Descartes' *cogito ergo sum* went too far. The only thing that is immediately and directly experienced is thought, so that all that can be said with certainty is that *thought exists*. This lack of certainty does not mean that we must retreat into solipsism. It is possible to seek, and to find, knowledge that is less than absolute. (2) On the second level, we seek knowledge through valid extrapolation from experience. You cannot know things *in themselves*, but you can know *things as they are perceived.* On this level you choose a methodology, a choice that is partly a leap of faith and partly a considered judgment on the basis of experience. I choose the history of concepts because it offers the best way of understanding a concept that is not firmly rooted in physical nature and therefore not open to scientific method. If you choose the history of concepts, you begin with your own experience, work out to the experience of others, move on to the manner of expression of that experience, and finally look for a traceable development, or tradition, of that expression. (3) On the third level, you establish what you can know on the basis of the methodology you have chosen. (4) On the fourth level, you integrate that knowledge into your life.

What do I know about the Devil? (1) I have had direct experience of a force that I perceive as evil, as having unity and purpose, and as coming from beyond myself. (2) This experience is quite common among sane people in many cultures, so it cannot be dismissed as madness. (3) The experience may appear to come from beyond myself because it arises from my unconscious, rather than because it objectively is beyond myself. (4) But the beyondness is part of the perception itself, and it is quite common in the perception of others, so that it must be taken seriously. (5) If the experience does come from beyond me, what precisely is the experience of? How describe the entity that occasions such an experience? Each person interprets the experience in terms of his own personal and cultural predilections, so that considerable variety exists in the content of reported perceptions. (6) My personal and cultural predilections should be adjusted and corrected in terms of what I have learned from the methodology I have chosen. (7) The methodology I have chosen shows a definable development of historical tradition, which asserts, at a minimum, the existence of a principle of evil. Naturally it can be objected that many people in many cultures do not share this view. I am here merely presenting my own grounds, as a human being, for my beliefs. Of course I am not certain that the Devil exists, much less what he is if he does exist. All reservations considered, however, I do believe in the existence of a personification and principle of evil, call it what you will.

Another important question must at least be raised. What is the *function* of the Devil today? Is belief in the Devil of positive value, or not? On the one hand, belief in the Devil is harmful, because attributing evil to the Devil may excuse us from examining our own personal responsibility for vice, and the responsibility of unjust societies, laws, and governments for suffering. It is also harmful in that people who experiment with Satanism open themselves to serious psychological dangers. On the other hand, there is at least one advantage to belief in the Devil. The old liberal belief that man is somehow, for some reason, intrinsically good, and that evils can be corrected by adjusting education, penal laws, welfare arrangements, city planning, and so on, has not proved its validity. Recognition of the basic existence of evil, and consequently of the need for strong efforts to integrate and overcome it, may be socially more useful as well as intellectually and psychologically more true. Further, theists at least should again consider a natural diabology. If a natural theology can be argued from the putative universal human experience of the good, then a natural diabology can be argued from the putative universal human experience of evil.

The story of the Devil is grim, and any world view that ignores or denies the existential horror of evil is an illusion. Ivan's one child crying out alone in the darkness is worth the whole creation, *is* in a sense the whole creation. If any world view, theist or atheist, minimizes her suffering, declares it nonexistent, gives it elaborate philosophical justification, or explains it in terms of a greater good, whether the name assigned that good be God or the People, that world view renders her life, and yours, empty and vain. Yet in spite of the reality of evil and amid the unceasing suffering of the world, Marcus Aurelius could write: "The cosmos is in love with creating whatever is to be. To the cosmos I say then: I will love with you."

Select Bibliography

The literature on evil and the Devil is vast, and unfortunately much of it is useless. I have included here the books and articles I have found most useful.

Abrahamsson, Hans. *The Origin of Death: Studies in African Mythology*. Uppsala, 1951.

Adkins, Arthur W. H. "Homeric Gods and the Values of Homeric Society." *Journal of Hellenic Studies*, 92 (1972), 1–19.

Ahern, M. B. *The Problem of Evil*. London, 1971.

Albright, William F. *Yahweh and the Gods of Canaan*. London, 1968.

Anthes, Rudolf. "Mythology in Ancient Egypt," *Mythologies of the Ancient World*. Ed. Samuel Noah Kramer. New York, 1961. Pp. 17–92.

Arendt, Hannah. *On Violence*. New York, 1970.

Armstrong, Arthur H. *The Architecture of the Intelligible Universe in the Philosophy of Plotinus: An Analytical and Historical Study*. Cambridge, 1940.

——, ed. *The Cambridge History of Later Greek and Early Medieval Philosophy*. Cambridge, 1967.

Bamberger, Bernard J. *Fallen Angels*. Philadelphia, 1952.

Barton, George A. "The Origin of the Names of Angels and Demons in the Extra-Canonical Apocalyptic Literature to 100 A.D." *Journal of Biblical Literature*, 30–31 (1911–1912), 156–157.

Baumbach, Günther. *Das Verständnis des Bösen in den synoptischen Evangelien*. Berlin, 1963.

Becker, Ernest. *The Structure of Evil*. New York, 1968.

Bellah, Robert. *Beyond Belief: Essays on Religion in a Post-Traditional World*. New York, 1970.

Berends, William. "The Biblical Criteria for Demon-Possession." *Westminster Theological Journal*, 37 (1975), 342–365.

Berger, Peter, and Thomas Luckman. *The Social Construction of Reality: A Treatise in the Sociology of Knowledge*. New York, 1966.

Bianchi, Ugo. "Dualistic Aspects of Thracian Religion." *History of Religions*, 10 (1970), 228–233.

——. "Il dualismo come categoria storico-religiosa." *Rivista di storia e letteratura religiosa*, 9 (1973), 3–16.

——. *Il dualismo religioso: saggio storico ed etnologico.* Rome, 1958.

Billicsich, Friedrich, *Das Problem des Uebels in der Philosophie des Abendlandes.* Vol. 1: *Von Platon bis Thomas von Aquino.* 2d ed. Vienna, 1955.

Böcher, Otto. *Dämonenfurcht und Dämonenabwehr: ein Beitrag zur Vorgeschichte der christlichen Taufe.* Stuttgart, 1970.

——. *Der Johannische Dualismus im Zusammenhang des nachbiblischen Judentums.* Gütersloh, 1965.

——. *Das neue Testament und die dämonischen Mächte.* Stuttgart, 1972.

Bonnet, Hans. *Reallexikon der ägyptischen Religionsgeschichte.* Berlin, 1952.

Borsodi, Ralph. *The Definition of Definition: A New Linguistic Approach to the Integration of Knowledge.* Boston, 1967.

Bosch, Frederik D. R. *The Golden Germ: An Introduction to Indian Symbolism.* The Hague, 1960.

Boyd, James W. *Satan and Māra: Christian and Buddhist Symbols of Evil.* Leiden, 1975.

Brandon, Samuel G. F. *Creation Legends of the Ancient Near East.* London, 1963.

——. *The Judgement of the Dead: An Historical and Comparative Study.* London, 1967.

——. "The Personification of Death in Some Ancient Religions." *Bulletin of the John Rylands Library*, 43 (1961), 317–335.

——. *Religion in Ancient History.* New York, 1969.

Brock-Utne, Albert. "Der Feind: die alttestamentliche Satansgestalt im Lichte der sozialen Verhältnisse des nahen Orients." *Klio, Beiträge zur alten Geschichte*, 28 (1935), 219–227.

Bruno de Jésus-Marie, ed. *Satan.* New York, 1952.

Campbell, Joseph. *The Masks of God: Occidental Mythology.* New York, 1964.

——. *The Masks of God: Oriental Mythology.* New York, 1962.

——. *The Masks of God: Primitive Mythology.* New York, 1959.

——. *The Mythic Image.* Princeton, 1975.

Caquot, André. "Anges et démons en Israël." *Génies, anges et démons.* Paris, 1971.

Carcopino, Jérôme. *La Basilique pythagoricienne de la Porte Majeure.* Paris, 1926.

Cassuto, Umberto. *The Goddess Anath: Canaanite Epics of the Patriarchal Age.* Jerusalem, 1951.

Cave, Charles H. "The Obedience of Unclean Spirits." *New Testament Studies*, 11 (1964/1965), 93–97.

Cavendish, Richard. *The Powers of Evil.* New York, 1975.

Charles, Robert H. *The Apocrypha and Pseudepigrapha of the Old Testament in English.* 2 vols. Oxford, 1913.

——. *Eschatology.* 2d ed. by George Wesley Buchanan. New York, 1963.

——. *Religious Development between the Old and New Testaments.* London, 1914.

Cherniss, Harold. "Sources of Evil According to Plato." *Proceedings of the American Philosophical Society*, 98 (1954), 23–30.

Chilcott, C. M. "The Platonic Theory of Evil." *Classical Quarterly*, 17 (1923), 27–31.

Christensen, A. *Essai sur la démonologie iranienne.* Copenhagen, 1941.

Corvez, Maurice. *Les Structuralistes, les linguistes.* Paris, 1969.

Costello, Edward B. "Is Plotinus Inconsistent on the Nature of Evil?" *International Philosophical Quarterly,* 7 (1967), 483–497.

Cross, Frank Moore. *Canaanite Myth and Hebrew Epic: Essays in the History of the Religion of Israel.* Cambridge, Mass., 1973.

Culican, William. "Phoenician Demons." *Journal of Near Eastern Studies,* 35 (1976), 21–24.

Dahl, Nils Alstrup. "Der erstgeborene Satans und der Vater des Teufels." *Apophoreta: Festschrift für Ernst Haenchen.* Berlin, 1964. Pp. 70–84.

Dahood, Mitchell. "Ugaritic Studies and the Bible." *Gregorianum,* 43 (1962), 55–79.

Dam, Willem C. van. *Dämonen und Bessessene: die Dämonen in Geschichte und Gegenwart und ihre Austreibung.* Aschaffenburg, 1970.

Daniélou, Alain. *Hindu Polytheism.* New York, 1964.

De Harlez, Charles. "Satan et Ahriman, le démon biblique et celui de l'Avesta." *Society of Biblical Archeology, Proceedings,* 9 (1887), 365–373.

De Jonge, Marinus. *Testamenta XII Patriarcharum.* 2 vols. Leiden, 1964.

Denis, Albert Marie. *Introduction aux pseudépigraphes grecs de l'Ancien Testament.* Leiden, 1970.

Detienne, Marcel. "Sur la Démonologie de l'ancien pythagorisme." *Revue de l'histoire des religions,* 155 (1959), 17–32.

De Vaux, Roland. *Ancient Israel: Its Life and Institutions.* New York, 1961.

Dexinger, Ferdinand. *Sturz der Göttersöhne oder Engel vor der Sintflut.* Wiener Beiträge zur Theologie, 13. Vienna, 1966.

Dhorme, Edouard. *Les Religions de Babylonie et d'Assyrie.* Paris, 1956.

Dodds, Eric R. *Pagan and Christian in an Age of Anxiety: Some Aspects of Religious Experience from Marcus Aurelius to Constantine.* Cambridge, 1965.

Dresden, Mark J. "Mythology of Ancient Iran." Ed. Samuel N. Kramer, *Mythologies of the Ancient World.* New York, 1961.

Driver, Godfrey R. "Mythical Monsters in the Old Testament." *Studi orientalistici in onore di Giorgio Levi della Vida.* 2 vols. Rome, 1956. I, 234–249.

Duchesne-Guillemin, Jacques, ed. *The Hymns of Zarathustra.* London, 1952.

——. *Ohrmazd et Ahriman: l'aventure dualiste dans l'antiquité.* Paris, 1953.

——. *La Religion de l'Iran ancien.* Paris, 1962.

——. *Symbols and Values in Zoroastrianism: Their Survival and Renewal.* New York, 1966.

Dumézil, Georges. *Archaic Roman Religions.* 2 vols. Chicago, 1970.

Dussaud, René. *Les Religions des Hittites et des Hourrites, des Phéniciens, et des Syriens.* Paris, 1945.

Eissfeldt, Otto. *The Old Testament: An Introduction, Including the Apocrypha and Pseudepigrapha, and also the Works of Similar Type from Qumran.* New York, 1965.

Eitrem, Samson. *Some Notes on the Demonology in the New Testament.* 2d ed. Oslo, 1966.

Eliade, Mircea, ed. *From Primitives to Zen: A Thematic Sourcebook of the History of Religions.* New York, 1967.

——. *Myth and Reality.* New York, 1963.

———. "Notes on Demonology." *Zalmoxis*, 1 (1938), 197–203.

———. *Patterns in Comparative Religion*. New York, 1958.

———. *The Two and the One*. London, 1965.

Erman, Adolf, ed. *The Ancient Egyptians: A Sourcebook of Their Writings*. London, 1923. 2d ed. New York, 1966. Originally published as *Die Literatur der Ägypter*. Leipzig, 1923.

Ernst, Josef. *Die eschatologischen Gegenspieler in den Schriften des Neuen Testaments*. Regensburg, 1967.

Evans, John M. *Paradise Lost and the Genesis Tradition*. Oxford, 1968.

Fascher, Erich. *Jesus und der Satan: eine Studie zur Auslegung der Versuchungsgeschichte*. Halle/Salle, 1949.

Feine, Paul, and Johannes Behm. *Einleitung in das Neue Testament*. 14th ed. by Werner Georg Kümmel, Heidelberg, 1964. Translated as *Introduction to the New Testament*. Nashville, 1966.

Ferguson, John. *The Religions of the Roman Empire*. London, 1970.

Festugière, André-Jean. *Epicurus and his Gods*. Oxford, 1955.

Frankfort, Henri. *Ancient Egyptian Religion: An Interpretation*. New York, 1948.

———. *The Birth of Civilization in the Near East*. London, 1951.

———, ed. *The Intellectual Adventure of Ancient Man: An Essay on Speculative Thought in the Ancient Near East*. Chicago, 1946.

———. *The Problem of Similarity in Ancient Near Eastern Religion*. Oxford, 1951.

Fridrichsen, Anton. "The Conflict of Jesus with the Unclean Spirits." *Theology*, 22 (1931), 122–135.

Fromm, Erich. *The Anatomy of Human Destructiveness*. New York, 1973.

Fuller, Benjamin A. G. *The Problem of Evil in Plotinus*. Cambridge, 1912.

Girard, René. *La Violence et le sacré*. Paris, 1972.

Glasson, Thomas Francis. *Greek Influence in Jewish Eschatology, with Special Reference to the Apocalypses and Pseudepigraphs*. London, 1961.

Gonda, Jan. *Les Religions de l'Inde*. Paris, 1962.

Goodenough, Erwin R. *Introduction to Philo Judaeus*. 2d ed. Oxford, 1962.

Gordis, Robert. *The Book of God and Man: A Study of Job*. Chicago, 1965.

Gordon, Cyrus. *The Ancient Near East*. 3d ed. New York, 1965.

———. "Canaanite Mythology." *Mythologies of the Ancient World*. Ed. Samuel Noah Kramer. New York, 1961. Pp. 183–215.

———. *The Common Background of Greek and Hebrew Civilization*. New York, 1965. Originally published as *Before the Bible*. New York, 1962.

———. *Ugarit and Minoan Crete: The Bearing of their Texts on the Origins of Western Culture*. New York, 1966.

———. *Ugaritic Literature: A Comprehensive Translation of the Poetic and Prose Texts*. Rome, 1949.

Gray, John. *The Canaanites*. London, 1964.

———. *The Legacy of Canaan: The Ras Shamra Texts and their Relevance to the Old Testament*. Leiden, 1965.

———. *Near Eastern Mythology*. London, 1969.

Greeley, Andrew M. *Unsecular Man*. New York, 1972.

Greene, William C. *Moira: Fate, Good and Evil, in Greek Thought*. Cambridge, Mass., 1944.

Griffiths, John G. *The Conflict of Horus and Seth, from Egyptian and Classical Sources: A Study in Ancient Mythology.* Liverpool, 1960.

Gross, Julius. *Geschichte des Erbsündendogmas: ein Beitrag zur Geschichte des Problems vom Ursprung des Uebels.* 4 vols. Munich, 1960–1972.

Gruenthaner, Michael J. "The Demonology of the Old Testament." *Catholic Biblical Quarterly,* 6 (1944), 6–27.

Güterbock, Hans. "Hittite Mythology." *Mythologies of the Ancient World.* Ed. Samuel Noah Kramer. New York, 1961. Pp. 141–179.

Guthrie, William K. C. *Orpheus and Greek Religion.* London, 1935.

Haag, Herbert, ed. *Teufelsglaube.* Tübingen, 1974.

Hager, Fritz-Peter. *Die Vernunft und das Problem des Bösen im Rahmen der platonischen Ethik und Metaphysik.* Berne, 1963.

Harden, Donald. *The Phoenicians.* New York, 1962.

Heidel, Alexander. *The Babylonian Genesis: The Story of the Creation.* 2d ed. Chicago, 1951.

Helfer, James S. *On Method in the History of Religions.* Middletown, Conn., 1968.

Hennecke, Edgar, and Wilhelm Schneemelcher. *The New Testament Apocrypha.* 2 vols. Philadelphia, 1963–1965.

Henninger, Joseph. "The Adversary of God in Primitive Religions." *Satan.* Ed. Bruno de Jésus-Marie. New York, 1952.

Herter, Hans. "Böse Dämonen im frühgriechisches Volksglauben." *Rheinisches Jahrbuch der Volkskunde,* 1 (1950), 112–143.

Hick, John. *Evil and the God of Love.* New York, 1966.

Hiers, Richard H. "Satan, Demons, and the Kingdom of God." *Scottish Journal of Theology,* 27 (1974), 35–47.

Hinnells, John R. *Persian Mythology.* London, 1973.

——. "Zoroastrian Saviour Imagery and its Influence on the New Testament." *Numen,* 16 (1969), 161–185.

Hinz, Walther. *Zarathushtra.* Stuttgart, 1961.

Hollinger, David A. "T. S. Kuhn's Theory of Science and its Implications for History." *American Historical Review,* 78 (1973), 370–393.

Hooke, Samuel H. *Babylonian and Assyrian Religion.* New York, 1953.

Inge, William R. *The Philosophy of Plotinus.* 3d ed. 2 vols. London, 1929.

James, Montague Rhodes, ed., *The Apocryphal New Testament.* Oxford, 1924.

Jeanmaire, Henri. *Dionysos: histoire du culte de Bacchus.* Paris, 1951.

Jensen, Soren S. *Dualism and Demonology.* Copenhagen, 1966.

Johnson, Roger N. *Aggression in Man and Animals.* Philadelphia, 1972.

Jung, Leo. *Fallen Angels in Jewish, Christian and Mohammedan Literature.* Philadelphia, 1926.

The Jung Institute. *Evil.* Evanston, Ill., 1967.

Kapelrud, Arvid S. *The Violent Goddess: Anat in the Ras Shamra Texts.* Oslo, 1969.

Kaupel, Heinrich. *Die Dämonen im Alten Testament.* Augsburg, 1930.

Kee, Howard Clark. "The Terminology of Mark's Exorcism Studies." *New Testament Studies,* 14 (1968), 232–246.

Kelly, Henry Ansgar. *The Devil, Demonology, and Witchcraft: The Development of Christian Beliefs in Evil Spirits.* 2d ed. New York, 1974.

——. "The Devil in the Desert." *Catholic Biblical Quarterly*, 26 (1964), 190–220.

——. "Demonology and Diabolical Temptation." *Thought*, 40 (1965), 165–194.

Kelsey, Morton. "The Mythology of Evil." *Journal of Religion and Health.* 13 (1974), 7–18.

Kerenyi, Karoly. *The Religion of the Greeks and Romans.* New York, 1962.

Kirk, Geoffrey S. *Myth: Its Meaning and Functions in Ancient and Other Cultures.* Cambridge, 1970.

Kluger, Rivkah Schärf. *Satan in the Old Testament.* Evanston, Ill., 1967.

Kockelmans, Joseph J., ed. *Phenomenology: The Philosophy of Edmund Husserl and its Interpretations.* New York, 1967.

Kramer, Samuel Noah. "Mythology of Sumer and Akkad." *Mythologies of the Ancient World.* New York, 1961. Pp. 95–137.

——. *Sumerian Mythology: A Study of Spiritual and Literary Achievement in the Third Millennium B.C.* 2d ed. New York, 1961.

Kuhn, Harold B. "The Angelology of the Non-Canonical Jewish Apocalypses." *Journal of Biblical Literature*, 67 (1948), 217–232.

Langton, Edward. *Essentials of Demonology: A Study of Jewish and Christian Doctrine, its Origin and Development.* London, 1949.

——. *Good and Evil Spirits: A Study of the Jewish and Christian Doctrine, Its Origin and Development.* New York, 1942.

——. *Satan: A Portrait: A Study of the Character of Satan Through All the Ages.* London, 1945.

Leach, Edmund R. *Lévi-Strauss.* London, 1970.

Lederer, Wolfgang. *The Fear of Women.* New York, 1968.

Lefévre, André. "Angel or Monster?" *Satan.* Ed. Bruno de Jésus-Marie. New York, 1952.

Leibovici, Marcel. "Génies et démons en Babylonie." *Génies, anges et démons.* Paris, 1971. Pp. 85–112.

Ling, Trevor O. *Buddhism and the Mythology of Evil: A Study in Theravāda Buddhism.* London, 1962.

——. *The Significance of Satan: New Testament Demonology and its Contemporary Relevance.* London, 1961.

Lods, Adolphe. "La Chute des anges: origine et portée de cette spéculation." *Revue d'histoire et de philosophie religieuses,* 7 (1927), 295–315.

——. "Les Origines de la figure de Satan, ses fonctions à la cour céleste. *Mélanges syriens offerts à M. R. Dussaud.* 2 vols. Paris, 1939. II, 649–660.

Long, J. Bruce. "Siva and Dionysos—Visions of Terror and Bliss." *Numen,* 19 (1971), 180–209.

Lorenz, Konrad. *On Aggression.* New York, 1966.

Lovejoy, Arthur O. *Essays in the History of Ideas.* Baltimore, 1948.

Lüthi, Kurt. *Gott und das Böse: eine biblisch-theologische und systematische These.* Zurich, 1961.

McCasland, Selby Vernon. *By the Finger of God: Demon Possession and Exorcism in Early Christianity in the Light of Modern Views of Mental Illness.* New York, 1951.

Macchioro, Vittorio. *From Orpheus to Paul: A History of Orphism.* New York, 1930.

McCloskey, H. J. "God and Evil." *Philosophical Quarterly,* 10 (1960), 97–114.

———. "The Problem of Evil." *Journal of Bible and Religion,* 30 (1962), 187–197.

MacCulloch, John A. *The Harrowing of Hell: A Comparative Study of an Early Christian Doctrine.* Edinburgh, 1930.

Mackie, John L. "Evil and Omnipotence." *Mind,* 64 (1955), 200–212.

Madden, Edward H. "The Riddle of God and Evil." *Current Philosophical Issues.* Ed. Frederick C. Dommeyer. Springfield, Ill., 1966. Pp. 185–200.

———, and Peter H. Hare. *Evil and the Concept of God.* Springfield, Ill., 1968.

Maier, Johann. "Geister (Dämonen): Israel." *Reallexikon für Antike und Christentum,* IX (1976), 579–585.

Maranda, Pierre, and Eppi Köngäs. *Structural Analysis of Oral Tradition.* Philadelphia, 1971.

Maritain, Jacques. *God and the Permission of Evil.* Milwaukee, 1966.

May, Harry S. "The Daimonic in Jewish History; or, the Garden of Eden Revisited." *Zeitschrift für Religions- und Geistesgeschichte,* 23 (1971), 205–219.

May, Herbert G. "Cosmological Reference in the Qumran Doctrine of the Two Spirits and in Old Testament Imagery." *Journal of Biblical Literature,* 82 (1963), 1–14.

May, Rollo. *Power and Innocence: A Search for the Sources of Violence.* New York, 1972.

Meeks, Dimitri. "Génies, anges, démons en Egypte." *Génies, anges et démons.* Paris, 1971. Pp. 17–84.

Meldrum, M. "Plato and the ἀρχὴ κακῶν," *Journal of Hellenic Studies,* 70 (1950), 65–74.

Ménasce, P. de. "A Note on the Mazdean Dualism." *Satan.* Ed. Bruno de Jésus-Marie. New York, 1952. Pp. 121–126.

Mendelsohn, Isaac, ed. *Religions of the Ancient Near East: Sumero-Akkadian Religious Texts and Ugaritic Epics.* New York, 1955.

Mensching, Gustav. *Gut und Böse im Glauben der Völker.* 2d ed. Stuttgart, 1950.

Michl, Johann. "Katalog der Engelnamen." *Reallexikon für Antike und Christentum,* V (1962), 200–239.

Montagu, Ashley, ed. *Man and Aggression.* New York, 1968.

Moreno, Antonio. *Jung, Gods, and Modern Man.* Notre Dame, 1970.

Morenz, Siegfried. *Egyptian Religion.* Ithaca, N.Y., 1973. Originally published as *Aegyptische Religion.* Stuttgart, 1960.

Munz, Peter. *When the Golden Bough Breaks: Structuralism or Typology?* London, 1973.

Mylonas, George E. *Eleusis and the Eleusinian Mysteries.* Princeton, 1961.

Natanson, Maurice, ed. *Phenomenology and Social Reality: Essays in Memory of Alfred Schutz.* The Hague, 1970.

Neumann, Erich. *Depth Psychology and a New Ethic.* New York, 1969.

Newman, John Henry. *Essay on the Development of Christian Doctrine.* London, 1946.

Nilsson, Martin P. *Geschichte der griechischen Religion.* 3d ed. 3 vols. Munich, 1967.

Noack, Bent. *Satanás und Sotería: Untersuchungen zur neutestamentlichen Dämonologie.* Copenhagen, 1948.

Nyberg, Henrik S. *Die Religionen des alten Iran.* Osnabrück, 1966.

Obeyesekere, Gananath. "Theodicy, Sin, and Salvation in a Sociology of Buddhism." *Dialectic in Practical Religion.* Ed. E. R. Leach. Cambridge, 1968, pp. 7–40.

O'Brien, D. "Plotinus on Evil: A Study of Matter and the Soul in Plotinus' Conception of Human Evil." *Downside Review*, 87 (1969), 68–110.

Oesterreich, Traugott K. *Possession, Demoniacal and Other: Among Primitive Races, in Antiquity, the Middle Ages, and Modern Times.* New York, 1930.

O'Flaherty, Wendy Doniger. *Hindu Myths.* Harmondsworth, 1975.

———. *The Origin of Evil in Hindu Mythology.* Berkeley, Calif., 1976.

———. "The Origin of Heresy in Hindu Mythology." *History of Religions*, 10 (1970), 271–333.

Olson, Alan M., ed. *Disguises of the Demonic: Contemporary Perspectives on the Power of Evil.* New York, 1975.

Otto, Walter F. *Dionysos: Myth and Cult.* Bloomington, Ind., 1965.

Penelhum, Terence. "Divine Goodness and the Problem of Evil." *Religious Studies*, 2 (1966), 95–107.

Petit, François. *The Problem of Evil.* New York, 1959.

Pètrement, Simone. *Le Dualisme chez Platon, les gnostiques, et les manichéens.* Paris, 1947.

———. *Le Dualisme dans l'histoire de la philosophie et des religions: introduction à l'étude du dualisme platonicien, du gnosticisme et du manichéisme.* Paris, 1946.

Piccoli, Giuseppe. "Etimologie e significati di voci bibliche indicanti Satana." *Rivista di filologia classica; nuova serie*, 30 (1952), 69–73.

Pike, Nelson, ed. *God and Evil: Readings on the Theological Problems of Evil.* Englewood Cliffs, N.J., 1964.

Pistorius, Philippus V. *Plotinus and Neoplatonism: An Introductory Study.* Cambridge, 1952.

Plantinga, Alvin. "The Free Will Defence." *Philosophy in America.* Ed. Max Black. Ithaca, N.Y., 1965. Pp. 204–220.

Pontifex, Mark. "The Question of Evil." *Prospect for Metaphysics.* Ed. Ian Ramsey. London, 1961. Pp. 121–137.

Pritchard, James B. *Ancient Near Eastern Texts Relating to the Old Testament.* 2d ed. Princeton, 1955.

Propp, Vladimir. *Morphology of the Folk Tale.* 2d ed. Austin, Tex., 1968.

Puccetti, Roland. "The Loving God—Some Observations on John Hick's *Evil and the God of Love.*" *Religious Studies*, 2 (1967), 255–268.

Radin, Paul. *The Trickster: A Study in American Indian Mythology.* London, 1955.

Raphaël, F. "Conditionnements socio-politiques et socio-psychologiques du Satanisme." *Revue des sciences religieuses*, 50 (1976), 112–156.

Reicke, Bo. *The Disobedient Spirits and Christian Baptism: A Study of 1 Pet. 3:19 and its Context.* Copenhagen, 1946.

Richman, Robert J. "The Argument from Evil." *Religious Studies*, 4 (1968), 203–211.

Ricoeur, Paul. *The Symbolism of Evil.* New York, 1967.

Ringgren, Helmer. *Religions of the Ancient Near East*. Philadelphia, 1973.

Roskoff, Gustav. *Geschichte des Teufels*. 2 vols. Leipzig, 1869.

Rossi, Ino. *The Unconscious in Culture: The Structuralism of Claude Lévi-Strauss in Perspective*. New York, 1974.

Russell, David S. *The Method and Message of Jewish Apocalyptic 200 B.C.–A.D. 100*. Philadelphia, 1964.

Sanford, Nevitt, and Craig Comstock. *Sanctions for Evil*. San Francisco, 1971.

Scheepers, Johannes H. *Die Gees van God en die gees van die mens in die Ou Testament*. Kampen, 1960.

Scheffczyk, Leo. "Christlicher Glaube und Dämonenlehre. Zur Bedeutung des Dokumentes der 'Kongregation für die Glaubenslehre' von Juni 1975." *Münchener Theologische Zeitschrift*, 26 (1975), 387–396.

Schipper, Kristofer. "Démonologie chinoise." *Génies, anges et démons*. Paris, 1971, pp. 403–427.

Schlier, Heinrich. *Principalities and Powers in the New Testament*. New York, 1961.

Schmid, Josef. "Der Antichrist und die hemmende Macht (2 Thess. 2:1–12)." *Theologische Quartalschrift*, 129 (1949), 323–343.

Schmidt, Karl Ludwig. "Lucifer als gefallene Engelmacht." *Theologische Zeitschrift*, 7 (1951), 161–179.

Schutz, Alfred. *The Phenomenology of the Social World*. Evanston, Ill., 1967.

Sesemann, Wilhelm. "Die Ethik Platos und das Problem des Bösen." *Festschrift Hermann Cohen*. Berlin, 1972. Pp. 170–189.

Shaked, Shaul. "Some Notes on Ahriman, the Evil Spirit, and his Creation." *Studies in Mysticism and Religion Presented to Gerschom G. Scholem*. Jerusalem, 1967.

Shiner, Larry. "A Phenomenological Approach to Historical Knowledge." *History and Theory*, 8 (1969), 260–274.

Simpson, William K., et al. *The Literature of Ancient Egypt: An Anthology of Stories, Instructions, and Poetry*. New Haven, 1972.

Soelle, Dorothy. *Suffering*. Philadelphia, 1976.

Sontag, Frederick. *The God of Evil: An Argument from the Existence of the Devil*. New York, 1970.

Soury, Guy. *La Démonologie de Plutarque*. Paris, 1942.

Spiro, Melford. *Buddhism and Society*. New York, 1972.

Stählin, Wilhelm. "Die Gestalt des Antichrists und das Katechon." *Festschrift J. Lortz*. 2 vols. Baden-Baden, 1958. II, 1–12.

Staude, John Raphael. "Psyche and Society: Freud, Jung and Lévi-Strauss from Depth Psychology to Depth Sociology." *Theory and Society*, 3 (1976), 303.

Stemberger, Günter. *La Symbolique du bien et du mal selon S. Jean*. Paris, 1970.

Storr, Anthony. *Human Destructiveness*. New York, 1972.

Strack, Hermann, and Paul Billerbeck. *Kommentar zum Neuen Testament aus Talmud und Midrasch*. 4 vols. Munich, 1922–1969.

Taylor, Richard. *Good and Evil: A New Direction*. New York, 1970.

Thornton, Timothy C. G. "Satan: God's Agent for Punishing." *Expository Times*, 83 (1972), 151–152.

Torczyner, Harry. *The Book of Job: A New Commentary*. Jerusalem, 1957.

——. "A Hebrew Incantation against Night-Demons from Biblical Times." *Journal of Near Eastern Studies*, 6 (1947), 18–29.
Vaillant, André. *Le Livre des secrets d'Hénoch: texte slave et traduction française.* Paris, 1952.
Van der Meulen, R. J. "Veraktualisering van de Antichrist." *Arcana Revelata: Festschrift W. Grosheid.* Kampen, 1951.
Vandier, Jacques. *La Religion égyptienne.* 2d ed. Paris, 1949.
Varenne, Jean. "Anges, démons et génies dans l'Inde." *Génies, anges et démons.* Paris, 1971. Pp. 257–294.
Verde, Felice M., O.P. "Il Problema del male da Proclo ad Avicenna." *Sapienza*, 11 (1948), 390–408.
——. "Il Problema del male da Plutarco a S. Agostino." *Sapienza*, 11 (1958), 231–268.
Vermaseren, Maarten J. *Mithras, the Secret God.* London, 1963.
Vermes, Geza. *The Dead Sea Scrolls in English.* 2d ed. Harmondsworth, 1970.
Von Petersdorff, Egon. *Daemonologie.* 2 vols. Munich, 1956–1957.
Wainwright, William J. "The Presence of Evil and the Falsification of Theistic Assertions." *Religious Studies*, 4 (1968), 213–216.
Wallace, Howard. "Leviathan and the Beast in Revelations." *Biblical Archaeologist*, 11 (1948), 61–68.
Watts, Alan W. *The Two Hands of God: The Myths of Polarity.* New York, 1963.
Wheelwright, Philip. *The Burning Fountain.* Bloomington, Ind., 1954.
Widengren, Geo. *The Great Vohu Manah and the Apostle of God: Studies in Iranian and Manichaean Religions.* Uppsala, 1945.
——. *Die Religionen Irans.* Stuttgart, 1965.
Willetts, Ronald F. *Cretan Cults and Festivals.* New York, 1962.
Williams, R. J. "Theodicy in the Ancient Near East." *Canadian Journal of Theology*, 2 (1956), 14–26.
Wilson, John A. *The Burden of Egypt: An Interpretation of Ancient Egyptian Culture.* Chicago, 1951. 2d ed. published as *The Culture of Ancient Egypt.* New York, 1956.
Winston, David. "The Iranian Component in the Bible, Apocrypha and Qumran. A Review of the Evidence." *History of Religions*, 5 (1965–1966), 183–216.
Wolfson, Harry A. *Philo: Foundations of Religious Philosophy in Judaism, Christianity, and Islam.* 2 vols. Cambridge, Mass., 1947.
Woods, Richard. *The Devil.* Chicago, 1974.
Zaehner, Robert C. *Concordant Discord: The Interdependence of Faiths.* Oxford, 1970.
——. *The Dawn and Twilight of Zoroastrianism.* London, 1961.
——. *Hinduism.* Oxford, 1962.
——. *The Teachings of the Magi.* New York, 1956.
——. *Zurvan, a Zoroastrian Dilemma.* Oxford, 1955.
Zandee, Jan. *Death as an Enemy According to Ancient Egyptian Conceptions.* Leiden, 1960.
Ziegler, Matthäus. *Engel und Dämon im Lichte der Bibel: mit Einschluss des ausserkanonischen Schrifttums.* Zurich, 1957.

Index

A

Adam and Eve, 182, 192, 227, 232, 241-242; Books of, 207-209
Aeschylus, 131, 136-137
Aeshma Daeva, 115, 215, 218
Africa, 65-66, 69
Ahriman, 58, 99, 102, 104-121, 152, 154, 204, 217, 219, 248, 253, 255
Ahura Mazda, *see* Ohrmazd
Ahuras, 58, 104
Aiōn:
    Greek, 152
    in New Testament, 232-235, 241
Alastor, 143
Alchemy, 67
Amahraspands, 112
American Indians, 58-62, 67, 75
Amesh spentas, see Amahraspands
Anath, 94-97, 253
Androgyny, 39, 45, 60, 111, 124, 138, 141
Angels, *see* Archangels, Fall of angels, Watcher angels
Angra Mainyu, *see* Ahriman
Animals associated with Devil, 70-72, 113, 116, 127, 217, 245-247, 254; *see also* Dragon, Goat, Ouroboros, Serpent
Anpu (Anubis), 77-78
Antichrist, 231, 243-245, 257.
Anunnaki, 90-92
Apep, 82
Aphrodite, 60, 124
Apocalyptic, 185-188, 191-198, 204-212, 217-219, 229, 231, 243, 246-247, 255; definition of, 175-176
Apocrypha, definition of, 175, 221
Apollo, 124, 127, 131, 134, 142
Apsu, 88-90
Aquinas, 146, 163
Archangels, 191
Ares, 66, 124
Aristotle, 149, 162
Artemis, 62, 69, 124, 127-129, 132
Arunta, 73
Asmodeus, 215, 218
Assyria, 84-87
Astarte, 94
Asuras, 58-59, 64, 104, 136
Atē, 130-131
Athene, 124
Augustine, 108, 146, 163
Az, 119
Azazel, 188-192, 197, 206-207, 211

B

Baal, 94-97
Babylonia, 84, 87-92, 217
Bacchanalia, 152
Beelzebub, 189, 228-229
Behemoth, 216
Belial (Beliar), 188-189, 193, 209-211, 213, 217, 219, 228-229, 243
Bene ha-elohim, 184-188, 191-198, 201, 203, 252
Blackness, 62, 64-66, 68, 76, 78, 141-142, 217, 246-247, 253

Blatty, William, 26
Blood, 84, 90, 133, 135
Buber, Martin, 102
Buddhism, 23-24, 32, 50, 67, 74-75

C

Cain, 192
Canaan, 84, 94-97, 184, 195, 215-218, 252-253, 255
Cerberus, 136, 143
Chaos, 66-68, 88, 135, 147, 217
Charun, 155-156, 159, 172, 254
Chicomecoatl, 62
Chimera, 136
Chinvat Bridge, 117-118, 255
Chronos, 97, 135-137
Chthonic, 78, 90, 139, 186, 254
    ambivalence of, 62-64, 126-127
    in Greek thought, 123, 126-127, 143-144, 172-173
    in Mazdaism, 118-119
Ciuacoatl, 62
Coatlicue, 62
Coincidence of opposites, 57-60, 68-69, 77, 95, 231, 251, 258
    definition of, 57-58
    in Egyptian myth, 80-84
    in Greek thought, 123, 128
    in Hebrew thought, 177-178, 183-184, 208, 219
    in Mazdaism, 107-111
Concepts:
    history of, 40-54
    nature of, 42-44, 46-51
Cybele, 127, 152, 172
Cynics, 144

D

Daevas, 58, 104, 120
Dagon, 94
Dayak, 68
Death, 64, 68, 75, 90, 92, 117-119, 127, 142, 172, 253-255; *see also* Eschatology, Hell, Mot
Demons, 73-75, 77, 123
    in Christianity, 236-237, 245-246
    definition of, 237, 252-253
    etymology of, 34, 142

    in Greece, 131, 142-144, 161, 167, 170-171
    Hebrew, 176, 215-217
    in Iran, 105, 115-120
    Mesopotamian, 42, 88
Deucalion, 134-136
Devas, 58, 104
Devil:
    definition of, 33-36, 237, 252-253
    etymology of, 34, 58, 174
    name of, in New Testament, 229
Diana, *see* Artemis
Dikē, 129-130
Dionysos, 45, 60, 137-142, 152, 170, 172, 253
Dostoevsky, Feodor, 17-18, 54
Doublets, *see* Coincidence of opposites
Dragon, 68, 89, 95, 116, 217, 243, 245, 254
Druj, 102, 116, 253
Dualism, 99-100, 251-252
    and Christianity, 227-228
    and Greek thought, 134, 137-139, 145, 160-161, 169-170
    and Hebrew thought, 183, 219, 220
    in Iran, 98, 101-107, 112
Dupré, Louis K., 50
Durga, 59

E

Echidna, 136
Egypt, 76-84, 97, 252-253, 255
Eliade, Mircea, 51, 58
Emma-O, 73-74
Enoch, Books of:
    Ethiopic, 186-188, 192, 194-196, 206-207, 217
    Slavonic (Secrets of Enoch), 194-195
Epictetus, 158
Epicurus and Epicureans, 158
Ereshkigal, 90
Erinyes, 127, 131, 143, 172
Eschatology, 255-256
    Christian, 233, 242-245
    Hebrew, 213-215
    Mazdaist, 117-120, 170
Essenes, 121
Etimmu, 92
Etruscans, 155-156

Eudoxos of Cnidia, 160
Euripides, 133-134
Evil, problem of, 17-35, 250-260
    in Christianity, 222-228
    in Greece, 122, 145-167
Exorcism, *see* Possession

F

Fall of angels, 210, 255-257
    in Christianity, 227, 241-242, 252-253
    in Hebrew thought, 185, 188, 191-197,
        206-209, 217
Fall of mankind, *see* Original sin
Female principle, 60-62, 92, 116, 124, 152,
    172-173, 253
Flint, 60
Flood, 90, 134
Frankfort, Henri, 52
Frashkart, 119-120
Fravashis, 113
Fromm, Erich, 23-24, 27-30

G

Gaia, 124, 135-136
Gayomart, 112-114, 117, 121
Gehenna, 77, 186, 240-241, 255
Genesis, Book of, 182, 184-185
Giants, 58, 184
Gnosticism, 99, 121, 139-142, 147, 170,
    235-236, 248
Goat, 125-126, 141, 151, 170, 215, 217
Gorgons, 143, 170, 253

H

Haag, Herbert, 36
Hades, 126, 143-144, 152, 172, 254-255; as
    Christian hell, 240
Hamestagan, 119
Harpies, 143, 253
Hathor, 82-85
Hecate, 127, 130, 172, 253
Hell, 64
    Asian, 73, 77
    Christian, 172, 186, 216, 240-241
    Egyptian, *see* Tuat
    etymology of, 62
    Greek, *see* Hades, Tartarus
    Hebrew, *see* Gehenna, Sheol

Mazdaist, 118-119
Mesopotamian, 90, 92
    see also Chthonic
Hephaistos, 124
Hera, 123, 152
Herakleitos, 67, 144
Hermaphrodite, 60
Hermes, 125-126, 170, 254
Hesiod, 132, 134
Hinduism, 23-25, 50, 55-56, 58-59, 64, 67,
    70, 73, 102, 114, 135, 220
Hittites, 97-98, 135
Homer, 129-132, 134, 142
Horns, 68-71, 73, 81, 83, 94, 103, 125-126,
    141, 177, 245, 249, 254
Horus, 77-82, 169
Hydra, 124, 136, 143, 170, 216

I

Incubus, 73, 194
Iran, *see* Mazdaism
Iroquois, 60
Isaiah, Book of, 195
Ishtar, 90-92
Isis, 80-81, 152, 172
Islam, 99, 208

J

Japan, 73-74, 100
Jeh, 112, 117, 253
Jeqon, 206
Job, Book of, 87, 131, 187, 198-204, 207
Joshua, Book of, 178-179
Jubilees, Book of, 192-194, 204, 206-207
Judas, 80, 231, 239-240
Jung, C. G., 29-33, 41, 46-47, 51, 56, 75,
    177-178
Juno, *see* Hera
Jupiter, *see* Zeus

K

Kali, 59, 62-63, 65, 68
Kelly, Henry Ansgar, 36
Keres, 142
Kings, Books of, 190, 202-203
Kogi Indians, 58
Kosmos, 232-235, 241
Krishna, 70

Kronos, *see* Chronos
Kumarbi, 97-98
Kur, 89

L

Labartu, 92, 253
Lamias, 143, 172, 253
Lateran Council of 1215, 34
Leviathan, 67, 216-217, 244
Lévi-Strauss, Claude, 41, 46-47, 51-52
Lewis, C. S., 102
Lilith, 143, 172, 215, 253
Lilitu, 92-93, 215, 253
Lotan, 216
Lucifer, 195-197, 207-208, 229, 257

M

Ma, 127
Ma'at, 76, 80-82, 102, 129
Maenads, 139-140
Magi, 104, 120, 152
Magna Mater, 127, 152, 172
Mal'ak Yahweh, 184, 197-205, 211, 213-214
Manicheism, 99, 105, 112, 120
Mara, 75
Marcus Aurelius, 158, 260
Marduk, 88-90
Mars, *see* Ares
Mashye and Mashyane, 113-115, 121
Mastema, 188-189, 193-194, 197, 204-205, 211
May, Rollo, 24
Mayas, 60, 62, 75
Mazdaism, 58, 98-121, 135, 178, 215, 231, 248, 253-255
    and dualism, 98, 101-107, 139, 145, 160-161, 213-214, 251
    eschatology, 117-120
    influence on Hebrew thought, 217-220
    myths of, 107-114
Mazdakism, 105
Mesopotamia, 84-92, 215, 252-255
Miasma, 132-133
Minotaur, 70, 143
Mithraism, 58, 120-121, 152-154, 256
Mithras, 70, 153, 155, 170, 172
Moira, 129, 131

Monism, 98, 145, 161-163, 168-169, 177, 228, 251-252
Moon, 69-70, 81, 94, 127-128
Moses, 177, 180-181, 198, 204; Apocalypse of, 207
Mot, 94-97, 253
Myth, definition of, 52-54, 56

N

Nahuatl, 67
Namuci, 64
Nemean Lion, 136
Nemesis, 129, 133
Neoplatonism, *see* Platonism
Neopythagoreans, 154, 159-160; *see also* Pythagoreans
Nephilim, see Giants
Neumann, Erich, 30, 58
Nonbeing, 66, 108, 146-148, 162-166, 224
Numbers, Book of, 190

O

Ohrmazd, 58, 104-121, 150, 152, 204, 254-255
Old Testament, definition of, 175
Ometeotl, 60
Oni, 73
Orgy, 64, 67, 140-142, 152, 172
Original sin:
    in Christianity, 227, 231-232
    in Greece, 134-135
    in Hebrew thought, 182-183, 196, 207-209
    in Iran, 113-115
Orphism, 137-142, 144-145, 147-148, 154, 159, 235, 248
Osiris, 78-82, 152
Ouranos, 135, 137
Ouroboros, 68-69

P

Pan, 73, 125-126, 151, 156, 170-171, 254
Pandora, 134-135, 137
Parmenides, 144
Paul, Saint, 64, 221, 232, 235-236, 245
Pazuzu, 91-92, 246
Persephone, 124, 127
Phanes, 137

Philo, 166-167

Plato, 134, 142, 145-149, 159-160, 162-163, 169

Platonism:
Middle, 160-161, 246
Neoplatonism, 161-166

Plotinus, 161-166

Plouton (Pluto), 64, 124, 126, 152

Plutarch, 142, 160-161, 170

Poseidon, 70, 124-125, 129

Possession, 230, 237-239, 249

Privation, theory of, 146-148, 162-166, 169, 205

Prometheus, 75, 136-137

Protagoras, 145

Pyrophlegethon, 144

Pythagoreans, 137-139, 144, 159, 169, 172, 246; *see also* Neophythagoreans

Q

Quetzalcoatl, 57, 67, 75

Qumran, 175, 179, 188, 194, 211-215, 217-219

R

Rahab, 216

Rakshasas, 73

Re, 76-78, 82-84, 150

Redness, 62, 64, 66, 78, 84, 217, 246-247, 253

Reshef, 94, 215

Rig Veda, 67

Roskoff, Gustav, 36

S

Salt, 133

Sammael, 188, 211, 216

Samuel, Books of, 189, 202-203

Sarx, 235-236

Satan:
as common name, 189-190
etymology of, 189-190
interpretations of origin of, 176
as leader of fallen angels, 188-189, 193-194
name of in New Testament, 229
in New Testament, 222-249
and Peter, 239

as plural entity, 206
as tempter of Adam and Eve, 196, 207-209, 231-232

Satanail, 188

Saturnalia, 68

Scylla, 127

Se'irim, 215, 217

Sekhmet, 78, 84-85, 97, 253

Semele, 53, 137

Semyaza, 188, 191-192, 206

Serpent, 68, 82, 116, 136, 170, 207, 217-218, 245-246, 254, 257

Seth, 77-82, 253

Shapeshifting, 116, 207, 247, 254

Sheol, 186, 195, 216, 240, 255

Shiva, 59-61, 65, 67, 69

Sin, 115, 119, 178, 181, 248

Sirens, 143, 253

Sisyphus, 143

Skeptics, 158

Skinner, B. F., 28-29

Snake, *see* Serpent

Socrates, 132, 142, 144, 148

Solzhenitsyn, Aleksander, 19, 22-23, 30-31

Soma, 235-236

Sophists, 145

Sophocles, 131-132

Soshyans, 120

Spenta Mainyu, 107, 112

Sphinx, 136

Stoics, 142, 144, 158

Succubus, *see* Incubus

Sumer, 84-86, 89, 92

T

Tammuz, 92

Tantalus, 143

Taoism, 76

Tartarus, 127, 136, 144, 172, 255

Taylor, Richard, 25

Teshub, 97

Testaments of the Twelve Patriarchs, 194, 209-211

Tezcatlipoca, 67

Themis, 129

Theodicy, definition of, 22

Thucydides, 133-134

Tiamat, 67, 88-92, 216, 244
Tibet, 65-66, 68
Time, 65, 108, 135
Time, 132
Titans, 58, 89, 135-141, 160, 191, 196
Tityrus, 143
Tlacolteutl, 62
Toltecs, 75
Trickster, 75, 82, 126
Trident, 70, 77, 129, 156, 254
Tuat, 76-77
Twinning, *see* Coincidence of opposites
Typhoeus, 124
Typhon, 136, 170

U

Ullikummis, 97-98
Utukku, 92

V

Vergil, 149-150
Vishnu, 70

W

Warfare among gods, 89, 97, 135-137

Watcher angels, 170, 188, 191-197, 206, 208, 241, 246, 256
Water, 88, 125, 133, 246; *see also* Flood
Whiteness, 65-66, 254
Wings, 87, 93, 126, 156, 170, 246, 254
Winnebago Indians, 60
Wisdom of Solomon, Book of, 200
Witchcraft, 64, 194
Woods, Richard, 36, 52

X

Xenocrates, 142

Y

Yester ha-ra, 176, 213, 236

Z

Zahhak, 116
Zarathushtra, 99-121
Zechariah, Book of, 190, 199-200
Zervanism, 99, 101, 105, 107, 109-111, 116, 119-120, 219
Zeus, 53, 102, 123-124, 127, 130-132, 134-137, 150, 152
Zoroastrianism, *see* Mazdaism
Zurvan, 110-111, 116